TURNING OVER THE PEBBLES

TURNING OVER
THE PEBBLES

A Life in Cricket and in the Mind

Mike Brearley

CONSTABLE

CONSTABLE

First published in Great Britain in 2023 by Constable

3 5 7 9 10 8 6 4 2

A CIP catalogue record for this book
is available from the British Library.

ISBN: 978-1-40871-596-3 (hardback)
ISBN: 978-1-40871-615-1 (trade paperback)

Typeset in Electra LT Std by SX Composing DTP, Rayleigh, Essex
Printed and bound in Great Britain by Clays Ltd, Elcograf S.p.A.

Papers used by Constable are from well-managed forests
and other responsible sources.

Constable
An imprint of
Little, Brown Book Group
Carmelite House
50 Victoria Embankment
London EC4Y 0DZ

An Hachette UK Company

www.hachette.co.uk

www.littlebrown.co.uk

To Luka, Alia, Maia and Lila

CONTENTS

I AM ME

It's the mid-1950s, and I'm walking along a corridor in the semi-basement of the City of London School that led to Room 20, where four years earlier we have been introduced to French pronunciation by Nicky Le Mansois-Field. I am now thirteen or fourteen. Through the high window, I see the corner of the building that lies on the other side of John Carpenter Street just before it meets the Embankment, and the bright sky above and across the River Thames.

It is, I now think, the middle of the day, around lunchtime, and, as I recall slanting sunlight, it must have been winter. More than sixty-five years on, I remember this moment, and my precise location and view, for its sudden epiphany – for the thought: *I am me*. I am for the first time aware of my identity as a separate self, capable of putting words (however few and small) to this experience. I suppose I mean something like this: I feel a conviction of myself as a centre of experience and a source of thought and action. *I am me*. I am unique and self-aware; not only part of a collective. The remarkable fact is, I exist. In the stillness, there is a self for me to listen to, and to do the listening.

And for the last forty years I have worked in my semi-basement consulting room in our house in London, with patients in psychoanalysis, with this same concept in the back (and occasionally the front) of my mind, an often obscure or unstated aim for me and them.

Decades on from this little scene, in the 1990s, I was talking to my analyst about being a late developer. As a teenager, I had been one of the last of my class to move into puberty, still wearing short trousers when, at fourteen, I got into the school First XI at cricket. And it took me a long time to grow fully into professional life, in cricket and as a psychoanalyst. What I was referring to in my session was being slow to achieve a psychoanalytic identity, as well as a more personal one. Quoting the regular remark of a character from a children's book: 'Better late than never,' I added, probably with some smugness, 'like Chippybobbie.' There was a moment's silence. My analyst responded drily, 'When are you thinking of beginning?'

When I spoke briefly along similar lines to another psychoanalyst, John Steiner, his comment was: 'You need to captain yourself.' 'A case we may assume of "physician heal thyself"', cricket broadcaster John Arlott once wrote about me and my batting: a similar notion.

In his poem 'Invictus', William Ernest Henley writes: 'I am the master of my fate, / I am the captain of my soul.' The phrase has a trace of Victorian pomposity. But the thought resonates. It also brings to mind a recent conversation on the phone, with a friend, someone with a considerable mind and presence, who had been diagnosed with dementia. In response to my conventional question about how she was, she said, painfully, slowly, 'It's hard. It's not good.' After a pause, I asked if she could say more about how she felt. She hesitated again, clearly struggling to articulate her thought. She managed to say: 'I can't get hold of myself.' I found this upsetting, but also poignant. Here was someone getting hold of herself sufficiently to be able to recognise she wasn't able to get hold of herself. I said something along the lines of 'Though it's very painful, it's truthful, and your getting there shows how brave you are and how much insight you have in knowing yourself.'

This book is in a sense a story of this quest, to get hold of myself, to be not too much a stranger to myself. To bring different layers to life, and closer together. To turn over the pebbles to see what lies underneath – murky detritus and/or richer patterns? While acknowledging the inevitability of selfishness, of over-sensitivity, or our all-too-human elements of destructiveness and indifference, we struggle to move towards the other pole. Part of such an ability consists in recognising our shadow-self, shadow-selves.

In the final Test of the cricket series in India in 1977, Dennis Amiss and I started England's first innings well into the third day. By close of play we were 99 for no wicket, and I was 68 not out. I'd played with more freedom in a Test match than before, or indeed afterwards. The next day was the rest day. That evening I was invited to dinner by someone I didn't know well at all. I checked that the meal would be early, so that I could go back to the hotel to sleep before continuing my innings. Reassured, I went. The party was crowded, smoke-filled, with much whiskey and beer drunk. I realised that I was there partly as a sort of trophy. The meal was not served until late. I ate quickly, went back to the hotel tired and frustrated. Next morning, I crept tensely towards the hundred I never scored in Test cricket. The Indian bowlers had changed their line on the slow pitch, which took some spin. They bowled to more defensive fields. As I approached the nineties, I played a leg glance off Chandrashekhar which was signalled by the umpire as four leg-byes. Eventually I was stumped for 91.

Here was an example of how a reluctance to look after myself and my obvious priority let me down. I can't of course know whether the outcome would have been different had I had the gumption to leave early, whatever the disappointment (as I imagined) to my host. But I do know that had I scored a century, this landmark might have enabled me to feel that I had come of age as a Test batter, and could have helped me to play as such subsequently. It has taken me a long time to be more steadily aware of this tendency to please others, to go along the easy path of acquiescing, and instead to have the courage to refuse to allow it to over-ride my sense that 'I am me'.

Captaining ourselves, like captaining a team, requires too a willingness to allow thoughts and feelings their space. It is not a matter of continuous conscious control. A skilled rider gives a horse its head, lengthening the reins. And then gathers the reins in again.

One thing life (and psychoanalysis) teaches us is that our unconscious ideas and basic assumptions play a part, sometimes a big part, in how things fall out for us. We self-sabotage. We open ourselves to malign influences. We close down on opportunities that might have opened up our lives. We repeat patterns that are bound to fail. We cling to, even nurse, grievances.

George Orwell wrote in his diary that by the age of fifty we have the faces we deserve. Nina Coltart commented that ten years, say, after qualifying, we psychoanalysts will be likely to have become set in our largely self-made moulds.

Some people go so far as to deny that there is such a thing as luck. According to the Existentialists, to feel controlled by fate or by past patterns of behaviour is to deny our freedom. If we do this, we are choosing, they say, to live like automata, following prescribed roles, our refusal to make a choice being itself a choice. I see this Existentialist/Orwell view as taking the part for the whole, but there is a kernel of truth that is exaggerated. Luck – bad timing, good timing – and environment play huge roles in all our lives. But to some extent, we are, too, authors of our fates, often without knowing it.

* * *

These are some of the themes that, I hope, will emerge. It will be a kind of memoir, reviewing from my present vantage-point various shifts and conflicts in my life. It is a book of second thoughts (with the risks of unhelpful complications, of losing touch with the capacity for wonder, curiosity and simplicity). Growing up includes coming to understand with more fullness things that were obscure to us earlier.

As for the title, my first writing collaborator, Dudley Doust, an American journalist who had moved from covering international politics to writing about sport, interviewed me during the 1977 Ashes series. We made a second appointment for a day of Middlesex's match at Lord's, against Surrey, which as it happened was rained off. We therefore spent the whole day together. Despite his knowing next to nothing about cricket, I so much liked him and his way of thinking about sport and writing that, soon after those two meetings, I asked him if he would co-write what would be my first book, a personal account of that summer's series. He taught me a great deal about writing and getting beyond the obvious. And he said of my way of talking, that 'it is as though he has been turning over pebbles, searching for the clearest, most unflawed, most precise, and above all the most balanced opinion to plop into the pool of conversation'.

I'm not so sure about the balance: but turning over the pebbles does offer a 'second bite of the cherry'. We have not only the original experience or thought, we have a new take on it. As the psychoanalyst Wilfred Bion said of a particular patient, 'It's fascinating how boring he is.' This is not only a second bite but a second orientation. We can be fascinated by how boring – or for that matter how seductive, how provocative, how contentious – someone is. We can be fascinated by how boring (etc.) we are ourselves.

At funerals and memorials, we speak with each other about the person who has died, who has gone for ever. We read (or occasionally write) obituaries. These record some externals of a life, but at best may also bring the person to life, sometimes in ways we haven't known about, sometimes in words that we could not have found. (I half-wish that obituaries were written before the person dies, for him or her to read; but I suppose they would then become more banal or ingratiating.)

Richard Holloway, once Bishop of Edinburgh, who left the Church in 1996, uses the same phrase in his nicely titled *Waiting for the Last Bus* about how these conversations and reflections 'bring to life' the person who has died. He goes so far as to suggest that this may be what 'resurrection' most aptly, and least literally, refers to. For him, as for many others who doubt the supernatural but are moved and touched by religion, this is as much as we know. 'As long as men can breathe or eyes can see, / So long lives this and this gives life to thee', Shakespeare tells us. Those we loved and have lost live on (in a sense) in our minds. Holloway takes his point further: 'All human art flows from this compulsion to represent or describe or make over again all the worlds we experience.' A symbolisation of, and reparation for, lacks, hatreds, fights, meaninglessness; a move from envy towards admiration and gratitude – second and subsequent thoughts are often more revealing and more substantial than first thoughts.

This book is, then, a 'memoir of the mind', of my mind, and its passions and moves, not a chronological, blow-by-blow autobiography. Looking back, I find memoirs of the future; in some cases, apparently trivial memories are etched in my mind because I somehow intuited that they would have meaning for me later, if not then. They are like screen memories, but more than that. An internal scriptwriter was already in residence and at work. Articulated second thoughts may occur almost instantaneously with first thoughts, but often they occur years later.

As a friend's teacher told him: 'Donkeys can't appreciate honey.' 'George Eliot's *Middlemarch*', the teacher added, 'is an adult novel. You boys won't understand, but you just may get a glimpse of something you'll understand more of when you grow up.'

I heard once of a patient, a woman who had no familiarity with psychoanalysis or therapy, lying down on the couch for her first session, saying: 'I have waited for this all my life.' She somewhere, somehow, knew this was an outcome that she had desired; she knew it long before she knew what form it might take. Narratives, personal stories, however nebulous early on, are central to our lives and to the person we are and become. Life has its strands, and they interweave.

CHAPTER 1

'IF YOU CARRY ON LIKE THIS…'

Five years or so before the episode in the school corridor, my mother, Midge, exasperated by my obsession with football and cricket, and no doubt with my treading mud into the carpet whenever I came (reluctantly) indoors, expressed her frustration with unusual directness. 'If you carry on like this,' she said, 'you'll do nothing but play football and cricket all your life.'

She may even have been speaking on the day after my first 'proper' game of football, as opposed to games in the local park with bundles of clothes as goalposts, or in the concrete school playground, or in the street outside our house where we used the arched yew around our long-missing front gate as a goal. I was playing for North Ealing Primary School – no idea who against – with real goalposts, pitch markings and a referee. It was on a Saturday morning; I have an inkling it was in Gunnersbury Park. My father Horace (we regularly called our parents by their first names) took me, and watched. The score was 2–1 (or 1–2; I don't know whether we won or lost). We wore blue shirts. I retain only one image from the game: I had a shot at goal, but the ball hit a player between me and the target (I've always been unlucky!). Much later, my father told me that on the Sunday afternoon I eventually said to him: 'Isn't there anything else we can say about the game?' It might have been then that my mother's frustration spilled out (in my memory I was nine on each occasion) as we toasted crumpets in the coal fire on extendable toasting forks.

And the answer to my own question, about whether there was anything else to say, not about that blocked shot or even that particular game, but about cricket or football in general, has been yes, there has been a lot more to think and to say.

Though there was to be little football in my life to come, my mother was at least partially right, not only in her prediction (or caveat) about my devotion to the strange game called 'cricket' – as one patient put it: 'How can a little boy like you, playing latency games with other little boys, have anything to offer a mature woman like me?' – but also in my long-lasting dilemma that was in part an argument between body and mind.

Early on, there was no conflict. I simply wanted to play. Play was wholehearted, in a way simple. I imagine myself as not unlike my six-year-old granddaughter Maia, who enthusiastically tries out football, cricket and ballet. She doesn't walk if she can avoid it, preferring more energetic motility, whether galloping, dancing, skipping or running.

As a last resort, scraping the bottom of the barrel, I would even get my mother's aunt to bowl at me in the back garden. I remember her quick but poorly directed underarm deliveries, the ball emerging from the maroon and grey draperies of her clothing.

Edie (we called her Dee-Dee) was unmarried. I think she had been the daughter who took on the duty of looking after her parents in their old age. I was told that Dee-Dee lived with us when I was a baby and toddler, before and after my grandmother died. She came to stay with us over Christmas and at other times, especially during school holidays. She would get up before anyone else to rake out the fire and set it up ready to be lit. She would remonstrate with me and my sisters by repeating in kindly, but I fear unproductive, tones, 'Come along, come along, come along.' I remember her pale veined hands, and crinkled lower lip, which we unkind children would mock, parroting 'Come along' through distorted apertures, and unkindly chanting, 'Can't blow the candle out'. I imagine she enjoyed her time with three teasing children, but probably breathed a sigh of relief to be back in her flat in Lancaster Road, Notting Hill, near where it crossed Ladbroke Grove.

This area, which had once been 'respectable', was known as a centre of 'counter-culture' in the 1950s and 1960s; a more accurate description might be that it was an area of racism, reverse-racism and exploitation. On my last day of school, in July 1960, my father and I went to visit Dee-Dee there. She told us about the Rachman-like pressures she was subject to, aimed at getting her out of the small flat where she'd lived for many years, presumably as a rent-controlled tenant. Shit was shoved through her letterbox.

Some years later, when the atmosphere in her rundown area had become increasingly threatening, she was forced to leave. She found, or was found, a small Home near us in Ealing, our borough, which my mother referred to as 'the Queen of the Suburbs'. Certainly, it was quieter, safer, more suburban than Notting Hill. Dee-Dee was bored. I remember an elderly Scottish resident with failing memory asking time and again, in a sweetly reasonable tone: 'Where's that noise coming fra?' – the noise being music from a portable radio. My parents helped Dee-Dee find a more congenial place. The last time I saw her, she was happily installed in a bigger Home in Twickenham, where she had become friendly with many other residents, including one particular person on the male floor. 'He's getting old, poor thing,' she said; 'he's seventy-three.' She herself was in her early nineties. She died when I was in California in 1967.

Dee-Dee was for me the nearest person to an ongoing grandparent. Three had carelessly died by the time I was eighteen months old; the fourth, my paternal grandmother, a redoubtable woman who had brought up eight children on very little money, lived in Heckmondwike, Yorkshire, near where her parents had kept a pub called the Shoulder of Mutton, in Liversedge. My father remembered her bridge technique; she would with increasing insistence bid and rebid her spades regardless of her partner's lack of support or enthusiasm. We saw her perhaps once every three years, Yorkshire feeling in those days as far away as Turkey does now. One memory of her is her treading dogshit into the house. I also recall the peculiar smell that clung to her clothes. She died when I was ten: on that day the person known in the patronising language of the day as 'the telegram boy' delivered the telegram. It had to be bad news, and it was.

Having four grandchildren of my own now, I value the grandparent relationship more and more, regret the lack in my own childhood, and remember Dee-Dee with gratitude, despite the fact that she couldn't bowl very well.

Dee-Dee's was not the only encouragement I had for sport. A Lancastrian who lived a few streets away, and had rigged up a miniature cricket net in his small back garden, would get me playing proper cricket shots, mostly defensive ones. My cousin Michael, on his occasional visits from Heckmondwike, would play football and cricket with me in the street – with a good deal of patience, I imagine, for this little boy five years younger than him.

Paul Swann, who was the goalie for my father's football team, Brentham, would chat with me while the ball was safely in the opposition half, as I stood by his goalpost. I sense now the pounding of boots on the ground as the game came closer, and recall the physicality of these big men. I remember feeling shame when the referee blew his whistle for a foul by Horace.

Doug Newman, who played for South Hampstead cricket club, and was a friend and opponent of my father's, would bowl at me on the outfield during the tea interval.

My mother too: she had played netball for London University, and then tennis at Brentham. She came to cricket matches, made picnic teas, fielded in family knock-arounds, and later kept cuttings of my games when scorecards and reports began to appear. She came to watch me play against Colet Court, the prep school for St Paul's. They had a lovely little ground, just the right size for small boys, ringed by a rope and deckchairs. I remember scoring 16, and being absurdly proud of the fact that this consisted of four boundaries. I also recall one of them, a hook that went directly to my mother's deckchair, jiggling over the rope between her legs. Why do I remember just that moment, and why, I now ask myself, do I use the word 'jiggling' for the little hop of the ball? I think the main reason for its enduring clarity is that it was a sort of present to my mother, and I sensed that she received it as such. I felt proud of myself in her eyes, imagining her pride in me. I am aware of the possible interpretation of more bluntly Oedipal ideas; a clichéd, even perhaps clangy, interpretation from my aged mind as I write.

But the principal encouragement came from my father, himself a fine cricketer and all-round sportsman, who would bowl and bat against me, and throw me catches to dive for. During our summer holidays in Bognor, he would bowl, or throw, balls at me on the beach, the breakwater for a wicket. He made sure he had the wind behind him, so that if I missed it, and it missed the breakwater, I would have to fetch it. I would sometimes persuade him to go to the local 'rec' on the Chichester Road, where a pitch had been cut and rolled in the middle of the field. The outfield was dry and bare, so I was discouraged from either missing the ball, or hitting it too hard, since once again I would have to fetch it wherever it ended up. These conditions made playing straight not only a virtue but a benefit.

As I have implied, it wasn't only the playing; there was also the talking that anticipated, accompanied and followed games. Horace would comment on games he (and later I) played in; on technique, on tactics. His standards required northern grit and shrewdness, as well as fair play as he saw it. He reckoned that defensive bowling wide of the off stump was against the spirit of the game (not an opportunity for scoring). I remember him once saying of Eb Schneerson, one of his team-mates, that when he flapped his hand in the direction of a fielder, the latter couldn't tell if he was meant to move to the left or the right, if he should come in closer or move further out. When I said of another, Dessie Parker, that he was a really nice man (he was friendly towards me), my father responded, 'But he is rather eager to please'.

I remember digging a hole in the back garden to get to Australia, doubtless already (I must have been five or six) the setting for the most glamorous radiance cricket had to offer. My parents, like psychoanalyst Donald Winnicott in relation to transitional objects, allowed the illusion; they did not challenge the naivety of this ambition, did not need to trim my fantasy to reality. (Amazingly, I got to Australia for cricket, even if by a different route.)

For many years, my father was my hero. He was proud of the picture taken by him with his homemade pinhole camera of three stumps painted on a wall in the back 'ginnel' (Yorkshire for lane or alley) behind the house he grew up in. For me it represented the romance of his childhood. I pestered him to make such a camera with me. We never did.

I also remember him coming home from a game against Winchmore Hill, in which he had broken his little finger in the course of scoring a hundred. The bowler was called Fox, and I have an image of a malign, lean, vulpine figure with a red moustache whom my father had overcome. His finger was crooked for the rest of his life, as is mine. Like him, I admired courage and fortitude in the game. Like me later, he enjoyed battles with skilful opponents, in his case Eddie Ingram and L. B. Thomson of Ealing Cricket Club, Henry and Doug Malcolm of South Hampstead, as well as the wicked Fox of Winchmore Hill.

My first professional hero, Jack Robertson, was an elegant, accomplished opening batter for Middlesex. I did not choose the incomparable Denis Compton or the dashing Bill Edrich, post-war stars for Middlesex and England. I think this must have had to do with Horace, also an opener, not often a dominating batter, but efficient, with a technique based on a sound defence. When I threw balls against the kitchen wall and then batted against the rebound, I *was* Jack Robertson, especially after his 331 in a day for Middlesex against Worcestershire in 1949, when I was seven. And eventually I became a Middlesex opening batter, not often dominant, but, like Robertson, a good county player.

* * *

So much for sport with its emphasis on bodily skills. There was also a slowly growing interest in ideas, and a vaguely sensed aspiration for a life of the mind. The conflict that my mother's words implied became more internal, though it did not become explicit for years. Certainly, it has taken a long time to resolve (if that is the right word: it is so only if 'resolve' does not denote finality). And the envy and contempt coming from (and imagined by me to be coming from) people on both sides have not disappeared.

When I first went to Cambridge, to read Classics, the conflict didn't trouble me much. Productions of Classical plays in the original Greek had taken place there, usually every third year, since 1882, and one was due in March 1961. As a sixth former, I had gone in for competitions in which boys and girls recited Greek and Latin poetry. Having enjoyed the drama, and the speaking in another language, I decided to apply for a part in the chosen play, Aristophanes' *Clouds*.

My friend from school, Michael Apted, who was soon to research and later direct, *Seven Up!*, the brilliant TV documentary following the lives of fourteen boys and girls from various backgrounds every seven years, and who later became a successful film director, suggested I learn two speeches from Harold Pinter's *The Caretaker* for my audition. These speeches were cruel tours de force through which Mick intimidates Davies, the so-called 'caretaker'. One begins 'You remind me of my uncle's brother' – not even my uncle, only my uncle's brother – 'always on the move, that man, never without his passport'; the second with 'You know, believe it or not, you've got a funny kind of resemblance to a bloke I once knew in Shoreditch.' The director was 'Dadie' Rylands, literary scholar, theatre director and aesthete. I was given the (important) part of Leader of the Chorus. Just when rehearsals were beginning, I was selected for the university lacrosse match to be played in Oxford later in the term, which happened to coincide with two or three performances of the play. I had to decide between them, but this was not a difficult decision. Of course I would play lacrosse! Sport over art; body, perhaps, over mind. When I told Rylands, he announced to the assembled cast that this 'young boy has decided to play netball for the university, so he can't be in our play'. And then he kindly asked if I'd like to come on, in any performances not clashing with the netball, as the 'deus ex machina' (the god from the machine), who is wheeled on to say two lines to round off the play. (Which I did, wearing sandals with spangly winged heels, representing Hermes, messenger of the gods, and being startled by the brightness of the lights.) I still recite (or mis-recite) the Pinter speeches as a party piece, and once, in 2009, addressed them to a cowering fellow-cricketer, Mike Gatting, roped in to be the bewildered Davies, in the Long Room at Lord's, as part of a tribute to Pinter, who had died the previous winter.

I was suitably embarrassed by the whole 'netball' scene but took Rylands's mistaking, deliberately or otherwise, netball for lacrosse as an expression of endearment. The gendered element did just about get through to me. Perhaps his hint of mockery was an intentional inversion of the usual direction of travel, a parody of the tendency of sporting hearties to think of themselves as quintessentially masculine and of netball as even more of a girls' game than lacrosse.

Not long after retiring from cricket, I was invited to speak to a conference run by the Marriage Guidance Council on the subject: 'Why do more women than men come for psychotherapy?' In my talk I referred to men's envy of women, using as an example my own reaction on discovering on a Saturday morning that my wife was pregnant, a much-desired outcome for us both; for the rest of the weekend, I wore (in the privacy of our flat) the Indonesian sarong I'd bought years before. I think this was my way of saying I wished it was me who could carry the baby. Without thinking further, I agreed to the Marriage Council's request that I put my talk in their annual magazine. What I hadn't counted on was that this detail would be picked up by two Australian newspapers, their articles headed in bold type: ENGLAND CAPTAIN WEARS A SKIRT.

The superiority and contempt between hearties and culture-vultures could be intense, though I don't remember being explicitly aware of it until I went to university, and rarely then. The admissions tutor at Christ's College in those days was Dr Pratt. He admitted dozens of sportsmen. Rumour had it that in his impatience with intellectual pretension among applicants, he resorted to the question: 'Do you see rhythm in a matchbox?' When one interviewee said, 'No, I don't. Should I?', Pratt is said to have responded, 'Thank God for that.' His question demanded a lot from nervous eighteen-year-olds.

I remember a seminar in which an English don, George Watson, said, in his halting, self-conscious way: 'The fact that I read twenty or twenty-five [he may even have said 'or thirty'] books a week doesn't make me bookish; there are times when I don't want to look at a book at all.' I thought it did, as I do now. In fact, I think his apologetic manner both hid and revealed a suggestion that he was rather pleased with his bookishness. We awe-ful (and awful) undergraduates were meant to feel like barbarians. But which books are they that one could read three or four of them in a day, every day?

A similar criticism, of pretentiousness, was made of a confession I made about my state of mind when batting against the fastest bowler I encountered, Michael Holding. I wrote that, trying to relax and not be hypnotised by his elegantly fluid, ominously quiet run-up – 'Whispering death' was how umpire Dickie Bird described him – I hummed the opening of Beethoven's Razumovsky Quartet, Op. 59, No. 1. This comment got me into *Private Eye*'s 'Pseuds Corner' (the only time – so far). Art critic David Sylvester told me that you're not a serious writer if you don't appear there. He claimed to have had a dozen or so credits in the column.

I was reminded too of the beginning of Evelyn Waugh's *Decline and Fall*, in which both elements, hearties and academics, reveal their vices. On one side the bullies ransack the rooms of undergraduates seen as arty or intellectual, smashing up one person's grand piano, dousing another's Matisse in a jug of water, tearing up Mr Partridge's black sheets, and debagging a serious-minded theology student on his way back from a lecture. On the other side, the dons are gleefully peeping out at the broken glass littering the quadrangles. They are interested only in the fact that the fines imposed would justify opening several bottles of Founder's port, maybe enough for a whole week of pleasurable drinking, if only the rioters would break the chapel windows. They do.

I had, however, misremembered a key detail of this fictional scene. The occasion is not, as I thought, the last day of Summer Eights week, that is, of the college boat-racing competitions. The hooligans were in fact members of the 'Bollinger Club' – 'epileptic royalty from their villas of exile, uncouth peers from crumbling country seats; smooth young men of uncertain tastes from embassies and legations, illiterate lairds from wet granite hovels in the Highlands . . . All that was most sonorous of name and title was there for the beano.'

'Bollinger' is a flimsy disguise for 'Bullingdon'. This actual club is infamous for its exclusivity and boorish behaviour. Founded in 1780, it was originally a sporting club, 'dedicated to cricket and horse-racing'. I had done the oarsmen (the sportsmen) a disservice, but I wasn't as far out as I thought.

* * *

Philosophical distinctions between body and mind are not restricted to abstract differences; they carry ethical or political weight. Which skill expresses the higher value – the sportsman's or the intellectual's, beauty of body or of mind? A parallel question occurs within categories of knowledge and belief: do we learn more from our senses or from our rational thinking, our intellect? Which is superior, sensory or intellectual certainty – that which is derived from the bodily organs of sense, combined with inductive reasoning, or conclusions from revelation, pure logic and deduction?

In Shakespeare's *Julius Caesar*, Brutus, sleeplessly suffering his inner 'insurrection' about whether or not to join the conspirators planning Caesar's murder, has a horrible nightmare. He says:

> I have not slept.
> Between the acting of a dreadful thing
> And the first motion, all the interim is
> Like a phantasma, or a hideous dream.
> The genius and the mortal instruments
> Are then in council; and the state of man,
> Like to a little kingdom, suffers then
> The nature of an insurrection.

Brutus's 'genius and the mortal instruments / Are then in council' means, I think, that his 'genius', his tutelary spirit, his immortal soul, his most human(e) self, is at loggerheads with his 'mortal instruments', that is, with agency whose motivation comes from parts of the self that will die and rot, ultimately from the unredeemed body. As usual, Shakespeare puts a difficult idea succinctly, and bluntly.

The conflict is both a cultural and a personal war. Plato was clear: among those attending the Olympic Games, he ranked spectators at the top of his hierarchy (athletes came second, vendors at the bottom). Christianity took up some of his ideas, of the immortality of the soul, and of its separateness from the body. In the Beginning was the Word. That is, the first duty of a Christian is to listen to the word, the Word of God; a mental duty, faith ahead of deeds.

But other theologians have emphasised Christianity's further claim; that the Word was made Flesh. Indeed, it tells the extraordinary story of the eternal God making himself human in Jesus, that is, embodied and mortal, subject to pain and the sufferings of the flesh. It is only through Jesus, these theologians say, that we can aspire to the being of God, an essence that has 'boiled over' into the flesh. As a result, flesh is not simply or only *opposed* to Spirit (as it is in the battles between the body's impulses and compulsions such as greed and lust, on one side, and conscience, which arises within the mind and is felt to come from the incorporeal part of the self – on the other). Flesh, the body, may become transformed if we come to respect and even worship it, using it not in a greedy, selfish, lustful and exploitative way, but seeing it, potentially at least, as the site of a spirit of giving, of loving, of being loved. Thus body and mind are, ideally, welded into one. The body is not only the scene or agent of sensuality and triviality, but of tenderness, empathy, loyalty; it knows and respects its own vulnerability and that of others. Through the body, we may express our better (in religious terms, our 'divine') nature and the divinity revealed to us. Sex can be sublime, as perhaps in the Garden of Eden. Word is made Flesh, but Flesh is also made Word.

These arguments are not dead; and they function at different levels. There is still a superiority in intellectuals that at times descends into scorn for more practical fields. The contrast or tension between bodily pleasures – gustatory, erotic, competitive – and mental pleasures such as contemplation and reflection is presented as fundamental. One form of culture war occurs between the sciences and the humanities. At another level, there is a division between practical skills (such as carpentry – never part of the regular syllabus at my school) and intellectual ones (solving problems in pure logic, arguing a case, analysing poems). Within the sciences and many arts there are distinctions between pure and applied (in mathematics, for example); the former seems more single-minded, more restricted to the thing itself, than the promiscuous, abundant, peripheral latter. Within a single discipline there are fights over priority.

Freud spoke of the narcissism of small differences, and there is no shortage of that in all these fields, and on each side of the arguments. I remember a professor of philosophy in California displaying in a graduate class contempt for students from what he called 'Aggy' (i.e. agriculture) colleges, and his almost sycophantic admiration for those he saw as academic high-flyers from Oxbridge or Harvard. I once had the courage to criticise him, privately, for this contempt; in his lecture on the following day he tried his best, asking in his most humble voice for 'Any questions?'; but the next minute his Cheshire-cat grin broadened as he pounced with sharp claws on the next tentative Aggy-student question.

A gloves-off version of the war between science and the arts in relation to culture and politics was waged between scientist C. P. Snow (who also wrote novels) and literary critic F. R. Leavis. Snow fired the first shots, in 1956, following up three years later with the publication of his book *The Two Cultures*. He addresses the ignorance, among most of the population, including those allegedly best educated, of basic scientific propositions; how many, he asks, would understand the concepts of mass or acceleration, or would know the second law of thermo-dynamics? There is, he suggests, a disturbing 'self-impoverishment' in this. Leavis responded with augmented acerbity, much of it *ad hominem*, claiming that Snow grossly misunderstood literary (and other) culture. There are barbarisms on both sides. A Republican Party governor in the USA pronounced not long ago that we 'need more welders and fewer philosophers'. In *Julius Caesar*, Caesar says of Cassius that 'He thinks too much: such men are dangerous.' And I recall the vice-chancellor of the University of Newcastle-upon-Tyne arguing in the 1970s that English literature was something you read on the train, not a field for serious intellectual study. He made this comment not long before the closure of the Philosophy department at the same university; English was too big a target, but philosophy could be picked off.

On the other hand, one reason for the success of a similar campaign at another university was the arrogance from those at threat, in this case too, philosophers. Their right to exist should not, they felt, have to be justified at all. They did not recognise the need to locate themselves within the academic community. After all, the queen of the arts and sciences is there by divine right! And I am told of a lecturer in an English department who argued as a matter of dogma that 'precept should precede practice', in other words that a student must have a ('pure') theory of reading before ('applied') actual reading.

Thus snobbery and counter-snobbery fuel each other.

In 2021, the vice-chancellor of Cambridge University, Stephen Toope, a human rights lawyer, commented on 'the need to abandon the idea that the arts are nice, but not essential'. If the view needs to be abandoned, it is still current: 'I think that focusing on what you can measure underplays value', he added – we know the cost of everything but the value of nothing. In another thoughtful article, political economist William Davies writes: 'The neoliberal position is that a humanities degree is a simple waste of money.'

I would argue, along with philosopher and psychoanalyst Jonathan Lear, that the value of the humanities is not to be thought of primarily in terms of economic and pragmatic factors, such as the value to the British economy of the arts or the value to the individual of an arts degree in terms of future employment potential. More fundamentally, and beyond what Toope argued for, the humanities call for the development of empathy and self-awareness, for a broadening of our emotional intelligence.

* * *

With versions of some of these arguments in the back of my mind, I chose in 1971 to leave my academic life as a lecturer in philosophy for a contract as a professional cricketer for Middlesex. My former supervisor, Renford Bambrough, responded to my request for advice with something like: 'This seems to be one of those occasions when what you feel you'd like to do [play cricket again] coincides exactly with what you ought to do.' (He may have been in part concurring with my estimation of myself as a philosopher.)

Several factors were involved in the decision. One was: I wasn't sure I am a real philosopher, with a strong vocation for the field. I liked teaching, my colleagues and much of the debating. But I felt I wanted something that engaged with others more personally and practically. Second, cricket is not only a physical activity, involving body skills, it is also a mind game. It is moreover a team game; and, among team games, it lasts longer than other games, involves one-to-one contests in the context of the team, and provides opportunities for good and bad practical reasoning. Like chess, it calls for planning, calculation of probabilities and intuition. One may punch above one's weight or below it. One may overthink or under-think; either way, thinking enters into performance. Cricket is, or can be, a thinking person's game. Third, I was to be captain. That gave my participation an extra dimension.

Finally, when sportsmen and spectators travel to a game, and especially when they leave it, like me after the football match in Gunnersbury Park, they talk about it; expressing hopes, expectations, and analysing high and low points, disappointment and elation. The talking is part of the game, certainly part of the love of the game. Style, skill, flair, determination – yes of course. But going to a game, or playing it, is a social, emotional and mental activity. It is not inevitably a mindless tribal excess.

Michael Henderson raises the question to himself as well as to his readers: 'Is cricket a part of your *sporting* life, or your other life?' If I understand him, I'm inclined to answer, with him, that it is, and has long been, a part of my life – of my life as a whole, not of one hived-off aspect of myself.

Later I made a further switch, to being a psychoanalyst. For some time I was liable to feel embarrassed when my cricketing past was alluded to by new colleagues or teachers. But as I get older, in my recent books, and in the writing of this one, I have been aiming to integrate these various fields, to bring closer together body and mind.

CHAPTER 2

FOOT-HAT OR HEAD-SHOE?

At the University of Newcastle-upon-Tyne, where I lectured in philosophy for almost three years, students could apply to do philosophy either as a stand-alone subject or in combination with other disciplines. In my last year, the professor, Karl Britton, asked me to interview, with him, a girl from London who was applying for the combined course with English. She had had an interview with the professor of English Language, a somewhat formidable woman who would sometimes dissolve in giggles, as when she recalled a recipe from a southern state in the US that started 'Have them beat you twenty eggs'. The applicant was unusually free in her responses to our questions. Comparing impressions after the interview, we found we were both well-disposed to her application. Just then, someone brought a note from the English professor: the applicant was 'all over the place and very vague'. Karl read this, frowning, then said; 'But such a productive vagueness, don't you think?'

What a difference in response between the two professors! No doubt in order to study linguistics and Anglo-Saxon an attention to detail, clarity and a capacity for clear and systematic thinking are crucial, as indeed I would say they are for studying philosophy and literature. But what about the space for imagination, for wide-ranging responses?

I love the speeches by Theseus and his wife Hippolyta near the end of A *Midsummer Night's Dream*. Theseus:

> Lovers and madmen have such seething brains,
> Such shaping fantasies, that apprehend
> More than cool reason ever comprehends.
> The lunatic, the lover and the poet
> Are of imagination all compact . . .
>
> The poet's eye, in a fine frenzy rolling,
> Doth glance from heaven to earth, from earth to heaven;
> And as imagination bodies forth
> The forms of things unknown, the poet's pen
> Turns them to shapes and gives to airy nothing
> A local habitation and a name.

And Hippolyta responds:

> But all the story of the night told over,
> And all their minds transfigured so together,
> More witnesseth than fancy's images
> And grows to something of great constancy.

* * *

I could not have said this of the discursive girl from London (perhaps Karl couldn't have either); but we did have hopes for something along these lines. Fantasies may apprehend more than cool reason and maybe not just a matter of fanciful images, but of growth towards constancy.

Vagueness may of course be unproductive. It may be, as Rebecca Solnit, quoting George Orwell, points out, 'blurring, evasive, meandering, avoiding'. But, she continues, 'thinking can also be too tight, too restrictive in vocabulary and connotation, when some words have been murdered and others severed from too many of their associations'. While bringing 'airy nothings' down to earth, 'bodying forth the forms of things unknown', metaphors allude to points of similarity, but don't necessarily specify exactly what the comparison is. Vagueness includes open-endedness, a range of possible meanings. It may offer space for the conversation to continue in the mind and voice of the other. It is not prescriptive or autocratic.

* * *

After O-Levels I had to choose subjects for the sixth form. In those days options were clustered narrowly. Schools tended not make it possible to timetable students to do, say, maths and French, or biology and religion. We had to settle either for science or for the humanities. Conventionally successful students like myself had been placed in the A-stream. At my school, there were in the three years up to O-levels five such streams, A to E. In 3A we had to choose between German and (Ancient) Greek, to go alongside the compulsory French and Latin. There were sets for maths, and in the fifth form year those in the top set were automatically put in for 'Additional' maths O-level as well as for the ordinary maths exam. We did not do separate physics, chemistry and biology; rather we were entered for 'General Science', for which our teacher taught biology for 60 per cent of the time, chemistry for 30 per cent and physics for not much more than 10 per cent. We surmised that he found physics uncongenial if not incomprehensible.

Thus, science was valued less than other subjects; it was only in the B-stream that you would be taught and put in for exams in each of the three sciences separately. Knowledge of dead languages was regarded as loftier than learning to speak and read living ones. Economics was absent from our pre-sixth form curriculum: history (with the exception of Classical history) was peripheral; and art, music, woodwork and the like were totally ignored, except as extra-curricular activities for a few.

The priorities were in accordance with the value system of nineteenth-century public schools. Students regarded as at the top of the tree were guided towards the pure logic of mathematics or the allegedly impeccable logic of Greek and Latin grammar, languages which were often taught like crossword puzzles to be solved, with an emphasis on parsing, conjugations and declensions. Classics was put on a pedestal, suitable, it was still supposed, along with cricket, to be the ideal preparation for running an empire or for entering the high echelons of the Civil Service. This was the royal road to intellectual and moral superiority. I was encouraged, though not pushed, to go into the Classical sixth form.

My school, far from being one of the 'great' public schools, but with some pretentions in that direction, was, more modestly, a good day school. There, we imbibed the kind of values-hierarchy that put rule-based learning ahead of imagination and practicality, a system that might have been approved of by Thomas Arnold, the famous headmaster of Rugby school from 1828 to 1842.

Writer Meg Harris Williams scathingly labels Julius Caesar in Shakespeare's play 'head boy, cricket captain' someone whom people would 'applaud though he had stabbed their mothers, such is the absence of any emotional reality in this context'.

I, too, have long been sceptical about this kind of emphasis on a top-down paradigm of learning and rationality rather than bottom-up. But broader values were not entirely absent. One feature of my education that I am grateful for was that, in English classes from the second form to the fifth, the second term of each school year was devoted to the reading of Shakespeare.

Moreover, many teachers did their best to make use of their passions, humour and love of their fields. For example, Revd C.J. Ellingham, our 5A class teacher, used one of the four or five Greek lessons each week for what he called 'Boneheads' versus 'Numskulls'; he would provide cyclostyled scenes that he had written in a mix of pigeon Greek and real Greek, which appealed to our teenage sense of humour. A boy called 'Ware' appeared as 'Phylax', the Greek for guard, while my moniker was 'Bontose', B plus 'ontose', the Greek for really. I remember one such skit, the day after the speaker at our annual prize day, who had family connection with the founder of the Boy Scouts, Lord Baden-Powell, had encouraged us all to become leaders. The next morning, we were reading about Phylax asking, in Greek, 'But sir, if everyone is a leader, who will be there to be led?'

I could have followed my maths-teacher parents by going into the maths sixth. I think one reason I didn't was that I wanted to do my own thing, not my parents'. I suspect that I also knew I was only proficient at maths, not passionate or creative; and perhaps I had a dim recognition of classics as a study of whole civilisations.

So, there I was in the Classical Sixth, an elite group of five in our year (two in the year above). We became skilled at translating Tennyson (and suchlike) into Greek verse. We were good at the optative and could tell a pluperfect from an imperfect.

I remember once, influenced perhaps by Ellingham's playfulness and traces of delinquency, risking a foray into extravagance of thinking. After two years, as part of our A-level testing, we took an exam called 'S-level', 'S' standing for Scholarship, a general paper that involved (I'm fairly sure) writing two essays in a couple of hours from a range of topics. I could not see anything that I knew much about in this list. What I did was to write first about Scientific Research, which I parodied by talking about dissecting an apple and getting to the core of the subject; the second was to argue against 'Industrial degradation of the environment' (or some such title) by describing rural electricity pylons as forming a chain of lacy jewels that was an aesthetic improvement on mere nature. I got a distinction in that paper.

Six months later I won a scholarship to Cambridge, a place I had no connections to or knowledge of. But it sounded good, and the university cricket team played against the first-class counties! Stanley Ward encouraged me to apply to St John's, on the grounds that this college valued all sorts of qualities, not only narrowly academic ones like parsing Virgil or accelerating particles. He thought Cambridge would suit me better than Oxford. I later appreciated his recommendations and came to understand what he meant. Renford Bambrough, who became my supervisor at St John's, once joked that, when he was in Oxford, he knew what people at Bristol felt when they were in Cambridge. My probably prejudiced idea is that perhaps still today, Oxford people are more obviously intellectually clever, and more socially assured, than those brought up in the more earnest Cambridge atmosphere. Could the difference in tone go back to the English Civil War, when Oxford was Royalist, Cambridge Puritan?

As we had been well taught at school in what was then the current style, arriving at university was not all that different. There was a sense of carrying on, without too much strain.

For decades I regretted the years spent on languages that were no longer spoken, and though I never did much about rectifying the lack (apart from trying to teach myself German during my two terms in the third-year sixth form after having got into Cambridge), I bemoaned my inability to speak and read any living language with even modest competence.

My wife, however, has helped me to see my situation differently. Brought up in India and in UK, she speaks fluent Gujarati and English, plus good Hindi and a smattering of French. But she never learned Latin or Greek, or for that matter Sanskrit, and regrets it. She envies me my knowledge of Classical etymology and of parts of speech: split infinitives, ablative absolutes, hanging participles and so on. From various angles, I have come closer to her view.

* * *

Probably inevitably, and perhaps necessarily, some of the teaching was a bit dull and mechanical. But I am now more inclined to think that what I should have been critical of was not the teachers but myself. I was not capable of going far in the direction of productive vagueness or the 'bodying forth of imagination'.

I find it hard to remember much of my life during the sixth form years, when I was aged sixteen to eighteen. I have a curious little problem these days that may or may not be relevant: when doing exercises and keeping track of how many I've done of each, I find that my silent counting goes: 'fifteen, sixteen, eighteen, nineteen…' I wonder if this jumping over 'seventeen' represents an elision of experience of what should have been an intense period of my life. That year or two seems to me now a somewhat closed book, an empty time, except to some extent with regard to sport.

I played for the rugby First XV for my last three years at school, as full-back or fly half. In my second game I broke my collar bone; the rugby master told me to circle my arms above my head and sent me back on the field. In my last year, I was a triallist and reserve for Middlesex schools. At Eton Fives, I was in the first pair, but disappointed the Fives master, Tom Manning, and the Head, by insisting on running in the House Cross Country on the day before we played against Eton, and then losing 3-2 after being 2-0 up. In 1959 I scored over one thousand runs for the school, including five centuries, though I can remember hardly any details.

I'm often asked how I remember incidents, passages of play, and sometimes scores from individual cricket matches over my career. I might remember a match where I was out for nought but not one in which I scored a century; or a match when we lost but not ones that we won. And sometimes what I remember is a single incident or delivery, but nothing else about the match at all – in these last cases, there may well be an emotional significance in the salient detail; in other cases, memory and forgetting seem more fickle, more random.

Recently I was surprised by being able to remember nothing of a particular match. In a WhatsApp group organised by Pat Pocock, who played for Surrey and England, Tim Lamb commented on a match he played in between Hampshire and Middlesex at Southampton in 1975. Barry Richards, he said, had played two wonderful innings of 59 and 70 not out on a spinner's pitch, against Fred Titmus and Phil Edmonds. 'Brears,' he added, 'will remember the match, which Middlesex won'. Being unable to recall ever playing at Southampton, let alone Richards's innings, I looked up the scorecard of the game. It turned out that I'd scored 70 and 114 not out in the match, and we had indeed won, by 135 runs. Nothing was jogged by the scorecard either.

Perhaps, I thought, I'm more likely to remember games in which individually and as a team we failed (just as bad reviews of books are sometimes more memorable than favourable ones). But no, I don't think so. In *Wisden* I now find the scores of a game Middlesex played a week or so after the victory at Southampton, at Old Trafford against Lancashire. We were beaten by eight wickets, and I scored a mere 13 and 20. I can remember nothing whatsoever about this match either.

There are of course events all those years ago that I do recall in detail, as my questioners implied. Some of them were themselves memorable, because of their high prestige or because of significant achievements or failures, But, as with family memories, another factor in my remembering them is that I and others have told the story repeatedly, and on occasion written about them. The question arises: do I remember the events themselves, or the events as reconstructed in the telling? Our grandchildren report with a pleasurable sense of participation that as babies or toddlers they refused to eat or got sick in the car; they speak as if they are remembering the event itself, but it seems more likely that what they so vividly describe is the story as they imagined it on being told it by their parents. I'm not sure which is the case with, for instance, my own 'memories', or 'imagined constructions', of having dreamt of tigers as a small boy, and standing up in bed rigid with terror.

Memories of Test matches are on the whole more authentic, but one factor is the writing them up that has contributed to making them features of my personal past. Every four years, when home Ashes series occur, I'm likely to be asked, by cricket writers and others, to provide old memories as if they are newly minted, or never before revealed. People are keen to hear from the horses' mouths what playing in these matches, that form part of cricket's tradition, mean and meant to past participants. The request feels sometimes like being wheeled out as a relic to carry a banner in this glorious pageant!

*   *   *

One of the classics dons in my college was Guy Lee, who taught Latin poetry. I think his way of thinking was too far ahead of me with my restricted literalness. John Crook, who taught classical history, was quirky, down-to-earth, and interested in social history. He wanted us to think for ourselves, including entering into the question what life was like in Rome, Athens or Sparta. He once wrote a comment on an essay of mine (on Theophrastus's *Characters*, I recall) that the content was as shallow as the writing style. But he also told me that he hoped I would get a first-class degree along with several 'Blues'.

My most striking memory of the concrete thinking that I was stuck in occurred in my second year. One morning, I emerged from the Mill Lane lecture rooms into bright sunlight. But I was in the dark. The lecturer has just suggested that 'beauty lies in the eye of the beholder'. A cornea, an iris, a pupil, a mote of dust, all these are indeed 'in' an eye. But beauty is not to be discovered by any microscope. I now find it hard to admit, even to believe, that I found this remark so hard to understand.

Years later I was able to figure out that a patient of mine had a particular unconscious view of emotions. She had the idea that they are like liquids, material substances, the use of which depletes one's store. For her, therefore, being emotionally generous risked running out of her precious stock of emotional resources, especially of love; and receiving love was like robbing someone else of theirs. She had to ration herself in both giving and receiving. Perhaps I had a similar 'theory'.

I also recall learning about, and recognising, concreteness of thought when reading in Homer of gods occupying people's bodies. Early in the *Odyssey*, the goddess Athena visits Odysseus's son Telemachus, who had been an infant when his father sailed off to Troy, leaving wife and son in Ithaca. Telemachus is now twenty-one. Suitors are besieging his mother and their home, rather as the Greeks besieged Troy. Athena, assuming the shape or likeness of Odysseus's old friend, Mentes, advises Telemachus to take a stand against the suitors. The goddess reinforces her influence later, taking the form of another man, with the similar name, 'Mentor', and recommending the young man to go to Nestor in Pylos and Menelaus in Sparta to enquire if they have any news of his father. The goddess strengthens Telemachus' self-confidence so that he can act as a worthy and active representative of his father.

Religious language exists at different levels of literalness. How did Homer, how did later Greeks, how do we, understand this idea of the gods' embodiment? Presumably there was a time when most people believed in such impersonations in a literal sense: that an actual deity took on the shape of living men, as when 'mentoring' the young Telemachus through the mouths of mortals. Later, perhaps there was an intermediate stage in which there was some ambiguity about what the writer was claiming about the material or metaphorical status of this kind of divine embodiment by a god or goddess. Later still, the story is understood in an 'as-if' sense: it is *as if* the caring fatherly help in Telemachus' growing to manhood was divine; perhaps it may even come from a masculine side of the feminine (Athena). Today, the story appeals to us in a purely metaphorical form; it has become a dramatic way of speaking of a change of heart, a growth of maturity. Running through all the versions, the words of the two mentors point to a transformative process going on within Telemachus.

It was through classics that my interest in metaphor and the opening up of my capacity for imagination (such as it is) began. 'All the story of the night told over . . . More witnesseth than fancy's images / And grows to something of great constancy.' Productive vagueness became more possible.

* * *

Another aspect of my journey towards a less literal-minded sense of things had some beginnings in the Classics. First came the recognition that the etymology of many English words is to be found in Latin or Greek. The word that comes most vividly to mind is 'supercilious', which derives from the Latin word for eyebrow. I love the image of a quizzically lifted or twisted eyebrow indicating disdain and arrogance.

These days I think of language itself as metaphor, with a range of applications. First there is the idea that language is a matter of putting something outside ourselves (by speaking) and also (as in hearing) taking in to ourselves; acquiring a new mode of 'taking in' – truth as food for the mind – and expressing – we express love or hate in words. Everyone understands the phrase 'shit-scared'. Words have an advantage over actions, avoiding physical injury or mess, and also being able to convey in more complex ways (articulately, that is, with joints – *artos* means joint in Greek) –what was once crudely expressed by a blow or a kiss. ('Sticks and stones may break my bones, but words will never break me'.)

Language may be thought of as carrying across by means of words what had previously been conveyed by physical somatic action. How we walk, our gait, may also tell people something deeper about our minds. Some meander through life, taking in the scenery, living out the message of the poem by W. H. Davies that starts: 'What is this life if, full of care, / We have no time to stand and stare.' (This reminds me of Henry James's 'gaping and idling'.) Some people march straight ahead, leading with their heads, driving themselves on, conveying that nothing will stop them. Others lurch from side to side, or sway seductively. One of the most painful descriptions of me during my cricketing days was that my walk was 'mincing'. I heard and still think of this as a comment on my personality, that in the eyes of this observer I was precious, small-minded and dainty. 'Mac', my honorary godmother, nicknamed me 'Baby Elephant' when I was eight or nine. I prefer to come across as the Saggy Baggy Elephant than the Mincing Mannikin. Many psychological terms derive from physical ones: 'understand' which is not always merely a matter of intellect but of bearing up, supporting; 'manipulate' which originally meant to handle with dexterity. (The list could be extended almost indefinitely.)

This links too with the notion of play. With my first granddaughter, Alia, we 'turned' the living room into a 'beach', called 'Ya Beach', where magical things could happen, starting with swimming and the creatures to be found in the sea. From being merely a prosaic 'room with two sofas', the space was turned into this magical place, 'Ya Beach'.

Second, individual uses of language involve the notion of carrying across, 'trans-lating'. As children grow, they start extending the application of words from the mother and other carers to people removed from them. They find in a favourite teacher an adored temporary substitute for mother. This is part of the process of becoming more social and more independent. And they extend their concepts.

Our granddaughter Lila, aged two, using for the first time a floating aid, said, 'Mummy, I'm cycling in the water.' Alia, just beginning to speak as a toddler, was getting dressed to go out on a winter's morning. She picked up one of her shoes and said 'foot-hat'. Analogical, creative thinking occurred in this recognition of a function or process common to shoes and hats, that of covering and protecting. She might with equal creativity have pointed at her hat and called it a head-shoe. Alia shows how words can have their uses extended.

Metaphors may either be dead, dying or alive. A dead, or near-dead, metaphor would be 'the ship ploughed the sea'. The phrase is so old, so much a *façon de parler*, that it is hardly likely to convey much more than 'makes its way through'. Dreams sometimes perform the function of bringing metaphors back to life. It is as if the regressed self (in sleep or in playful speech), hits on old metaphors to express deeper meanings. For example, I once dreamt of myself *driving a big truck, and coming to a T-junction. I didn't know whether to turn right or left.* The context of the dream made it clear that the dream was saying that I had a difficult decision to take and didn't know which way to 'turn'. (I once treated a taxi driver who, when trying to put into words an emotional problem, would physically change his posture, at the same time moving his hands and arms as if making a U-turn in his taxi.)

Metaphor can be conscious and playful. A colleague, Kannan Navaratnem, tells me a story from the early 1980s, when he was first getting interested in psychoanalysis. He was making his way to the old Institute of Psychoanalysis building, Mansfield House, in New Cavendish Street, London. Mistakenly, he entered the twin-building next door. He asked the rather grand, but quickly understanding, commissionaire whether he was in the right place. 'No', came the friendly reply; 'This is the Institute of Petroleum. Your place is next door.' Kindly escorting him to the right place, he added: 'They do a bit of digging there, too'.

The commissionaire knew the difference between literal and metaphorical digging, and clearly respected the latter kind. The metaphor for him was still alive. As for dead metaphors, we can 'breathe life back into them'.

Metaphors may also convey a rich range of possible meanings. Ernest Hemingway's *Old Man and the Sea*, in which the old man has to go far out to sea to pull in a huge marlin, which he then ties to his boat, describes the sharks repeatedly plundering his catch, ramming the carcass and the boat in their feeding frenzy. By the time he manages to get back to the shore, the magnificent marlin has been reduced to a battered skeleton. Part of the story's power is the range of possible meanings it suggests. At one level, it is a simple story about an old man and his loss of potency. More broadly, it suggests the pathos of human endeavour; our hard-won achievements do not last and are not recognised (or not for long). The story makes us feel the heroism involved in his 'failure'. It may strike us as even more poignantly autobiographical; had Hemingway created an analogy for the fate of his own endeavours? The sharks may be the critics and others who ram his achievements, and/or the self-inflicted depredations on his wellbeing as a result of drink and omnipotence.

* * *

Nowadays I give greater place to the fact that doing Classics at school and university introduced me, via the history of Greece and Rome, to debates about democracy, slavery, empire and tyranny, and to discussion of some of these themes in drama too. We read Aeschylus, Sophocles and Euripides; I remember the horror of Agamemnon's death at the hands of his wife Clytemnestra and her lover Aegisthus, and of the revenge murder of Clytemnestra by her son Orestes, with the help of his sister Electra, and the subsequent debates about whether revenge is ever justified. We read in *Alcestis* about a young woman who allows herself to be sacrificed so that her husband Admetos could live. Most vividly of all, I recall Sophocles' trilogy, which starts with Oedipus, king of Thebes, initiating an investigation into the question: 'Who by his sins has brought drought and blight to the city-state?' By the end of this investigation, it has become plain even to Oedipus himself that he himself is the man, having killed his father and married his mother. She, Jocasta, hangs herself, and he blinds himself with the brooch on her dress. In the second play, Antigone, one of his daughters, accompanies him to Colonus, near Athens, where he has a religious conversion. In the last of the three, Antigone, in burying the body of one of her brothers who had been killed in the civil war that followed this turbulence, has disobeyed the edict of her uncle, Creon, and later hangs herself.

Classical studies may in some ways have been too much like exercises in grammar and composition, but they contained underlying violence, passion and debate.

During one university long vacation, two friends and I drove to Greece in a Mini. A few days after reaching Greece, we took a boat to the island of Skiathos. We walked from the harbour along a cliff path to a smaller town to find a place to stay. The sun was hot, and the sea as still as a mirror. I remember saying that it was difficult imagining anyone drowning here. That evening we went back to the town for supper, sitting in a café on the terrace looking out onto the wide harbour. Suddenly there was a kerfuffle, an atmosphere of drama and agitation with people standing up, staring out on to the water. A few minutes later, a middle-aged man, dressed in working clothes, arrived and told the crowd what had happened; apparently a boat from the warship anchored in the harbour at a distance from the shore had capsized, two sailors (who, amazingly, could not swim) had got into trouble. They were being rushed to a doctor. One died. The man spoke with passion and drama, not that I could understand his words, of course. But I was struck how the Messenger in ancient

Greek plays must have created an atmosphere as electric as this dramatic storyteller, with his utterly gripping, intense and powerful rhetoric. For me, Sophocles and the other dramatists were brought to life in a new way.

* * *

Another reason I now feel grateful for having studied the classics is that it was through this route that I made, or found, my way to philosophy.

I recall two lecturers within the Classics department who taught philosophy. John Raven lectured on the pre-Socratic philosophers. He had a saturnine look, unmoving with his statuesque pale face and raven-black hair. I think he viewed the pre-Socratics as a rather odd lot. He spoke, drily, about Heraclitus' view that one cannot step into the same river twice. He quoted an obscure remark from the same philosopher: 'it is a pleasure to souls to be wet'. My incomprehension about this wetness was no doubt largely due to my limitations, but it was not, as far as I can remember, addressed, let alone dissipated, by the lecturer. Looking back now, and reading some of Heraclitus' other fragments, I see the remark as part of an attempt to give a psychological account of human nature, and of the conflict between pleasures of the senses and intellectual delight. Drunkenness may be a – wet – pleasure of souls, but such pleasure is bought at a cost. The drunkard can't think straight and is prone to stumble. He has to be led by a boy. His self-control has been dampened, weakened. Soul, the seat of reason, is more like fire – mobile, perhaps, and warm. Fire is put out by water. Raven was dry, but scarcely fiery.

A very different experience came from Bambrough, who also taught ancient philosophy in the Classics Department. It was my good fortune that he was a Fellow of St John's; as a result, I had two or three supervisions or seminars with him for this part of the

Classics syllabus, and later much closer contact. Unlike Raven, who was a historian of ideas, Renford was a real philosopher, who made sense of the strange questions, and even stranger answers, that many philosophers raise. He showed how the pre-Socratics, for example, arrived at their obscure and sometimes apparently paradoxical utterings. And there was vastly more to be said about Socrates, Plato and Aristotle.

Bambrough's clarity and care, and the kind of philosophy he understood, gave me the idea that maybe this subject would help clear away the clouds of my confusion, epitomised by my bewilderment about the nature of beauty. I may well have been disabused of this particular bafflement fairly quickly, but it shows not only my intellectual naivety, but also how concrete my thinking was. 'In', as in 'in the eye of the beholder', had to have exactly sense it has when we say there are beans *in* A can. My mind was a can of worms. Bambrough was a major factor in my beginning to consider a shift to philosophy.

Another nudge came from a fellow undergraduate, Edward Craig. We had been playing cricket together for Cambridge since our first year. In that season, I kept wicket, while he was the regular fielder alongside me at slip. He was already reading philosophy, or 'Moral Sciences' as it was called. Having plenty of time fielding, often without too much to do, he and I were able to have conversations about philosophy, or rather one or other of us would ask or quote naive, sceptical questions, and he would report some of the answers that were on offer. For instance, we can only really know with certainty the contents of our own minds, all else is inference without certainty (solipsism). Or: we can never know the mind of another person, all we can know is their behaviour or their bodily reactions (behaviourism). Ethics and aesthetics are purely subjective, and religion is either nonsensical – there being no method of verifying the existence of God(s) – or meaningful only in a reduced sense.

Or, ethical statements are merely expressions of feeling or 'persuasive definitions'. And so on.

I found these ideas provocative and fascinating. Like Renford, Edward was a good teacher, whose career culminated in his being the Knightsbridge Professor of Philosophy at Cambridge. He introduced me into the sorts of arguments that people were putting forward in his seminars and reading.

After that summer term when I had my taster in Greek philosophy, and having taken the Part One Classics tripos, I decided to change subjects for Part Two. To be fair to myself, I think there was a real curiosity as well as this element of game-playing. There was an effort to get to some of those 'more things in heaven and earth' not (yet) dreamed of by Horatio.

Classics has, then, been for me not only a setting for mere cleverness, for following rules, for producing things to please teachers or markers, it has also been, in the longer run, and perhaps always to some degree, a setting-off point for layered thinking and for appreciating and using language in ways that are both vague and productive. As I said, as indeed Orwell said, there is unproductive vagueness, but there is also dried out precision. We need both ways of thinking. Vagueness and precision, wide focus and narrow.

CHAPTER 3

MORE THINGS IN HEAVEN AND EARTH

In my last year at school, I played Horatio in the school play. Hamlet, by the way, was played by John Shrapnel, who was already in the National Youth Theatre and later became a leading actor, while Michael Apted was Claudius. I kept in touch with both until their recent deaths. I miss them. Shrapnel came to City of London School for the sixth form, along with others from the Mercers' School, which had, in 1959, just closed down. I was in awe of his father, who wrote on politics and social affairs for the *Guardian*. Apted and I arrived at the school on the same day, aged eleven and ten, from opposite ends of the District line, and were in the same class.

I had played one or two tiny parts in previous years – as a Christian in Shaw's *Androcles and the Lion*, as the traitor Sir Thomas Grey and the Duc d'Orléans in *Henry V*, and as Hermia in a short extract from *A Midsummer Night's Dream*, minor roles that reflected the fact that my talent for acting was yet to be detected.

My first foray into acting was when I was eight. In a skit also scripted and directed by three of us boys, we played a comedy in which two boxers are fighting. The literal punch line, which we thought was hilarious, occurs when one boxer ducks, and the referee (played by me) gets punched, laid out and carried off. Shortly after the school *Hamlet*, I was involved in a similar exercise, when a small group of us cast, rehearsed, negotiated with the Guildhall School of Music and Drama who kindly allowed us to use their theatre, and put on for at least two performances *The Frogs* by Aristophanes (in English). I remember a moment in the first performance, when I got a gesture and timing right, and there was a ripple of laughter from the audience; this was wonderful. When, however, I tried to copy this moment in the second show, it all fell flat. I learned from this, if I hadn't known it before, that I was not destined to be an actor, and how hard it is to achieve a repeated impression of naturalness.

In the early 1980s, I joined a neighbour, Ken Ellis, who invented and ran 'Tube Theatre'; he and others would create a minor stir in a tube train, and innocently improvise an ensuing scene. Later still, Ian Rickson, an excellent director, discussed some of his productions with me, and invited me to attend (and contribute thoughts to) rehearsals with the cast. I loved this, and learned how hard actors work at their characters and at mutual interactions. Rickson used table tennis as a warm up, and as an aid to cooperation and quickness of uptake. He got the actors to try out, in many different ways, different ideas. I was privileged to be included.

To return to the school production of *Hamlet*: I imagine my being cast as Horatio was in part a joke and tease of my father, called Horace, sometimes referred to as 'Horatio', who was a colleague and friend of Geoffrey Clark, the director of the school plays. The reference to Horatio that I have been struck by ever since is Hamlet's saying to him: 'There are more things in heaven and earth, Horatio, / Than are dreamt of in your philosophy.' Was this a comment directed both at my father and me? I was, as people told me, a 'chip off the old block'. I find it illuminating and amusing to think of Clark playing with what he no doubt knew about both of us at that time.

The actual Horace was a down-to-earth Yorkshireman who had little time for castles in the air, especially religious ones. He described himself as agnostic, but was at the atheistic end of that spectrum. Nevertheless, decades later, when I was training to be a psychoanalyst, he asked me for something to read in the field. His comment on the book I gave him as a taster (Klein's *Envy and Gratitude*) was 'She does seem to be rather sure of herself.' I suspect he found it unduly speculative, but I was grateful to him for taking it, and me, seriously.

I find much to value in his orientation, but was apprehensive of his scorn for what he regarded as sentimental, fanciful or irrational.

So, whenever I had a hankering after any of the 'more things in heaven and earth' I was nervous. As a twelve-year-old, for instance, I was fascinated (and embarrassed about my fascination) by TV coverage of the American evangelist Billy Graham, with his fervent perorations and expression of conviction to large crowds at Wembley Stadium. He said he was more certain that he would go to heaven than he was of standing there in front of the audience, adding that teams of horses, whether actual horses or metaphorical ones, could not have dragged him from his position. I remember feeling a sort of awe at such hyperbolical belief. How could that degree of passion be based on a delusion? Now I know better. 'The best lack all conviction, while the worst / Are full of passionate intensity,' Yeats wrote.

As a child, I would occasionally go to the local Methodist church, prompted on Low Church high-feast occasions by my mother, though I managed to get out of Sunday school in order to play games of cricket or football on the street outside our house or by the River Brent, or watch my father at play. The Christianity I was exposed to seemed, or seems in retrospect, milk and water, comforting rather than challenging. I don't remember being afraid of God, or his judgement.

My mother was nervous about strong opinion or histrionic behaviour. Soon after the school *Hamlet*, Clark invited some of the cast to his house for supper. We listened to the tape of the play, and, feeling important, stayed until the early hours drinking and talking.

45

Our teacher drove us home to various parts of London in his Jaguar. As it happened, I was the last to be dropped off, and when we arrived at my home in Ealing, dawn had arrived and my parents were already up, preparing to drive for their Easter holiday to Cornwall. The melodramatic Geoffrey wanted to kiss my mother in apology for making her anxious for my wellbeing. As he approached her, she backed away round the table.

My mother felt more comforted by the idea of everlasting reassurance than by this too-pressing attempt by Geoffrey Clark to relieve his guilt.

At fourteen or fifteen I decided to be confirmed, a ceremony that took place in St Paul's Cathedral, the school's 'local' church. The preparation was done by the headmaster, Dr A. W. Barton, a man who held rigidly and without humour to certainties in many areas of life. (Refereeing a rugby match for the Under 14s against St Dunstan's School, he ruled my attempted dropped goal valid, when I could clearly see it to have missed the outside of the post. When I hesitantly told him it missed, he ordered me not to argue with the referee.) In the confirmation classes, I remember only one detail: he told us bluntly that Jesus Christ was 'either the Son of God, or the greatest megalomaniac the world has ever known'. Take your pick! A menacing sort of message, I felt – and feel now – in that one is either in touch with the truth or deluded (though I have to admit that Jesus did make quite a claim).

But there were other, more subtle, more benign influences. Whenever, in the absence of Barton, Mr Nobbs, the deputy head and also head of Maths, took Assembly, the prayer he read out (after the Jewish boys had trooped out for their own ceremonies) was the one that reminds us that: 'We have erred and strayed from thy ways like lost sheep. We have followed too much the devices and desires of our own hearts. We have left undone those things which we ought to have done; and we have done those things which we ought not to have done. And there is no health in us. But thou, oh Lord, have mercy upon us, miserable offenders.'

I recall this not only with admiration for the language of the Prayer Book, and for Mr Nobbs's appropriately sepulchral intonation, but also, as with the prayer, for the reference to sin or error, to the incisive 'devices and desires', to repentance, and to the possibility of and hope for forgiveness – prominent features of Christianity. Jesus chose as his disciples not wealthy, respectable Pharisees and Sadducees, but fishermen and doubters; he shocked many by the company he kept, the poor, prostitutes, refugees, whose feet he washed.

* * *

In my first year at Cambridge, Martin Smith and I found ourselves in neighbouring rooms. He had been the winner of the public schools racquets competition. As a doctor, he would become Medical Director of the Royal Surrey County Hospital in Guildford, in which role he was described as being a 'steadying presence' which 'belied his ferocious competitiveness'. Through Martin I met Revd Edward Maycock, vicar of Little St Mary's Church on Trumpington Street. For perhaps a year, I went to services there, partly because the building was so beautiful, as were the priestly garments and the stained glass windows, and above all for the plainsong, which I was hearing for the first time. The idea of organised religion as offering a sort of aesthetic meditation on the potential beauty of life was perhaps dimly glimpsed by the young me.

Playing bridge with Smith, Maycock and the Bishop of Ely, gave me an insight into clerical competitiveness. But between hands, Maycock told an enigmatic story from the time of the Second World War. His brother was in West Africa. For some days, Edward was unaccountably anxious and depressed. His thoughts went to this brother. He was unable to reach him by telephone. When, a fortnight later, he got through, he learned that his brother was just beginning to recover from blackwater fever, from which he had nearly died. He saw this as evidence of supernatural communication. I didn't know what to make of it. Thirty years on, when my daughter Lara was thirteen, I witnessed a similar event. Gautam, her maternal grandfather, at his home in India, was due to phone us back at the hotel, where the three of us had been for twenty-four hours at the start of a week's holiday in Corsica. They had been chatting but at great expense, all this occurring long before mobile phones and WhatsApp. He said he would phone back in a few minutes. In the meantime, Lara took a shower. When she came out, she was sobbing uncontrollably. She didn't know why, but she had never felt like this before; it was 'as if there was no meaning in anything'. Just then, Gautam's sister phoned; he had collapsed and died a few minutes before, presumably while Lara was in her shower. There was no sign, as far as we knew, of a weak heart or of ongoing illness. I still don't know what to make of such coincidences, if that is what they are.

In the Classical Sixth Form, we read, stumblingly, several books of the *Iliad* and the *Odyssey*. The *Iliad* starts with the line 'I tell the anger of Achilles.' Achilles, we learn, insulted by Agamemnon, the commander-in-chief who stole his concubine Briseis, has taken umbrage (and vengeance) by withdrawing himself and his troops from the campaign to destroy Troy. By Book 9, his refusal to fight has led, along with the dastardly machinations of Zeus, to near-disaster for the Greeks. Defeat looks imminent. The Greek leaders meet to persuade Agamemnon to make amends for his greedy and foolish treatment of Achilles, in effect to apologise in word and deed. Agamemnon agrees, offering not only Briseis, but also gold, tripods, horses, even the right to choose one of his daughters as a wife. The delegation visits Achilles to persuade him to come back to fight, on these terms. Three men plead with him to do so. Achilles refuses. He says he can see their point, but the rage that occupies his chest (like an alien entity) is so strong that he cannot and will not be appeased. At the end of the speeches, he makes one small concession: if the Trojans get to his own ships, he will re-join the Greek forces. Until such time, he will continue to 'sulk with Patroclus in his tent'.

One of the delegates, Phoenix, a man who had been ejected by his own father and brought up like a son by Achilles' father, Peleus, makes a more thoughtful point. Rage, arrogance and stubbornness are, he says, follies or sins. Even the gods change their minds. Given Agamemnon's ample restitution, the gracious thing would be to accept, and thus be reunited with and fight alongside his erstwhile comrades and friends. For, Phoenix continues, 'Sin goes racing around the world doing harm, while Prayer, represented by the daughters of Zeus, old, lame and half-blind, follows them at a distance, trying to catch up and put things right.' (I like Basil Hume's parallel remark, 'You know more than you understand. Understanding comes slowly, trailing behind knowledge.')

In 1957, Stanley Ward had recently arrived at the school as head of Classics. He was a small, shy man with a warm smile. My strongest memory of his teaching was his inviting us to reflect on the moral development expressed in Phoenix's argument. We often do commit wrongs by rushing into action without thinking. We are hasty and unreasonable. Our first instinct in response to humiliation is to retaliate or run away. Only later, Ward suggested, do we have second thoughts and stirrings of conscience about our over-the-top reactions, and climb down from our high horses. Like the daughters of Zeus, we find it hard to see what we've been doing, we're slow to give a hearing to these more reason-based responses. Homer, through Phoenix, proposes a shift from a notion of prayer as purely self-serving: the prevalent form of prayer in Homer – '*Do ut des*', Latin for 'I give [to you, gods] in order that you give to me', a kind of contract of appeasement between gods and men – is replaced here by an idea of prayer as a form of reparation through the work of conscience. This was a moral leap.

Indeed, it now makes me wonder if Homer had read Klein, for whom one important shift is from the paranoid-schizoid position (in which difficulties are entirely someone else's fault) to a depressive position (where guilt and responsibility may be felt and reparation made). Not that this is all that is invoked in Phoenix's moral arguments, for he adds that such a shift is in itself a healthier and more satisfying state of mind; if Achilles were to act in this way, he would himself be better off in the long run, not least because of his enhanced wealth and prestige.

I'm interested that this story has remained with me. Out of all the hours of Classical and other studies, why does this moment and idea stand out? One reason may have been that I sensed Stanley Ward's own passion and conviction. I learned not long ago, after his death, that after retiring as a teacher he trained and worked as a parson. But another factor may have been that it was for me a sort of memoir of the future, a hint of what would become important to me later. Not so much the religious part, though that was there too, but I appear to have been ready to give house-room to the psychological and moral point of the story. We easily become unforgiving. In religious language, we are closed to the path of repentance. The daughters of Zeus are often lame and blind, and we are too impatient to take them seriously. Indeed, in these post-modern or post-post-modern times, with their overvaluation of subjectivity, reminders from Phoenix and the daughters are timely. We are all liable, like Achilles, to remain stubborn.

In 2008, a Christian prayer reminded me of all this. I went to the funeral of my good friend, Dudley Doust. I was amazed at the end of the service, at St Leonard's Church, Butleigh, Somerset, to hear a prayer in which God is represented as a super-psychoanalyst.

Here it is:

Intimate God,
You are able to accept in us
What we cannot even acknowledge;
You have named in us
What we cannot bear to speak of;
You hold in your memory
What we have tried to forget;
You will hold out to us
A glory we cannot imagine.
Reconcile us through your cross
To all that we have rejected in ourselves,
That we may find no part of your creation
To be alien or strange to us.
And that we ourselves may be made whole,
Through Jesus Christ, our lover and our friend

I found out where it comes from – Revd Stephen Wilson, SSC (the Society of the Holy Cross), told me that it is printed in a supplementary volume of *Common Worship* entitled *Pastoral Services*. Wilson added that 'the standard of content and style of the material in *Common Worship* is, in the opinion of many, high . . . Some may feel that departures from this such as "Intimate God" are liable to seem contrived and mawkish.' I don't agree. The God addressed in this prayer is strikingly different from the jealous God of the Old Testament. He is, one might say, more humane, even, more human.

Phrases from the Bible come back to me, especially comments and parables referring to hypocrisy and to the conflicts between the outer and the inner person. Jesus often emphasised how having the right spirit should trump ritual and law, as when he proposed that 'the Sabbath is made for man, not man for the Sabbath', and how 'spirit' should be given its proper domain when he advised people to 'render unto Caesar the things which are Caesar's, render unto God the things which are God's'. He often criticised those mysterious Pharisees and Sadducees for legalistic self-righteousness. When he was provokingly invited to throw the first stone at the woman taken in adultery, his response, after giving himself time to think by bending down and writing in the dust, was both shrewd and humane: 'Let him who is without sin cast the first stone.' On adultery again: 'Whosoever looketh on a woman to lust after her hath committed adultery with her already in his heart', thus drawing attention to the continuity between wish and act, without either condoning the act or denying the important differences between fantasy and action. Jesus was notorious for consorting with the down-and-out, and with outsiders (like the Samaritans). He could be tough; famously turning over the tables of the merchants doing business in the courtyard of the Temple at the time of Passover, accusing them of being a den of thieves in their unbridled commercialism.

Hypocrisy, according to La Rochefoucauld, is 'the tribute vice pays to virtue'. It is a nice question whether we are better off with or without it. Without it we might be more cynical, disengaged or corrupt; with it we lose our authenticity and risk becoming sanctimonious.

Such universal messages strike me as moral and psychological, not specifically religious. They are also examples of Jesus' professed aim: 'To fulfil the law, not to abolish it.' That is, in putting at the top of his agenda a recognition not only of unworthy actions, but of the reality and importance for us all of empathy and a questioning of ourselves, he was filling out the notion of moral law.

These comments reveal too his opposition to the views of fundamentalism of many kinds. Jesus repudiated the views of those who, relying on ancient precedent and prejudice, insisted on the letter of the law. His stance is not specifically Christian, nor is it omniscient or megalomaniac. It is down-to-earth, in the spirit of tough love.

* * *

As for formal religion, despite Billy Graham and his fervour, I have never been a believer in the supernatural. I have come down on my father's side on these ontological questions, but I think that religion is one mode of raising deep psychological questions and enquiry into whether and how life has meaning.

Of course, I wished things might be as Graham asserted with such confidence, that there might be 'underneath, the everlasting arms' of a God who 'sees the meanest sparrow fall'; that something bigger lies behind, that there are things in heaven that give significance to life here on earth; and what's more, that life on earth is not all there is but a preparation for resurrection after bodily death.

I'm also aware that belief in God is often determined by one's broad culture, and by more familial influences. For many centuries, perhaps even for millennia, belief in God, or gods, went virtually unquestioned. Today, we have grounds for assuming that in the so-called Western world, most people, especially the long-educated, would describe themselves as agnostic, even if in times of crisis they call, outwardly or inwardly, for help from God – it was said that there were not many atheists on the Western Front in the First World War.

As for family influences, two stories come to mind. One was told me by Harold Stewart, a psychoanalyst who supervised my work and became a friend. In hospital not long before he died, he talked about occasions when as a young boy he was allowed to join his father at meetings of Jewish men held in a room in the East End of London. My impression is that even though the men wore prayer shawls, they spoke not only about obviously religious but also of many other matters. Harold conveyed a sense of belonging and a seriousness of engagement that he was drawn to all his life. This represented an important part of his Jewish identity.

Another friend, whom I knew through cricket, Michael Melluish, once told me that when he was a young boy growing up in Surrey, he and his father used to ride to church on horseback, tying up their horses to the churchyard railings. I joked with him that I couldn't think of a better argument for the existence of God; it was not entirely a joke.

As for me, I see religion as raising and keeping in front of us eschatological questions. Religion offers a framework in which to talk and think about mortality. The idea of God as the 'ground of our being' is a way of emphasising values and the inner life, reminding us of a world where love has a central place, encouraging a frame of mind in which there are grounds for hope and for belief in something good, in life having meaning. Many religious people would find my view reductive. But talk of life after death in any literal sense strikes me as magical thinking. I like the slogan of the charity Christian Aid: 'We believe in life before death'. Despite the air of paradox, we might paraphrase this as, 'I believe in life after death before death' – in other words, the first 'death' in the sentence means living death, deathliness, deadliness, while the second refers to becoming a corpse.

*　*　*

It is hard to know how to understand the writing of some religious visionaries, people who have experienced trances, who write in mystical terms, often with vivid imagery. One such man was Ezekiel. Exiled to Babylon after the fall of Jerusalem in the early sixth century BCE, he raises the question: 'Can these white bones live?' and answers it in the affirmative. Where there's life there's hope, we say. But is there hope beyond death?

There are many ways of understanding Ezekiel's question and his response to it. His writing is obscure, powerful and disturbing. He reports visions, including the one about the valley of bones. But what did he mean by these stories? How are we to view them?

54

There is a range of possible readings. First, he may have been referring to a literal resurrection; that the dead human bones lying in the grave will be reconstructed, clothed again in actual flesh, covered in skin, imbued with breath. After all, religious people have believed, and many still believe, in the resurrection of the body. Or, second, is his intention purely metaphorical? Is he saying that our deadly ennui or our life-inhibiting guilt may be repaired, that we may have a change of heart, that the spirit of life may be revived from the depths of despair? Is his 'vision' of the dead bones reanimated thus to be thought of as a creative, imaginative dream? A third interpretation falls between the two extremes – that there is a mysterious force that comes from an outside reality, a God or spirit, which breathes into us a divine spark? And a fourth: Ezekiel might interject, 'Please don't ask that question' – rather as we don't ask of the toddler's transitional object, their rag or doll, whether it is objective or subjective. For Donald Winnicott, this transitional space is the fluid base for cultural life, with its creative use of illusion, where new realities are invented/ discovered. Finally, a fifth possibility is that he is out of contact with reality, like the man who confessed that he had to be terribly careful about what he thought, as he knew that all those killed in the Troubles in Northern Ireland died because of his 'bad thoughts'. Was Ezekiel, in other words, suffering from a psychotic delusion, conflating in a symbolic equation the bones comprising the skeleton with symbolic bones of a desiccated life?

'The lunatic, the lover and the poet' – to some, Ezekiel and his ilk are the lunatics, madly leading us astray into mystical nonsense. To others he is inspired, whether by divine truth or as a poet, 'of imagination all compact'.

There is a continuum from naturalism (that only scientific, material explanations such as the laws of gravity have any validity), to a belief in the supernatural; in between are accounts in terms of intentions and purposes (human and perhaps animal aims), and mythology, where some ambiguity about the supernatural is permitted.

Child psychotherapist Priscilla Green has a further take on Ezekiel. She notes that he oscillates between two extremes. 'Much of the text', she suggests, 'consists of storming tirades, full of self-righteousness and savagery. The reader may well feel revulsion . . . and a conviction of the writer's insanity; but Ezekiel also contains passages of . . . beauty and profundity', where she finds 'traces of a mind whose insane outpourings seemed to be the result of a deliberate creative act, a mind capable of great clarity and self-abnegation'. She comes to the view that the poet/prophet enters into the (pre-verbal) state of the toddler having a tantrum or the psychotic person racked by the experience of an extremely harsh superego that deadens and maddens, but Ezekiel then emerges from such states into the mindset of a poet/ healer, thus giving indications of how such deadness may be transformed. A person who experiences such trauma and some of its consequences, and conveys something of such an experience, risks being overwhelmed by it, even maddened by it. But Green persuades me that the whole book is a poetic story of integration of parts of the self that have become split off from each other.

There is a delicate balance between risking too much in this kind of internal encounter with early traumatic states, and on the other hand living a numbed inner life. But there are those who take this risk, not only on their own behalf. At best psychoanalysis shares something of this, providing a site where such experiencing of trauma may be suffered and transformed. Religion offers a language and a context for such processes.

* * *

I think psychoanalysis in small and large ways sometimes offers the means to understand disordered feelings and then revive. Here is a small-scale example. While struggling with writing about Ezekiel, I got up one morning fully intending to continue, but felt flimsy, without energy, for the whole day. I felt I lacked the inner resources to embark on it. That night, I had a dream, part of which was: *I am in a small city in Japan, trying to get to Tokyo to catch a flight home. I'm lost, though I can see a long-distance, metalled version of moving walkways in airports; it ran through the old chaotic city with its narrow streets, tiny shops, foreign (to me) shop signs – all a hive of activity. I am carrying with difficulty a lot of little packages and bundles of papers, but am unclear which are relevant. I can't find or hold on to my ticket, nor can I read the writing on the various documents, as it is in an Oriental script, which I take to be Japanese.*

Also in the dream were allusions to *two potential helpers, one knowledgeable in Japanese, the other an old cricketing friend, Doug Insole, who said to me that he had a bag full of things he used to know but can't any longer access. Within the dream I was not able to be helped. But the hint was there.*

Thinking further about the dream, I see that it expresses my fear about not knowing my way around, or how to get to my true home. Being in this space where speech and writing are incomprehensible to me is frightening. Does this foreign land and language stand for religion itself (writing about which was the task I could not face the previous day)? Was this difficulty the underlying cause of my lethargy? 'Metalled' reminds me of T. S. Eliot's 'In appetency, on its metalled ways' – possibly I was seeking to understand religion in a too mechanical way?

Or is my dream a form of recalling an ongoing experience of my early childhood? 'Infant' means 'one who can't speak', an incomprehension that could have made me feel left out and rejected. (I greatly admired our grandson, Luka, for his equanimity as a two-year-old when faced with not following what we adults were discussing between ourselves; 'What we talking?' he would ask cheerfully, already assuming that he was, or would be, included. He was not paranoid about being left out, not too anxious about failing to understand.)

A darker interpretation of the dream is that the state of incomprehension refers to Alzheimer's. I am well aware of this haunting fear; it is the disease that distorted the end phases of the lives of both my parents. Might the dream even be an indicator of this insidious process already having begun? Again, there is a less pessimistic view – my wife suggests I get a hearing aid, as sometimes my getting the wrong end of the stick is a result of mishearing. And there are the good figures in the dream. Maybe I could learn from my own analyst (expert in the inscrutable unconscious, the 'Japanese')? Maybe I could open the bag of things I already know, even if the Insole-self of my dream couldn't?

As Freud said, the problem of self-analysis lies in the counter-transference; as must be evident, I'm unsure how sure I can be about any of this. Certainly I'm familiar with the feeling of not knowing my way around, and aware that this can lead to self-lacerating panic.

But I was able to write the next day. The dream and the reflection on it helped to clear my mental air.

＊　＊　＊

Rowan Williams was Archbishop of Canterbury for ten years from 2022. I first came across his work in his short book, *Writing in the Dust*, where, after describing his experience of having been led through the dust-filled streets close to the Twin Towers on 11 September, 2001, he reflected on how we may be able to move from initial reactions to atrocity of fear and revenge towards attempting to understand. As newly appointed Chair of the section that arranged such talks at the psychoanalytical society in London, I wrote to ask him if he would consider coming to speak to us. He agreed, and, having at first to postpone for a year after being elevated from Archbishop of Wales to the head of the Anglican Church worldwide, came not once but twice.

I was impressed and warmed by his clarity and empathy. The discussions following his talks at these meetings stand out for me now as they did then. He is able to take in fully what an audience member says, sometimes bringing out more than the questioner himself is aware of, and then in a simple and clear way give his own views on the subject. I also met him at a conference called 'Trialogue', which brought together people from the fields of religion, literature, and psychoanalysis.

So I was privileged and fortunate, as well as slightly nervous, to be invited by the Camden Psychotherapy Unit to have a conversation as part of a webinar. In the webinar we spoke about the overlap between religious thinking and that of psychoanalysis, while being aware of the ways in which religion has a philosophy that goes beyond that of psychoanalysis; making bigger claims and offering more exalted hopes than what therapy proposes. For him, God underpins the metaphorical and puts it into context.

We had a considerable area of shared terrain. As a poet and psychotherapist, he fully acknowledges broad readings of religion. There is much to be learned in each direction between the two disciplines.

Some of these issues emerged in our discussion about Marilynne Robinson's latest novel, *Jack*, a religious novel that could also be seen as a psychoanalytic one. The novel's atmosphere and context are explicitly religious: both Jack, the 'black sheep' of a family of eight children, and Della, a black schoolteacher, have fathers who were or are ministers of the church. The other prominent feature of the setting is racism, which permeates life in the America of the 1960s, and in particular the atmosphere of the city of St Louis, where Jack and Della live. They become lovers, a large part of the book consisting of their conversations and thoughts about each other.

Jack has his problems. He has long been, recurrently liable to periods of joblessness, drunkenness and homelessness. As a child he provoked critical attention, stealing in apparently pointless ways, setting fire to mailboxes. He got a girl pregnant, and allowed his brother to sit exams for him. He became at times the unnamed embarrassed subject of his father's sermons. Jack is a character in an earlier novel by Robinson, *Home*, set later in time than *Jack*, when he returns to Gilead, his home town, to find out for himself if Iowa might be a place where he could bring Della as his wife, along with their young son. Late in that book, he tries calling his father 'Dad'. His father barks back: 'Don't call me that. I don't like it at all. It sounds ridiculous. It's not even a word.' His father had tried, according to his lights, to 'rescue' Jack, and to understand his own role in the difficulties, but finds himself, despite these efforts, unforgiving. Both father and son are uneasily preoccupied with each other, angry, guilty and confused.

Jack's mind is fidgety. His ruminations get going easily, and are usually persecutory towards himself. He can't fully own a thought or feeling, can't stay with it long enough to 'suffer' it. He quickly feels he is a risk to the wellbeing of the other, whether he engages with them or not. He frequently feels it safer to err on the side of caution, avoiding contact, desire and love. Much of his restlessness consists of internal dialogues with his hypercritical conscience or superego. His inner world is characteristically a sort of pandemonium, troops of demons coming at him from all sides. He has what his author calls a 'quivering nerve of pride, ready to heighten the misery of any occasion'.

Della is a much easier person, less tormented, less touchy. In particular, she is not unduly anxious about damaging those she loves. At one point she says that once in one's life we may see the soul of another, the inner reality of a person, and be aware of its goodness directly. She is not blind to Jack's difficulties either. She can be tough with him, frank, but never punitive, dismissive or contemptuous.

A central theme and question of the novel is: can Jack be saved? Can Della, with her love that passes human understanding, save him? This is a novel in which redemption is lived out, with all its uncertainties. The novel is a battle for Jack's soul.

By similar tokens, the relationship has echoes of a psychoanalytic therapy. As in psychoanalysis, the relationship is asymmetrical, though also mutual and ongoing. No detail is too small to carry a weight of significance. 'Giant miseries and hopes can carry on their wars in the merest cranny.' Jack refers to 'being caught at some trifling stupid thing which always became a reflection on the whole of his character'.

Della listens, takes him seriously, hears the better person through the complicated ramifications of his mind. She believes in him and his potential. She does not deny the negative, but nor is she put off by his hesitations and backslidings. Living in a racist society, with racist laws, they take a chance together. The novel ends on a note of cautious hope for their relationship, as it does for Jack himself.

* * *

Psychoanalysis may become a religion in a bad sense, puffing itself up, relying too much on its rituals rather than the emotional substance. But at its best it too supports the good in the person – a colleague, Gordana Batinica, describes the analyst as a 'miner of precious metals' – while being prepared to face, and offer patients the chance to face, their destructive and self-destructive sides. Remember Homer: 'Sin races round the world while prayer follows after, lame and old.' Della, like a good analyst, offers the other a firm but fair superego, not a harsh one. We all hope for what Ivo Andrić alludes to in *Signs by the Roadside*: 'If people knew *what a struggle* living my life has been, they would be more willing to forgive all my wrongdoings and all the good I have failed to do, and still have a shred of compassion left over for me.'

There are many areas of agreement and congruence between Williams's and my respective belief systems and the challenges we share in our 'pastoral' work. We both recognise the need for empathy, for putting ourselves into the shoes of the other, for allowing ourselves to enter, temporarily and of course partially, into their world with its pain, conflict and trickiness. We recognise that we are bound to feel feelings such as anger and revenge, but see the need to work on them, to go beyond hostility at least in trying to understand how it arises, and with what justification and mitigation. We aim to make judgements, that is, to think clearly, but to avoid judgementalism.

We recognise that narcissism and selfishness are part and parcel of us all. We recognise the inevitability of and need for moral and psychological struggle. We agree that identity is to some extent (but not only, not infinitely) fluid; has to be struggled towards, and is never fixed. Value judgements too are often provisional; having reached some good-enough-for-the-time-being conclusion, every human being will then find new problems, and be liable to react in ways that create new difficulties. We may also come to realise that our framework has been limited, that there are wider or deeper considerations than those we had based earlier insights on. We (repeatedly) have to grow up. We agree that it is only through suffering our experiences (in the sense that Jesus suffered the little children to come to him) that many of us move towards a greater maturity, that it is only with humility that we become less selfish and controlling.

We may manage to change in our lives. Human beings are complex creatures caught between love and hate, generosity and meanness, kindness and cruelty, self-respect and self-inflation or deflation. We are troubled by these and many other tensions. Good qualities may ignore or oppose other good qualities, and may tip over into self-righteousness. We all get things wrong, we all lack much in our orientations. We all have our mad or depressed or manic or perverse sides. Indeed, we need some degree of mania to kickstart us into life; we need some depression to bring us down and to recognise the harm we have done; we need some acquaintance with psychosis, as we saw with Ezekiel. But we may also come to be ourselves in ways that feel authentic without denying, or infringing too much on, the identity of others.

Williams and I would agree about the centrality of love, and of the efforts that need to be made not to be stuck in hate. We agree about the difficulty of knowing ourselves, and of combining such understanding with action.

We would agree about the need for loving attention, from parents to children, mutually in relationships, in therapy and from priests to people struggling with their lives. Compassion without superiority. 'There but for the Grace of God go I', or indeed, 'There go I'. We are both convinced that bringing up children is often thwarted by grown-ups having too rigid an agenda for what their children should do, how they should be. This does not mean there should be no firmness, no teaching of manners and confronting with selfishness and so on.

We would, I think, share many attitudes to judgement, mercy and forgiveness.

Yet of course there are differences. For Williams, the moral and psychological are embedded in a religious worldview. The body is to be respected because God became incarnate. The provisional nature of identity and values is based on the belief that in comparison with God's our views are partial and flawed; we see 'through a glass darkly'. For Williams, like Robinson, evil is, I think, a privation of the good, rather than a reality in itself; hence the idea of 'meeting a soul' that has not yet been polluted or corrupted by the world. (My own, provisional, view is that there is an inbuilt tendency to destructiveness just as there is an instinct for love and communality.)

In their focus on human beings in our complexity and suffering, I see religious studies and psychoanalysis as central to the humanities. At best, they also help others (and ourselves) to deal with life in a fuller, more truthful, way.

On the face of it, Rowan Williams and I occupy radically different positions on religion. But when we get closer in, our areas of agreement are, I think, shared to a remarkable degree.

CHAPTER 4

'NO, NO, NO, NO . . . NO, ON THE WHOLE NO'

It was in 1962 that I changed to Moral Sciences (a misleading term for philosophy) for the second part of my degree. One outcome was that I would take four years as an undergraduate rather than three. I was happy about this; I was enjoying myself, and in no hurry. I never felt pessimistic about eventually finding a path. Nor was I worried about a steady income. In those days, the state was generous in funding time spent at university, and I supplemented the grant with occasional small fees playing cricket for Middlesex Second XI. Material wealth did not interest me; I was careless if not carefree in this aspect of life.

With Renford Bambrough's encouragement, I attended John Wisdom's first lecture of that academic year. Eager to receive the goodies about to be poured into my vacant mind, I sat in the middle of the front row of desks. The professor made some noises and gestured, spoke for a while, then raised Descartes's doubts about the possibility of knowledge. Looking puzzled, he stopped talking, put his elbows on the desk, and gazed with his clear blue eyes directly into mine, inviting me, along with the roomful of bright young students, to risk an answer. I was unable to think, paralysed by what felt like a powerful and impossible expectation. This was not what I had signed up for!

John Wisdom was tall and elegantly lean; he wore old but fine countryman's suits, or creased, even crumpled, cream-coloured light jackets. His trousers were tailored to curve round his heels. He sometimes sported a green-ish countryman's cloth cap. He owned a horse and liked to ride. He put a jacket round the horse in the winter. He had a handsome, sensitive face and a bald head. He lectured at 9 a.m., when most of us students were still half-asleep. He offered an open invitation to come to tea (poured shakily by him into fluted, pink, willow-patterned cups) on Friday afternoons in his flat, overlooking a fen. When teaching he would grasp his head as if in anguish and extreme puzzlement. He put himself into the shoes both of the sceptic and of the person who reacts against the sceptic. He was said to have given a lecture in New York, at the end of which he was asked a verbose, over-intellectual question. Wisdom was silent for some time, clutching his head. Eventually he came up with his emotionally modulated response. 'No, no, no, no,' he said, his voice descending as if in grief: adding with a sense of upbeat after a slight pause, 'No, on the whole no.' And then waited for the next comment.

As I got to know him better, I learned how tolerant he was of apparently naive questions. He respected philosophical doubt as the starting point for philosophical thought, and the faltering efforts made by us students to express it or respond to it. One Californian woman used to ask the same question week after week, in a tone of plaintive perseveration, regardless of whatever he and others had said last time: 'But surely, Professor Wisdom, it's all subjective?'

One factor in Wisdom's patience was his philosophical view of what philosophy is. He saw the questioning of common sense, the doubting of everyday grounds for knowledge, as akin to neurotic anxiety. He likened philosophical argument and debate to psychoanalysis (one of his books has the title, *Philosophy and Psycho-analysis*). Philosophical 'treatment' involves facilitating the capacity to allow into awareness what we in a sense already know, a process that may lead to a stage

66

where, having expressed more clearly and fully what we inadequately knew, we are not condemned to permanent paradox or uncertainty.

For example, Descartes doubted that we can know for certain that anything exists in the external world. We may be dreaming the world we see. Is there anything beyond our own minds? Wisdom gave house-room for such doubt. Do we 'really' know? Do we have guarantees of knowledge? Clearly, we may be deceived; mirages occur in deserts; while dreaming, we feel as terrified as in waking life. Could everything be a dream? But then Wisdom would remind us how strange and unrealistic it is to question in this total way what we do in fact know. I remember two of his examples: 'Looks like cheese, smells like cheese, tastes like cheese: but is it cheese?' With this question he reminds us what life is like, what knowledge actually is. And second – in response to the idea that we never know the mind of another – 'What, never know that a child is unhappy? Never know that a deer has heard a sound when, along with the rest of the herd, it becomes extremely alert?' This last point was accompanied by his index fingers as ruminant's ears pricking up above his head, his eyes wide open in mock alarm. We then imagine the cheetah lurking downwind in the long grass. 'We never know the mind of another! – Really?'

Part of his teaching method, linked as it was to his conception of philosophy, was his 'living' the feelings and thoughts, entering into the anxieties, owning them. In his hands, philosophy was not a dry intellectual activity, it involved passion; it included feelings and convictions that seemed to clash, but which, having become more articulated, may be reconciled. Philosophical anxiety could thus, sometimes, be assuaged, largely by case-by-case discussion.

I remember another of his thought experiments. This one was designed to remind us that it is not primarily the nature of brain function that concerns us when we consider the personal qualities of others and ourselves, including the capacity to think. Imagine, he said, your best friend is undergoing brain surgery. The surgeon opens up the skull. What does he find? Nothing but hay! What should he do? He puts the skull bones back together and leaves well alone.

Wisdom retained a childlike ability to experience the familiar, the ordinary, in fresh, lively ways. He retained his sense of wonder. When I was at the Irvine campus of the University of California in 1966, I arranged for him and Bambrough, who were both at the time visiting professors in Oregon, to come to talk to our faculty and students. Outside, as we rounded one of the university's handsome concrete buildings, we saw against the blue-white sky kites being flown. I have a vivid impression of John shading his eyes with his hand, peering up, and saying with wholehearted delight and amazement: 'Look how high they are!'

Wisdom taught us that there are indeed different categories of thought, each with a different type of verification. Something may taste to me like cheese (a subjective statement) but not be cheese (an objective one). The 'claim' about the material world ('here is some cheese') has, by virtue of its being about a shared world, more ways of being disproved than the former ('this tastes to me like cheese'). 'It is colder today than it was yesterday' requires more for its validation or falsification than 'It feels to me colder today than it did yesterday.' To know something outside our minds to be true requires more than believing it to be true. This is the truth behind the sceptic's bizarre, misguided claims ('we can never know the "external" world'). The verification process is more complex, more demanding, than it is for the subjective. The sceptic distorts the differences into grounds for generalised doubt, but the process of addressing scepticism calls for respect for the doubts. Wisdom wrote of these doubts (or these philosophers): 'There is good in them, poor things.'

The difference between verification of assertions about our own minds and those about the minds of others has been similarly misconceived. We know our own minds differently, but this difference is precisely what makes a statement what it is – whether it is about one's own mind or about someone else's. And we have come to understand

68

that though knowledge about our own minds is not infallible (we self-deceive), we are in a (logically) unique position – privileged, but not infallible – with regard to our own minds – as is everyone else in relation to theirs.

Wisdom wrote about various ways in which it is not only by discovering new empirical facts that we come to new knowledge about the world, but by reflection on established facts. For example, the slave in Plato's *Meno* is helped without new practical input to realise that the area of a square field is not doubled but quadrupled when the length of each side is doubled. Similarly, by logical, numerical reasoning the accountant shows us that we, like Mr Micawber, are spending beyond our means. Wisdom went on to consider less arithmetical routes to new perceptions and new realisations, as when case-by-case examples settle a disputed argument – a lawyer may demonstrate, for instance, without telling us anything that we didn't already know (though in most cases he or she would attempt to do that as well), that a husband's persistent violence and intimidation towards the wife who, after twenty years of abuse and violence, could bear it no more and killed him, may be as much a justification for acquittal of murder as loss of control due to medical abnormality; in each case the killer may be seen to have been acting with diminished responsibility. A cartoonist or comedian shows us truths by means of exaggeration. It was partly by reflections on what was already known that Freud was enabled to posit unconscious intentions.

(Strangely, when I met Gautam Sarabhai, my future father-in-law, I discovered that he too had been taught by Wisdom, in 1938–9, and spoke of him fondly.)

* * *

At the time when in 1962 I gingerly stepped into the strange terrain of philosophy in its particular instantiation in Cambridge, Ludwig

Wittgenstein had been dead for eleven years. He had been, and still was, a forceful presence there, ever since turning up unannounced, aged twenty-two, in October 1911, eager to learn and discuss mathematical logic with Bertrand Russell. The latter saw him at first as 'threatening to be an infliction', but soon as a genius. The inflictor would radically change philosophy.

One central element in Wittgenstein's philosophy is the manner of his approach, which results both from his personality and from his ideas about what the point of philosophy is. I find it hard to write about his ideas without tending to lose a sense of the urgency of his commitment to truthfulness.

Throughout the First World War, Wittgenstein fought in the Austro-Hungarian army, serving in Russia and Italy. He was decorated for bravery. He carried in his knapsack the draft of the only book he published in his lifetime, the *Tractatus Logico-Philosophicus* (1921). After being freed from an Italian prisoner-of-war camp, he returned to Austria for eight years, teaching small children in remote villages. Explaining that he 'prostituted his mind talking to intelligent people in Cambridge', he would go off from time to time to work in isolated mountainous places, including in western Norway, where in 1918 the small hut that he had designed was built on a rocky outcrop overlooking a fjord.

He was enticed back to Cambridge in 1929 (partly as a result of conversations with philosopher and mathematician Frank Ramsey). He would be allowed to work there only if he had a degree. For this purpose, Russell and G. E. Moore interviewed him to ratify the *Tractatus* for a PhD. After the *viva* (the interview at which a thesis is assessed), Wittgenstein is said to have clapped both interviewers on the shoulder and told them: 'Don't worry, I know you'll never understand it.'

He was made a fellow of Trinity College, and a lecturer in philosophy. Ten years later, in 1939 after Moore's retirement, he was appointed professor.

In the next war, he worked as a hospital porter at Guy's Hospital in London, and then as a laboratory assistant in Newcastle. In 1945, he went back to Cambridge, where he died six years later.

Wittgenstein's lectures became legendary. He would put out deckchairs in his room in Trinity College, and discuss with colleagues and students the nature of philosophy, the philosophy of mind, ethics, religion, psychoanalysis and other topics. He was particularly concerned with language and how it conveys meaning. There was a passionate intensity in his attempts to express and sort out his own often-conflictual thoughts and feelings.

Wittgenstein could be impatient, conveying that *how* one did philosophy was as important as *what* one did in the field. Georg Henrik von Wright, who was appointed to succeed Wittgenstein when he in turn retired from the professorship in 1948, wrote: 'Each conversation with Wittgenstein was living through the day of judgement. It was terrible.' Narrowness and shallowness infuriated him. The voice of conscience inside was excoriating, and was also directed outwards. What is the point of life, he asked, if sin and error can be facilely forgiven? Hence his identification with 'Hebraic' religion and its absolute condemnation of heresy: 'If what we do now is to make no difference in the end, then all the seriousness of life is done away with.'

He longed for friends, perhaps rather for 'soulmates', with whom he could be intimate, but knew that this was hard to attain and sustain. When he lived in Austria in the 1920s, he wanted to come back to England to see Maynard Keynes, but insisted that they spend weeks together; a single chat would be of no use. He was strenuous and demanding.

For Wittgenstein, doing philosophy with total commitment was a spiritual pilgrimage.

The Russian poet Osip Mandelstam described the poet as 'the one who "disturbs meaning"'. Wittgenstein's philosophical work was likewise experienced as 'disturbing meaning'; his struggles to think and live up to his aspirations were, to him and to some of his interlocutors, a matter of life and death. Three of his four brothers killed themselves; he himself was at times close to suicide; 'Often it is as though my soul were dead,' he remarked.

*   *   *

Many philosophers believe he transformed the subject, not once but twice: first with the *Tractatus,* which claimed to be the last word in philosophy, then again with his overturning of those ideas in *Philosophical Investigations,* published in 1953, two years after his death.

There were others who thought his later approach esoteric, that he had not directly or in traditional ways argued for or against major positions in the history of the subject.

His followers also fought each other. Their arguments were based in part on the issue of who was the true inheritor of his life-work, who most closely represented the 'true' Wittgenstein. I gathered that, during my time at Cambridge, faculty meetings to decide degree classifications were almost interminable, as teachers backed students who were closest to their own views and affiliations.

I'm reminded of the story of the blind Hindu sages who, when asked to describe the nature of this strange animal (an elephant), answered in terms of the bit of the animal each had hold of – trunk, tusk, ear, leg or tail.

This scenario has much in common with the 'Controversial Discussions' in the British Psychoanalytical Society following the death in 1939 of Sigmund Freud. Divisions between three main groupings came to a head. More generally, political and family disputes arise when longstanding patriarchs or matriarchs die. Earlier tensions that had been suppressed while they were alive emerge with renewed sharpness, each group claiming to be the most loved and regarded by the ghost of the dead patriarch, and thus the most entitled of the next generation.

❊ ❊ ❊

So: what was it that came through so strongly from the man himself? What gave him his powerful appeal to some, what elicited the frustration and ambivalence of others?

I'm struck by Wittgenstein's capacity for awe and reverence. He quotes one of Bach's dedications, of his 'Little Organ Book', to illustrate 'what I would have liked to say about my work – "To the glory of God and that my neighbour may be benefited thereby"'. Even trivia had to be lived out wholeheartedly – on Midsummer Common in Cambridge, he enjoyed being the moon circling the earth, itself circling the sun. He liked going to the cinema, where he would sit in the front row to get the full impact of the drama.

His commitment to truth and his scrutiny of what we (especially in philosophy) are inclined to say 'must' be the case, was part of this urgency. 'Don't think, look,' he wrote. Looking, really looking and really seeing connections, is like hearing music: 'The meaning of a piece of music cannot be described by naming anything that the music "stands for".' 'Understanding a sentence is much more akin to understanding a theme in music than one may think.'

Seeing, making connections and truthfulness are all extremely hard to achieve, and require courage and discipline, but also a willingness to disrupt oneself by giving up established frames of thinking. He was suspicious of any over-easy answer. He writes: 'If one has toothache, it is good to put a hot-water bottle on your face, but it will only be effective as long as the heat of the bottle gives you some pain. I will chuck the bottle when I find that it no longer gives me the particular kind of pain which will do my character any good.'

Born into a family that was one of the richest in Austria, Wittgenstein gave all his money away and lived simply, even poorly. He was suspicious of luxury of any kind – a box of chocolates would be an unwelcome gift, as he would not know how to stop. During the 1920s, he supported himself on his meagre teacher's salary; he wanted to come to England; to do so would entail finding a paid job; perhaps he could be a gardener? He spoke about it being essential for him to have a 'proper' job, with no 'wangling'. He encouraged others to give up philosophy to do ordinary work with ordinary people.

Truthfulness was for him an exacting moral quality. His passion and stringency at times came close to tyranny, disdain and arrogance. One drawback of his personality was that he created followers who were so devoted as to be disciples, who sometimes jeered when the name of any other philosopher was brought up.

I was myself in awe of this genius, and knew that I would have been reduced to silence if I had ever met him. But his attitude and view of the world appealed to me, underlining my sense of the shallowness of my thought, at least in comparison. I remember dreaming of a grey conventionality, something to do with the way the old *Times* newspaper presented itself, with, I seem to remember, no news on its front page, only advertisements and announcements of the births and deaths of the social elite. Grey clothes, grey thoughts. Wittgenstein was anything but.

What he also conveyed, to me at least, was that everything could be the focus of deep attention. Some people complained that 'analytical' philosophy, as done in most British universities in the post-war period, was trivial. Wittgenstein seemed to be a leader of this analytic emphasis, but his reflections on the ordinary were new and vivid.

The central locus of his later work was language. The revisionist author of the *Investigations* showed that ordinary language was not essentially confused. It serves its purposes well. Rather, it was philosophers who introduce the confusion. Wittgenstein writes that it is the job of philosophy to clear up confusions that they, including his earlier self, have introduced into their accounts of ordinary language. I recall David Hume writing that it was more likely that there were errors in his own sceptical arguments than that we can't know much of what we take for granted as knowledge. This is not, of course, the end of the argument, but it is an important beginning, one that we need to keep in mind throughout. There is a healthy streak of pragmatism and common sense in the British empirical tradition.

In the *Investigations* Wittgenstein imagined a primitive language game, a thought experiment through which he explored what this might reveal about language in general. A builder has an assistant; the language consists of instructions and responses: the builder says 'brick', the assistant brings him a brick. What makes this the beginnings of language? One feature is that it takes its place as part of a shared activity. We don't need to posit mental or mysterious entities in order to account for the assistant and the builder understanding each other, for having the same concept of 'brick'.

Philosophers, he said, have the idea that there must be one underlying element that explains all meaning, something 'crystalline', perfect, a sort of key for which words stand. This view relies on a false notion that the meaning must somehow reside in the word, or in the user's mind, *at the moment of use*. Wittgenstein offers the compelling analogy, that this is like thinking that the meaning of 'check' in chess is to be found in the moment of its occurrence, whereas its meaning is given by means of the rules of the game, which spell out and prescribe the way the term is used when people play chess. The language game is played; it provides a social context in which words are used. This setting is ignored in highfalutin' philosophical discourses.

Wittgenstein hated the triviality of much philosophy; he spoke about how it had become a mere 'skill', rather than an arduous struggle to avoid confusion and pretentiousness. He wrote to Norman Malcolm, 'What *is* the use of studying philosophy if it doesn't improve your thinking about the important questions of everyday life?' He spoke of the way philosophical theorising is liable to misuse words, forcing them to spin like wheels in a machine without connection to the machinery. I am reminded of Leavis's description of the style of some of Henry James's late writing – that it was 'meretricious word-spinning'. (I'm not saying I agree about the application, but I like the notion.)

I don't believe that the use of small examples makes the subject trivial – examples like: 'What makes it wrong not to return library books?' or, a question that Wittgenstein himself was puzzled by as an eight-year-old, 'Why should one tell the truth if a lie has good consequences for oneself?' Triviality is more a matter of how such examples are used. Philosophy helps us to see the differences between categories of thought – mind and body, knowledge about oneself and knowledge about others, ethics and matters of fact, the past and the future – without having to resort to hierarchies of reality and knowledge ('we can never know the mind of another', say, or 'ethical statements are either nonsense or merely disguised expressions of emotional preference').

In his later work, Wittgenstein argued at length, and with many challenging examples, how meaning derives from the context of the words in the shared life of the language speakers. On the face of it, words look the same as each other; a fact that tempts us to think they must all have meaning in the same way, by 'standing for' a thing or a concept, but he reminded us that they have meaning in different ways. Like levers in a signal box, they look alike, but their functions are varied.

'I point out differences', he said, 'in things that look alike.'

* * *

I ask myself: why did I turn to philosophy? Why then? I suspect one source of my interest lay in unhappiness and anxiety.

From the beginning of the 1970s, Bryan Magee had been a lucid expositor of philosophical positions, interviewing on radio and television philosophers of many schools. In 2018, he gave what turned out to be his last interview. Here Magee made it clear that his interest in philosophy derived from major existential worries, especially 'Why should there be anything rather than nothing?' I was struck by this, and by his dissatisfaction with what he considered his own modest contribution to philosophy. 'Not good enough' was his verdict. His not being a great thinker, not one of those who change a discipline for ever, meant for him that he was a failure. He failed to live up to his ideal self, to being an intellectual superman, which, sadly, meant that his real achievements, especially his clarity and his giving philosophy a widespread public appeal and interest through interviews and books, appeared to carry little weight with him.

In this interview he also told a story about his mother, that when he and his sister were quite small, she would say to them early in the day: 'Get out of the house, get out of my way; I don't want to see you till dark.' He did not appear to consider that there might have been a link between his terrors of nothingness and this unavailable mother, nor that his interest in philosophy might have had something to do with feelings of rejection and loss (not to mention, no doubt, helpless rage).

One fear I had as a small boy (aged perhaps seven or eight) started when I was informed that the sun and other stars are bigger than the earth. This terrified me. It took time for me to come to see that there was a false basic assumption that led to terror: I had the idea that the universe is a rectangular room, the earth being its floor, the stars and sun painted on the ceiling. If a star was bigger than the ceiling – and therefore also than the floor – chaos and danger threatened;

it was natural, even rational, that I felt alarmed. I was afraid of vast, destructive implosion from above.

Another childhood fear of mine was that the sounds of planes coming in to land at Northolt airport (not far from where we lived in west London) were the prelude to them crashing into my bedroom. In fact, one bomb did destroy a house near us in 1945, and caused our ceilings to crack. I have a memory (or perhaps a fantasy) of our having a large wooden table, under which we were to hide if bombs were dropping; my concern was whether we would be safe there even if a bomb landed right on top of it.

Other fears included nightmares of being confronted by tigers – my parents told me they would find me standing bolt upright in bed, with my eyes wide-open in panic – and separation anxiety. I was also frightened of heights.

I think most if not all of us have had large or small traumas in our lives, which are among the causal factors in long-lasting anxieties and in efforts to resolve or repair them. My parents were totally different from the mother Magee described. But I think philosophy and religion had this purpose or function in my life, as I suspect they did for Magee.

As a psychoanalyst, and ex-patient, I am also aware of the dual nature of the fears and traumas. On one hand, there were external dangers from the air; my mother was evacuated from London with her baby son (me). I presume this occurred in the first months of 1944, the period of the 'Baby Blitz', while my father was still abroad in the navy (as a naval instructor-lieutenant he was posted to South Africa, where his job was to teach ratings navigation and meteorology). But on the other hand, there were also my own fantasies of dealing with the problems of life by becoming a superior and powerful bomber myself, someone who then fears not only falling from a height, but also becomes at times an explosive bomber, whose anxiety is increased by guilt and who also worries about omnipotently throwing himself down to prove his (i.e. my) invincibility.

I was strongly affected by a story I heard soon after the war of an RAF pilot whose parachute failed to open when his plane was shot down over a forest in Europe. The pilot miraculously survived by having his fall cushioned by the springy branches of a giant fir tree.

I am sure my fears of falling were also fears of jumping.

There was a whole range of doubts and uncertainties, and my wishes to resolve them, that may have been factors in my interest in philosophy.

* * *

My move to philosophy, my little rebellion against accepted truths, must also have been in part a response to changes in the Zeitgeist, coinciding as it did with what social historian David Kynaston refers to as 'the nation's turning point in its post-war trajectory'. The year 1962 marked the first concert by the Rollin' Stones (as they were then called) and the second appearance on radio of the Beatles. In the same year, in a desperate and failed attempt to 'buy the party out of its electoral troubles', Harold Macmillan sent packing a third of his cabinet in 'The Night of the Long Knives'. Next year, he departed without a fanfare. The year 1962 saw the final Gentlemen vs Players cricket match, indeed January 1963 saw the end of the whole official distinction in cricket between amateurs and professionals. It also heralded the beginning of the satirical TV programme, *That Was The Week That Was*, presented by the young David Frost, which was, to say the least, irreverent to authority and the Establishment.

It was at this stage that I discovered *Beyond the Fringe*, also mocking of Macmillan and his aged forgetfulness (with Peter Cook lugubriously intoning: 'I had meetings with the German Foreign

Minister, Herr, Herr . . . here and there'). Wanting to see it a second time, I managed to get a standing-room ticket at the back of the stalls, where I had room to double up in laughter.

We were entering an era in which there was less blind obedience to written and unwritten rules of life. My shift to philosophy and its challenges to conventional thinking may have been one tiny tremor emanating from this social earthquake.

* * *

Another element in my motivation for pursuing these second-order, meta-disciplines such as philosophy (and psychoanalysis) was meeting people who inspired me, who became mentors and paradigms. No doubt the same is true of many vocations and career choices.

Karl Britton impressed me from my first meeting with him when, as Professor of Philosophy at Newcastle, he chaired the panel of four people that appointed me as a lecturer there in 1968.

Early in that interview, I was asked a question by the professor of law. It went something like this: 'The law of hearsay states that reported speech does not count as evidence of the event reported unless the topic of the words is the state of mind of the speaker. Is there any philosophical ground for such a distinction?' I started tentatively, hesitantly. The questioner quickly cut across me with an authoritative, perhaps even domineering, 'No, no, no.' Britton instantly intervened, cutting across him sharply. 'Let him finish,' he said. I regard this as a crucial moment in my life. Without it, I may well have decided that the law professor was completely right about me, not only on the matter in hand; I might have dried up, crushed by an inner voice that could have ganged up with him against me. Instead, I had the reassurance that at least one person in the room believed I had more to say. Even if I had no clear notion at that moment of what this might be, Britton was right – I hadn't finished. I was able to say something more or less sensible in answer to the question: I spoke about the central feature of psychological statements being that the grounds we have for them are different from those that attribute thoughts or feelings to others, and from words that describe public events. These self-expressions are not 'hearsay' evidence, they are not rumours overheard, they are more relevantly evidential than hearsay about someone else's inner life. Confidence restored (or engendered), I got one of the two jobs on offer.

Nine years later, in 1977, I was vice-captain for England in the Centenary Test against Australia in Melbourne. Tony Greig was captain. (It was during this match that, along with media mogul Kerry Packer, he made final arrangements for the launch of World Series Cricket, which was a challenge to the official bodies administering cricket worldwide. It was directly as a result of these secret machinations that, a few months later, I was appointed captain in his place.) On the night before the Centenary match, we were having the customary team talk after our team dinner. One of the younger players, Derek Randall, started to make a comment. Tony Greig cut across him. I said what immediately came to my mind: 'Let him finish,' doing for Randall what Britton had done for me. It may well be foolish, even arrogant, to suggest that my intervention made any contribution to Randall's wonderful 174 in the second innings of that match; but who knows?

As I got to know him, I much admired Britton, who came across as shy, kind, honest and impressive. He wrote a book about the meaning of life in which he moves between the meta-questions – what might we mean by 'meaning'? – can we speak about meaning if we believe that death is the end of personal existence? – and a consideration of potential answers to the first-order question, such as that the ultimate meaning of life is to prepare ourselves for another life, after death.

During my last year in the department (1970–1), feedback to lecturers was for the first time required in British universities. Until then, a laissez-faire attitude had prevailed. Karl told me that he'd better start with me, as I was the junior member of the department; so, sitting quietly in the back of the room, he attended a lecture of mine (on Descartes, I recall). I spoke for forty minutes, then asked for questions or comments – there were none. I filled the remaining ten minutes with more lecturing. I think all of us in the room – students, professor and me alike – were anxious. Britton made only one comment afterwards: that when I paused for questions, he was reminded of the banns being read out during the wedding ceremony, when the congregation is told: 'If any of you know cause or just impediment why these two persons should not be joined together in holy Matrimony, ye are to declare it' – in other words, 'speak now or forever hold your peace!'

Shortly before I left Newcastle, I gave a short paper to students and colleagues, questioning the assumption that homosexuality was inevitably abnormal or pathological. I learned later that Karl was uncomfortable with this. I think he thought it provocative for the students. With longer hindsight, and following subsequent shifts in social attitudes, I now think that perhaps it was twenty years ahead of its time. Today it would be more provocative to question the conclusions in my paper than to assert them.

My second influence was Michael Scholar. For several years, he and I followed each other in various ways. Michael remembers us having met during the scholarship exams at St John's College while we were still at school, which I don't recall. In my mind, our first meeting was in the first week of our first term, both of us studying Classics, outside the rooms of R. L. 'Bonzo' Howland, who had put the shot in the Olympic Games of 1928. Brought together in this small seminar group, Michael and I have been friends and influencers of each other ever since.

My example in moving from Classics to philosophy was a significant factor in his doing the same a few weeks later, and I followed him in going on to do postgraduate work in philosophy. He finished his PhD – on Aristotle; I never finished mine on 'The Explanation of Action'. We both got positions in universities, he at Leicester, I at Newcastle. We both became interested in joining the Civil Service, and had found work experience in different departments, mine being at the Ministry of Labour. Both of us took the exam and were successful. At this point we diverged, he taking up what became a successful career in public service, in which he ended up as a Permanent Secretary in the Department of Trade and Industry, while developing his passion for playing the organ and piano; I going off to play cricket professionally and later to train as a psychoanalyst.

We have branched out in our own ways. But Michael is someone whose views, thoughts and feelings have always had weight with me. When we were younger, I was perhaps slightly in awe of him. He seemed to be more of a piece than me. I think that this, along with his self-questioning and humour, resulted in his having a similar impact on other people besides me.

Philosophers are not always noted for their practical common sense. I once went to a lecture in a large auditorium at a philosophical conference in Philadelphia. A crisis loomed when the microphones failed to work. A sort of panic set in. Experts were phoned. At last, a man with long white hair stumbled down from the back of the room. He traced the wire back from the microphone to the plug. He turned the switch on. Lo and behold, sound! A year later I recognised him as Geoffrey Midgeley, my new colleague at the University of Newcastle.

CHAPTER 5

HENRY JAMES'S RUINED SHOES

In my early twenties, I was walking with Michael Scholar towards the Sidgwick Site, an area of newly built lecture rooms and libraries, some designed by James Stirling, in the Newnham area of Cambridge. We were speaking of books we'd each read. Michael asked me if I'd read Henry James's *The Portrait of a Lady*. I hadn't. He said: 'I envy you reading it for the first time.' I can't recall anything else of this conversation. I do know I'd read *The Europeans*, James's wonderful comic novel about a European brother and sister visiting their American cousins with the aim of finding a wealthy husband for the sister. So I was ready for Michael's recommendation and took his hint. *The Portrait* fulfilled all expectation, both in the first reading, when I fell in love with the book and with Isabel Archer, and in subsequent ones, in which I could reflect on her self-damaging shortcomings of naivety and stubbornness, qualities closely allied to her strengths of character and her charm.

Michael can't recall this conversation; but what he remembers is being surprised and delighted at my response to the novel itself. Another mutual friend to whom he'd recommended it had scathingly dismissed it, referring to the first scene, depicted in a leisurely way, of a small tea-party on the lawn of a beautiful house beside the Thames.

This friend, I imagine, found the whole novel slow, unduly contorted and unnecessarily long.

What was it that I loved about it? And why do I now turn to James to be my prime example of the impact of novels on me? It's not that if I were to be dispatched to an island at the end of *Desert Island Discs* I'd choose this or any other novel by James as the one book I would take besides the Bible and Shakespeare. But there is something about James's stance and writing that strikes me as peculiarly relevant for a future psychoanalyst. I think it's to do with James's focus on the inner worlds of his characters. Standing back from action and thought, imagining what might lie behind both, he does what psychoanalysts do: he gradually builds up a portrait of his characters, revealing more and more of their underlying unconscious motives and personality. The journey taken by the reader, as by the characters, is indeed slow, sometimes indirect, like the sentences in which the story is told. We readers may, like analyst and patient, feel at times lost. But the picture gathers density and at times a devastating clarity.

We are taken into the mind of the striking, spirited, independent young American woman, Isabel Archer, who becomes wealthy as a result of a bequest from her cousin Ralph, which he decided on when dying of lung disease. He wants her to be relieved of all money pressures so that she can be entirely free to marry the person she loves, whomever that may be. Ironically, her choice, manipulated by the scheming Madame Merle, is to avoid the opportunity of marrying the solid and decent friend of Ralph's, Lord Warburton, and to turn down her passionate and persistent Boston admirer, Caspar Goodwood. For her, we surmise, they are too 'safe', too socially respectable and predictable. Instead, she marries the languid American dilettante and art collector Gilbert Osmond, living in Florence, a man who combines with his arrogant superiority a deadening conservatism and possessiveness. He hates and controls Isabel's independence of mind and action. What's more, the whole liaison turns out to have been set up by M. Merle, her supposed friend, to ensure a wealthy future for Pansy, the secret child of her own earlier liaison with Osmond.

I would have come to *Portrait* sooner or later without Michael's recommendation. But what is the difference between a first and a subsequent reading? In life, the first time we meet a person we soon fall for, there is a kind of dazzle. An idealisation, no doubt. Subsequent readings, like meetings, will deepen and complicate first impressions. We may be disillusioned. We may continue with our infatuation despite knowing the person is not 'our type', not really someone we could live with. Or again, the initial passion may grow to include less perfection, we love and are loved 'warts and all'.

As Freud said, loving one woman is a sort of madness, an insult to all other women! But how odd and disconnected would a man be who proposes marriage in terms such as: 'On the one hand I know you are a good and kind person, on the other I realise you have a series of faults, and I know you feel similarly about me, but would you care to tolerate such feelings and be my wife?'

As for the book itself, the shock of coming, gradually, like Isabel herself, to realise both the malign tricks played on her, and her own high-minded naivety, is powerful enough to sustain and enlarge several readings.

* * *

As a young child, I would go to the library in Pitshanger Lane, Ealing, on Saturday mornings and get books for the week. We had some books at home, too. At one stage, perhaps I was five or six, my favourite was about Miskoo, an Eskimo boy who got carried away by an ice floe, taken to Lapland, where he met reindeer, and was eventually taken back to his family in the far north. I came across my old copy recently, a hardback, with delicate pictures of Arctic settings in pastel shades of grey, yellow, pink, burnt sienna. I was enchanted by both the story and the pictures. The book stayed with me, and then thirty years later I met Mischa, who became my stepson, and loved to play and roll in the snow.

From nine or ten, I read boys' books. *Just William*, later *Stalky & Co.*, the Billy Bunter stories. I went for a day to the Test at Lord's; when rain stopped play, I bought for my sixpence or a shilling a little book of England-Australia Ashes Test scores going back to the 1870s, with names like Bannerman and Spofforth, Grace and Ulyett. In my first year at the City of London School (aged ten and eleven) we read in class three books that I remember: *The Cricket Match* by Hugh de Selincourt (a revelation to me, that there could be a story about the game I was already obsessed with): 'The Truth about Pyecraft', a short story by H. G. Wells about a man who wanted to lose weight, but didn't appreciate it when instead of getting slimmer he became lighter, a balloon floating against the ceiling – a cautionary tale about the risks of getting what we wish for. The third was 'A Horseman in the Sky' by Ambrose Bierce, set in the Civil War in America. A young man and his father fight on opposite sides. The boy becomes a scout, and is ordered to make sure no enemies enter the valley he is guarding. He falls asleep. To fall asleep on duty was to risk being shot for desertion. Awaking in terror, he sees a man seated on a beautiful horse, on a promontory opposite his hiding place. The man is silhouetted against the sky. He remembers the necessary procedure – shoot the horse in the chest, the horse will jump. He takes careful aim. He shoots. He has recognised the man. The man is his father.

I was fascinated by this story, no doubt partly by unconscious ambivalent feelings towards my own father. When Freud introduces the Oedipus concept, he at once also proposes a theory of aesthetics, suggesting to his friend Wilhelm Fliess that one reason the play *Oedipus the King* appeals to us is that we are all little Oedipuses in our unconscious.

By the time I heard about *The Portrait of a Lady*, I had been influenced by F. R. Leavis, who was still a lecturer at Cambridge when I was an undergraduate. I once went to a lecture of his. He was not immediately charismatic. Small, almost (apparently) shy, he mumbled, his words running along without much emphasis. His accent was demotic, not in any way affected. The lecture I attended came in the middle of a series (whose topic I can't remember); I had little idea what he was talking about. But I did buy some of his books, and read him. And was amazed at the clarity and power of his reading. He was opinionated, perhaps even narrow in the range of those he admitted to his literary canon. But I could begin to see for myself the kinds of reasons for his choices.

So, I read Jane Austen, George Eliot, Joseph Conrad, D. H. Lawrence and James, who constituted Leavis's 'Great Tradition', alongside other discoveries: Tolstoy and Dostoyevsky, Hemingway and Dickens. And life grew deeper, more meaningful, more available for attention and intensity.

My own literary pantheon embraces many modern novelists, including Marilynne Robinson, Elizabeth Strout, Hilary Mantel and Sebastian Barry; I love *The Leopard* by Giuseppe di Lampedusa. But the list has at its pinnacle nineteenth-century novelists, including those mentioned above, plus Chekhov.

* * *

The writing of fiction, like many other forms of writing, involves standing back from experience, reflecting on it and making use of it, re-viewing and reshaping it. The novelist turns over the numerous pebbles of his life to see what else was or is going on, what else might be imagined to be going on. (Dudley Doust remarked that I should call my next book 'On the Other Hand', giving me the credit of a link, however loose and flimsy, to such an attitude.) And this orientation in what underlies, this valuing of the examined life, is what most obviously links literature, philosophy and psychoanalysis.

All writers in these fields have this capacity and tendency, no one more so than Henry James. In his late-life *Autobiographies*, he refers to his own early-developing fascination with 'gaping and dawdling'. He refers to 'the quality of our [his immediate family's and his cousins'] inward life'. He notes the 'early groping' towards what became of value to him personally throughout his life – observation and imagination. The word 'gaping' recurs numerous times in these memoirs. Open-mouthed, open-eyed, almost simple, though also indubitably complex.

One such gap or gaping relates to his brother William, almost a god in Henry's eyes. '[It was] as if he [William] had gained such an advance of me in his sixteen months' experience of the world before mine began that I never for all the time of childhood and youth in the least caught up with him or overtook him'. Henry refers to 'that play of genius in him of which I never had a doubt from the first'. Adam Gopnik describes succinctly Henry's sense of this fraternal bond: 'how his brother's intellectual dominance forced him into a lesser role as attendant observer; but how, in that lesser, watching role, he eventually found his vocation in life, a vocation defined by its disabilities'. James himself writes: 'He', his future self, 'was to go without many things . . . as all persons do in whom contemplation takes so much the place of action.'

Yet what a miracle this gaping receptivity was converted into! It was partly a matter of Henry's own tenacity. 'The more I squeeze the sponge of memory the more its stored secretions flow.' 'The truth is doubtless much less in the wealth of my experience than in the tenacity of my impressions, the fact that I have lost nothing of what I saw, and that . . . the various items surprisingly swarm for me . . . [I wish] at the moment only to make my point of when and how the seeds were sown that afterwards so thickly sprouted and flowered.'

He has come to terms with the fact of his 'disability for action'. 'If success in life may perhaps be best defined as the performance in age of some intentions arrested in youth, I may frankly put in a claim to it.' That is, one should have faith in the 'day-dreams of infant ignorance'. He refers to them also as 'divinations'; predictions, but also (I suggest) as verging on intentions, however provisional, however inchoate, for the future. These early fascinations and tendencies applied not only to his way of thinking and writing, but also to his love of particular worlds, of theatre, of art, and of London – this last he links with the smell of print in some of the first books he came across. 'He [Henry himself] was to enjoy more than anything the so-far-from-showy practice of wondering and dawdling and gaping. He was really, I think, much to profit by it.'

James wrote of the 'pale joy' of only understanding that one doesn't understand. But he also was 'much to profit' by this wondering and watching. Later, the gap will be filled, the mouth that gaped will swallow and digest. The tenacious work will be done. A lack is turned into a deeper gain.

When I read Colm Tóibín's *The Master*, his novel about a fictional Henry James, I began to think more about James's detachment, I thought I recalled reading that James had described looking through a fence into a playground, watching other children play and act. Failing to find this in the *Autobiographies*, on re-looking I came across what I think must have been what I had, hazily, in mind. James remembers a large house at the north-eastern corner of 18th Street and Broadway, whose grounds were 'peopled with animal life . . . I have but to close my eyes, in order to open them inwardly again, while I lean against the tall brown iron rails and peer through to a romantic view of browsing and pecking and parading creatures'. He will always be looking in, through railings. What I had partly mis-remembered conveys, I now think, the message: James compensates for his being outside animal life by the passionate, nose-against-the-railings, looking in, both onto the world of action and sensuality in others, and inwards into his own pecking and browsing.

The intense dramas of Henry James's inner life contrast with the conventionality and stability of his outer, social life.

And now I read by chance, in novelist Alan Hollinghurst's review of *Germs*, the memoir of philosopher Richard Wollheim, about a similar but less transparent fence, in Wollheim's case with more explicit hints of wildness and animal brutalities beyond:

> There is a brilliant section about a fox-terrier . . . and of their walks together in a semi-wild area of sand, gorse and blackberry bush known as the Black Fence, from the tall corrugated-iron fence that closed off the undeveloped tract beyond it. Nobby's escapes under the fence, and his returns bloodied by adventures the young Richard can only imagine, are occasions for much fear and frenzied prayer. But it is the unremarkable landscape itself that endures for Wollheim, remembered in every detail, and becoming indeed the pattern for thought in later life, 'the involuntary backcloth to much thinking in my mind, particularly of an abstract kind'.

Tóibín's novel is about a fictionalised but persuasively realistic Henry, and he brings out the detachment, that involuntary backcloth, in one episode after another.

Here is one of them. Henry, who like William had avoided fighting in the Civil War, is visiting badly wounded soldiers in New England. They were in what was called a 'field hospital', which consisted merely of 'canvas tents and improvised shanties'. The men 'lay inert, half dead'. Henry talked to a few, in particular to one boy whose 'calm bravery, his whispering readiness for what was coming', touched him. On his way back to Newport, sitting on a deckchair on the steamboat, 'he felt involved for once in an America from which he had kept himself apart'. He wanted to aid and console the young soldier, 'but he also knew that he wanted to be alone in his room with the night coming down and a book close by and pen and paper and the knowledge that the door would remain shut until the morning came and he would not be disturbed.' (The 'ands' and the lack of punctuation suggest both a breathless urgency of wish and the anticipation of an uninterrupted sequence of time.)

The gap between the two desires filled him with sadness and astonishment at the 'mystery of the self, the mystery of having single consciousness, knowing merely its own bare feelings and experiencing singly and alone its own pain or fear or pleasure or complacency'. Suddenly, Tóibín continues, the realisation 'how deeply real and apart this self was came fiercely home to him; how intact and separate this self was once the knife was cutting ruthlessly into the flesh of someone else . . . He realised that his own separateness was complete, inviolate, just as the young soldier could never know the comfort and privilege which came from being the son of Henry James senior, who had been kept away from the war.'

'I am me.'

James had been protected, and protected himself, from the clamour and clash of engaged life. Most of us become involved, willy-nilly, in the jangling animation of social life. We shout and play, we interact and marry. We go to war, say – if we have to – jubilantly or sombrely. From time to time, even in some cases almost contemporaneously, we stand back, more or less, but first we plunge, or teeter, in.

I have had the great good luck to have never had to go to war or, except for my first three years, suffer it on my doorstep. In my youth, I rushed to be part of things, of a group. I did not particularly like loud extroverts, but I did love the camaraderie and participation of teams.

I realised later that I could take the somewhat dubious pleasure of being the number two, slightly on the fringe, following the leader but allowed to avoid his or her responsibility. I learned this from a psychodrama event, one of weekly sessions that the nursing staff at Northgate Clinic in London , where I worked for two winters in the 1970s, arranged for ourselves. On this occasion, 'God' told us that we were to be members of an island-dwelling tribe; we had no language, and each of us could take on any role. My choice was to become a child, who could go where he liked and be 'in', or half in, everything. In the next scene, 'God' decreed that we should be endowed with speech. Finally the tribe should select a leader. Gender played its part throughout this process. One man declined to take the role of leader despite being encouraged to do so. Two others became ambitious rivals, ending up fighting for the throne. I grew up from being aged four, say, to fourteen, but only to become the number two to whoever won, thus being with the women in the domestic sphere and avoiding stark conflict. (When things fell apart, the women took over in more practical, less hierarchical and conflictual ways.)

As protagonists and partisans, we are participants and combatants in the interpersonal activities of life. But then, perhaps, we shut the door, and become aware of ourselves. We have our momentary realisation of 'inviolate' separateness. We are not only social beings; we are also unique, private, separate.

Henry James had this quality of separateness to an extreme degree, and it was central to his becoming the writer he was.

Each tendency has losses and gains. The cutting off may be either escapist or creative, or both. It is a withdrawal, a defence – there is always a 'sense of doom which comes with loving and attachment', James writes. He 'was at times', as novelist Elizabeth Lowry wrote of him, 'guarded even in his own most intimate relationships, and wary of overly-demanding entanglements'. In fact, he fled from them. He failed to go to friends, women, who asked urgently for his help. Lowry also points out how he 'seems to have drawn back, time and again, from the moment of consummation'. But his withdrawal is also, markedly, an entering into the deepest and subtlest motivations of the other and himself. With his often-convoluted sentences, the entanglements that drew him in most persistently and intensely were mental and linguistic.

Here is a second episode, from Tóibín's first chapter. Henry is visited by an old friend, a Russian princess who has lived most of her life in Paris. She has come to London to tell him that she is about to return permanently from Paris to Russia, to a life of subservience to her domineering husband, in which she will be compelled to live in a dilapidated palace deep in the countryside. She has prepared for her ostracism by 'seeing everyone who is still alive' and by reading over the letters of all those who are dead. She has burned the letters of one Paul Joukowsky and also met up with him.

We learn that Henry and this Paul, both now around fifty, had not met for twenty years. Henry had not even allowed himself to think of Paul, and 'no-one had ever come like this and mentioned his name'. Now, the princess's apparently casual but implicitly knowing reference to Paul brings him back to a significant event from the time of their last meeting, an event that is a key to his whole way of being. Henry had at that time returned to Paris, where he received a note from Paul intimating that he would be alone that evening in his third-floor flat. Gazing upwards, Henry had been rooted to the spot outside, straining to see Paul's face at the window.

'Night fell, no one came or went . . . He had stood there for hours, wet with rain, brushed at intervals by those passing by. Then he walked slowly home. He was on dry land again. His clothes were soaking, his shoes had been destroyed by the rain.' He wonders now 'if those hours were not the truest that he had ever lived', perhaps the clearest statement of the central dilemma of his life with its sad, melancholic, lonely outcome that was transformed into animation and richness by his writing.

Tóibín has his character writing, for the first time, and for strictly private purposes, the story of what might (had he been different) have happened: what if (we imagine him imagining) he had 'alerted Paul to his presence and Paul had come down and they had walked up the stairs together in silence? . . . His hands were shaking. He had never before allowed himself to go, even in imagination, beyond that point. It was the closest he had come, but he had not come close at all!'

Paralysed with terror, he had been unable to move towards the other, to his potential lover. He could, though, write, and even twenty years on, this imagined alternative makes him shake.

The story is not invented by Tóibín (though the ruination of the shoes may have been). James's friend Edmund Gosse, staying one summer at Henry's house in Rye, and walking together in the garden as twilight deepened, suddenly 'found that in profuse and enigmatic language he [James] was recounting an experience, not something repeated or imagined'. He was 'standing on the pavement of a city, in the dusk, and gazing upwards watching, watching for the lighting of a lamp in a window on the third storey . . . Through bursting tears he strained to see what was behind [the lighted lamp], the unapproachable face. He stood there for hours, wet with the rain . . . '

Others have unearthed references to a Russian young man, Z, probably Zhukovsky, with whom Henry James swore eternal friendship. Was Zhukovsky Joukowsky? We are given to think he was.

As for transformation of memory into fiction: in one of James's late novels, *The Ambassadors*, Strether, the not-so-young 'ambassador' from America, is attracted in Paris by the milieu of the young Chad, whom he had been sent to recall or rescue from a life of suspiciously Bohemian looseness. There are hints that Strether is attracted also to Chad himself. In one scene, he looks up at a balcony in the dusk and sees a young man smoking, who turns out not to be Chad but his friend, who, Strether comes to realise, spots him looking up. The scene is repeated in reverse later, when Strether himself is on a balcony alone. Both passages suggest Strether's being outside some desired (and feared) scene or person, looking and being looked at, dawdling and gaping, but it not being the real thing, just looking in and out, cut off from the kind of youthful romantic and erotic yearnings and enactments that Paris represents and that Strether had missed out on. Strether's reflections end with a qualified reconciliation; he refers to a 'perched privacy' (remember the birds perched in the menagerie on 18th Street?) as the 'only domicile, the only fireside, in the great ironic city, on which he had the shadow of a claim'.

* * *

Henry James is, typically, the third, the one outside, the observer looking in and out. Novelists take us inside their characters. And thus a little further inside ourselves.

Tolstoy has a masterly passage in *War and Peace* that shows how tension and awkwardness may arise between two people as a result of their unconscious or semi-conscious ideas. The author/narrator is able to observe with conviction these kinds of moves of the mind, these kinds of interaction.

The episode concerns a first meeting between two women characters who later become close friends. Mary (or Maria) is the sister and Natasha the fiancée of Prince Andrew (Andrei) Bolkonsky. Natasha's father has brought her to Mary's father's town house for the meeting. Natasha is being introduced to her fiancé's family. Both women are subject to troubling unconscious thoughts and emotions, and to their defences against them. The result is a meeting characterised by touchiness and strain.

Mary, the sister, who is not a conventional beauty, is unmarried (in this milieu, to be single in her late twenties meant being 'left on the shelf', that is, almost an old maid). She lives at home in the country looking after her much-loved but brusque and difficult father. Mary is

97

inwardly critical of Natasha. She finds Natasha 'too fashionably dressed, frivolously gay and vain'. Tolstoy explains: 'she did not at all realize that before having seen her future sister-in-law she was prejudiced against her by her involuntary envy of her [Natasha's] beauty, youth and happiness, as well as by jealousy of her brother's love for her.'

Tolstoy uses the word 'involuntary' here, both in the sense of unwilled, out of her control (that is, she wishes that these difficult feelings didn't come up in her, no doubt feeling ashamed of them), and also in the sense of unconscious – she 'did not at all realize' that she felt envy and jealousy. These unconscious and involuntary emotions, which she cannot clearly recognise, but which she doesn't want to reveal, make her tense and unnatural.

On the other side, Natasha is mortified, that is, embarrassed and humiliated, by her father's nervousness at the possibility of having to meet Mary's father, a man whose reputation for being trenchantly opinionated is well-founded. Natasha's shame on behalf of *her* father – she 'blushed for him' – turns into anger and off-handedness, a sort of cold indifference. Tolstoy describes this shift as follows: 'She suddenly shrank into herself, and involuntarily assumed an off-hand air which alienated Mary still more.'

Natasha thus cuts off from herself and from Mary, becoming hard and prickly, as her way of dealing with, and denying, her shame, as well as her incomprehension and hurt that Mary's father has made it known that he is opposed to the marriage. Her reaction is due also to her sensitivity to the older character's hostility. Mary in her turn reacts touchily to Natasha's alienating touchiness.

'Neither knows why they do certain things or why the conversation became irksome. Neither knows what she herself feels. Mary doesn't know why it's so difficult to speak of the marriage, and Natasha doesn't know why she glances at Mary ironically and critically.'

In these few pages Tolstoy shows his acute observation and understanding both of unconscious thoughts and emotions, and of the kinds of defences, also unconscious, that are used to push away awareness of them; the combination of which creates the mutual dislike that he describes so acutely.

Novels expand my idea of the self and its depths. I was, and am still, excited by this opening up of vistas, inside myself and outside. Indeed, one special feature of novels for both reader and writer is getting into the minds of others, real and imaginary. There is joy in this expansion.

Perhaps this is an example of my looking through the railings into the life of a novelist who is doing the same.

CHAPTER 6

'PLEASE LOOK AFTER MY DOG'

I guess it was in 1965, when I came back to Cambridge to do post-graduate work – by then I'd begun to get interested in psychoanalysis – that I joined the Samaritans, a national phone line for people who are depressed or suicidal. Samaritans did four-hour daytime shifts, and occasional all-night ones, 'manning' the phone and responding. I don't recall my reasons for joining, except for the vague interest in helping, and a sense that this would be a route towards contact with people in emotional trouble.

There was a ten-week introductory training and assessment period. The last two of these sessions involved staged calls, to which we applicants took turns to respond. In one the 'caller' said that he would be away for a while; would the Samaritans be willing to look after his dog? The voice sounded depressed. When the potential Samaritan responded as if this was a limited, literal request, the tone became more insistent. Blandly benevolent, the trainee on the phone repeatedly failed to entertain the idea that there might be a hidden, more drastic subtext in the message. To the rest of us, listening in on the loudspeaker system, this was painful, even embarrassing. It was also salutary; people asking for help may not admit their despair explicitly, yet they phone. They both want and don't want the intensity of their depression to be known. And we too, at the other end of the phone, may be reluctant to experience such distress, with the often-accompanying anger. We had better be alert to it.

In the course of my phone-answering as a Samaritan, I found that people did not readily ring off: I learned I could listen in a way that felt to them that I was in some degree in touch with them. The experience made me curious to understand more. Why did life become unbearable for some? How was it that a listening ear and presence could, at least in the short term, make a difference between wanting to die and regaining hope and the will to live?

I'm reminded of a story told me by Neville Symington, a psycho-analytic colleague and friend. One winter evening he landed in Aarhus, Denmark's second city, where he was to give seminars over the following days. The taxi driver, having asked him what brought him there, then told him about a recent experience of his own. A man had got into his cab late one evening. He asked to be taken to the harbour. The driver was receptive to the somewhat obscured message that his passenger planned to throw himself into the icy water. The driver took a stand. He locked the doors, and told him that he wouldn't go along with this; he would not let him out of the cab until he had at least told him what it was all about. The man then disclosed that he had lost his wife and daughter in the course of a few weeks, one I think from cancer, the other from a road accident. He could see no point in carrying on. They spoke for some hours in the quiet, dark car. At last, the passenger asked to be dropped at his home, not at the harbour.

As Symington said, the driver became this man's temporary therapist. Locking the door was the first step. He turned his taxi into a life-saving consulting room. He did not fail to see the depth of despair, nor did he retreat from it. Like the 'Good Samaritan', he did not hesitate to offer himself in the crisis. The passenger needed someone to be there, empathic, taking him seriously without being judgemental. Most people will never go to formal therapy, but we all need this kind of receptivity and care at difficult times.

Close listening is at the heart of what psychoanalysts offer. We do more; but this is a *sine qua non* of the capacity to help, not only in moments of crisis, but sometimes through thick and thin. We have to bear distress with the patient.

In 1968, I left Cambridge to take up my position in Newcastle, where the workload for a first year of lecturing was heavy. I did not attempt to re-join the Samaritans until returning to London (and to professional cricket) in 1971, an arrangement that left me with winters to fill and the opportunity to explore possible careers for whenever my cricket playing would come to an end. I applied to a local branch of the Samaritans. I would not need to repeat the assessment seminars, but I would have an interview with one of their trainers, who turned out to be a young psychiatrist. Predictably, he asked me why I wanted to do this work. Among other reasons, I said I wanted to learn more about myself through this process. I was turned down. I had failed the interview. I had enough self-respect and, I think, realism not to feel mortified, but rather to protest and to ask for the grounds for the decision. I was told, in effect, that I had been selfish. In a second interview, with another person, I said I thought stopping me from re-joining was a mistaken response. I did wish to help others, but I sensed also that being aware of my own feelings, and paying attention to them, could contribute to that task. Moreover, why should I not learn things for my own benefit too? I was invited to join – and did.

* * *

I have at times fared well in interviews, while in other situations I've done myself no favours. My success in the Newcastle interview was down to me in that I had to be resilient enough not to fold up when the law professor assumed I had nothing of value to offer. But it was facilitated by the presence of a person who made clear that he thought I had something to say – 'Let him finish.' To believe in myself, I needed – and was able to make use of – that sort of confirmation.

A differently helpful element in the two-and-a-half-day interview process for the Civil Service in 1964 had been my own uncertainty about whether this was what I really wanted to do. Naturally, I was keen to succeed; but as I didn't too much mind failing, I could freely be myself – more freely at any rate than if I really cared. Less was at stake. At the end of this process, I learned I'd come equal top for the year.

I also contributed to some failures. One tendency I have is to put people, activities or ways of being into categories, ranking them. When I admire, I tend to idealise, attributing exaggerated qualities to the other while seeing myself as small in comparison. This leads to loss of confidence and of access to my own ideas. I become too eager to please, and then stilted. I may feel I'm an imposter. By contrast, and to leap over that compliance, I overvalue myself (though it doesn't feel like that at the time) and enact this superiority. One result has been my feeling compelled to prove that I am not conformist by being provokingly, self-destructively, different. I then appear to think I know more than my interviewers, and thus subtly undermine them. They're not impressed. Perhaps there was an element of this with the young psychiatrist.

This damaging pattern of thought and behaviour goes beyond simply doing badly at interviews. It has led to my refraining from taking on with full vigour people who I felt were better than me in whatever field. For example, though I played the great fast bowlers of my day with courage, it was a stiff-upper-lip brand, a matter of gritting my teeth and surviving. Batting at that highest level I became tense and constrained. This rigidity was not only a matter of technical or inbuilt limitations (though they were real enough). It was also that in the atmosphere of Test cricket I would play with less freedom than against the same bowlers in county cricket, that is, at the next level down. And as a psychoanalyst, I have not chiselled out my own views about theories or eminent practitioners, nor have I always been willing to risk making explicit my doubts or disagreements. I have been too frightened of making a fool of myself in public, and have in subtle ways avoided the fray.

* * *

Becoming, and being, a psychoanalyst has been deeply rewarding. I rather marvel that I had this idea, even this aspiration, at a time when I had little knowledge of what it might involve. In my family no one among our acquaintances was a patient, a therapist or an analyst. The whole area was foreign to our experience and worldview.

By 1965, I had done two years of philosophy at Cambridge, had played cricket professionally for eighteen months, and had passed the Civil Service exam. What to do now?

Certainly I was in a general way looking for the 'more things in heaven and earth' than were dreamed of in Horatio's philosophy. But why *these* more things, that is, self-examination and psychotherapy? How did I get to this *terra incognita*, this off-the-map intuition?

Literature was for me an introduction to the emotions, including to our tendency to deceive ourselves and be driven by unconscious assumptions. Religion offered a glance towards the esoteric, along with an enquiry into what the point of it all is.

As for the Civil Service, one prejudice of mine was viewing that work as uncreative, as opposed to that of philosophers. I remember an Indian meal in Newcastle with the Scholars, at which I spoke, pretentiously I imagine, along these lines. Angela Scholar argued strongly. There are different kinds of creativity, she said. She was right. But I'm glad the career I got into involved the personal so closely and individually.

As it happens, I had another bite of a Civil Service cherry in the late sixties. A letter arrived from a department of the Foreign Office, asking me if I'd be interested in an interview with them. Arriving at the grand old house off Pall Mall, I was directed to a large room, where a small man emerged from his seat behind an enormous desk. The room was extremely quiet. An old-fashioned grandfather clock ticked sombrely in the background. The interviewer was serious, careful, with a soft voice that I had to strain to hear. I would have a regular position in the Foreign Office, he told me, but this would be a front for my main work, which would be reporting on matters that might be significant as intelligence about the country to which I was posted. This might be a friendly country or otherwise. It was important to know what both categories – friends and foes – were up to. I expressed misgivings about the constant air of deception that would pervade the work. My interviewer said that for him it had been a fine feeling to have contributed to negotiations that avoided a war. 'We have never lost one of us,' he added. (I didn't check how broad a category 'us' was.)

The clock ticked ominously. If I was not convinced at that moment that this was not for me, I was shortly afterwards when, walking on that crisp winter's morning through St James's Park, I saw seagulls devouring a more or less torn-apart duck. Being a psychoanalyst is being for much of the time in the dark, trying to get further into someone's psyche. But the big difference is that the patient is not someone who only needs or wants to keep secrets from me, as well as from him- or herself, they also, at some level, want to know. There are therapeutic alliances as well as anti-therapeutic resistances. Being a spy would mean, I felt, living in a world of constant deception, with potential for menace and ruthlessness.

After the interview I challenged Renford Bambrough, my former philosophy supervisor, whose recommendation, I learned, had played a part in this invitation. He said that our country, like others, needs

intelligence, that is, spies, just as we need butchers. He could understand that I wanted to be neither. That was up to me.

⁂ ⁂ ⁂

Back to 1965. As I've described, John Wisdom (the man who also
taught my father-in-law) was a key figure in my tenuous but persistent
hankering after psychoanalysis. He asked, with an air of bewilderment,
how can it be that we don't know the contents of our own minds, that
someone else may at times know us better than we do? He wrote
about an episode from Dostoyevsky: in the middle of the night a
man suddenly wakes up to find himself in an intense state, creeping
up towards his sleeping wife with a knife in his hand; shocked, the
man infers or comes to recognise that he must be in the throes of an
unconscious intention to kill her.

Psychoanalysis too might enable a patient to realise, not only infer-
entially (like the man with the knife), but with fuller consciousness
or self-awareness, that he or she is or has been not only loving but
jealous, driven by hatred. Wisdom, who had been a patient himself,
writes:

> You loved your sister. Of course there were occasions when you
> lost your temper with her, but these were temporary aberrations
> when perhaps she broke your best soldiers or tore your best book.
> So far so good. It is only later, perhaps, that the adequacy of this
> picture begins to be suspected. You love your wife. You are of
> course sometimes angry with her. And here you are sorry to say
> you are sometimes extraordinarily angry with her, unreasonably
> angry, much angrier than you would be with someone else who
> had done what she did. Perhaps of course she has done the same
> thing before. But sometimes she has not. And anyway why were
> you so angry with her from the first? You might be tempted to say

107

sometimes that you detest your wife if it were not that you love her and love her very much. And now you come to think of it, though sometimes your sister was very provoking it is also true that you were sometimes angry with her about very little, and no less when grown-ups in a certain tone of voice *again* said that she was smaller and weaker than you. Did you really detest her for the love she won so easily? The suggestion is preposterous. But is it pointless? Isn't it in fact extremely pointed?

As I've said, Wisdom developed hints of Wittgenstein's that the scepticism that characteristically sets off philosophical activity has something in common with neurotic uncertainty and anxiety, but at a more abstract and intellectual level. And he takes this further, suggesting that the appropriate treatment of the philosopher's quasi-neurotic uncertainty could, or should, be akin to that of psychoanalysis.

*   *   *

Wisdom agreed to supervise my PhD. My topic was 'The Explanation of Action', with a focus on the different kinds of explanation of action (or of states of mind or of bodily movements) by the material sciences from those offered by novelists, psychoanalysts and all of us in everyday life.

The most striking difference is between accounts formulated in objective terms, as in physiology or neurology, and accounts that are subjective in that they refer to the agent's personal reasons. In the first type, no one, including the subject, is in a unique place to understand what moves them; while in the latter, each of us is in a unique (though not, especially since Freud, an infallible) position. In explanation of the first kind, one's agency as such does not enter the explanatory narrative. An example is Oliver Sacks's explanation of the person who saw his wife as a hat in terms of damage to the right hemisphere of the brain. This kind of explanation and account contrasts with: 'The reason I'm going to the supermarket is to get some cheese'; or, more complexly in Hanna Segal's example, the violinist who 'can't play in public because he sees his violin as a penis'.

Another central aim of my thesis was to offer an account of unconscious as opposed to conscious reasons. The former, of which Segal's is an example, often feel like causes, but may become owned and thus be recognisable as reasons for actions – recognisable, that is, as factors that are after all 'my' reasons, that are explanations that I am uniquely placed to recognise. Whether conscious or not, basic assumptions are intentional in a way that damage to the brain is not.

Clearly I was already trying to find ways of thinking about the unconscious.

I did not finish my PhD. In those days it was possible to get a job as a university lecturer without one, which I did in 1968 at Newcastle. And then I was too occupied with preparing lectures and so on to pay much attention to the thesis.

For the second of my three years engaged on this intellectual effort, I applied for and was accepted for the position misleadingly described as 'Research Assistant' at the University of California, Irvine; misleading in that what I did was hardly to be described as research, nor did I assist anyone. One of the teachers there was Daniel Dennett, who has since gained fame in the field as a philosopher of mind who embraces physicalism, that is, the claim that there is nothing over and above physical matter. One day in the 2000s I received a package from him in the post. It contained an essay I'd done for his class in 1967 on 'Knowledge and Belief'. He had come across it while clearing out cupboards, had re-read it, and thought it had qualities that went beyond those of usual graduate essays.

This was of course gratifying; but I wasn't sure I could have gone much further.

* * *

During this second period at Cambridge, I asked Wisdom for information and advice about becoming a psychoanalyst. He offered to introduce me to a real, live practitioner, John Klauber, a friend of his who became president of the British Psychoanalytical Society. (He also, I discovered much later, had analysed Symington.)

Klauber kindly invited me to visit him in his elegant house in Elsworthy Road, London NW3. I remember a room full of books, and a man of charm and sophistication.

It was only after getting a degree in Modern History at Oxford that Klauber himself had decided to become a psychoanalyst. To this end, he studied science up to A level, got into medical school, qualified as a doctor and specialised as a psychiatrist, before finally training as a psychoanalyst. (This was, incidentally, the same path as Wilfred Bion's.) I learned, or calculated, that he must have started on this medical marathon when he was at a similar age to mine at the time – twenty-four or twenty-five. Incorrectly, I got the impression that he was telling me that a medical degree was a prerequisite of becoming a psychoanalyst; rather, he was, I came to realise, recommending the journey he himself had taken.

For years there had been non-medical analysts in the British Society, though in the 1920s and 1930s they had been treated as second-class members, not allowed to do initial consultations (only medically qualified analysts were thought competent to do these), and precluded from certain committees. Indeed, in contrast to Freud, who expressed full support of 'lay' psychoanalysts in his paper of 1926, Ernest Jones, president of the British Society, advocated in the following year that the (preferably small) proportion of 'lay' members 'should not engage in practice independently of the medical profession'. With that background, it was not surprising that non-medical persons seeking training would be directed first towards medical training.

The accredited training institutes of the American Psychoanalytic Association took this further. For decades, they insisted on applicants being qualified as doctors before even being considered for training. Only after an anti-monopoly lawsuit initiated in 1985 were these bodies legally obliged to open their doors to non-medical applicants.

As for me, I couldn't countenance becoming a student for another ten years at least, at which point I would still not have started to train in psychoanalysis. I now believe that much of what I would have learned in medicine would have been irrelevant, at times even misleading, to the work of a psychoanalyst. I left Klauber's house in some awe, but also disappointment. Despite his help and generosity, the outcome of our informal talk might have been my permanently giving up on my quest.

* * *

After this visit, I stayed on in philosophy for another five years before returning to professional cricket at the age of twenty-nine. I had learned that my inference from the meeting with Klauber was wrong. A year later, I had also had an unexpected acquaintance with one branch of the psychiatric world. Someone to whom I was close spent a summer in Halliwick Hospital, suffering from depression. I learned a lot from her. At Halliwick, I went to art therapy classes led by Elspeth Weir, who would invite us to draw or paint as the mood took us; she then initiated discussion on what our productions might say about ourselves.

It was clear to patients there that the people who helped most were not necessarily the psychiatrists; it might be the night porter, the cook, the art therapist or a nurse who made insightful comments or showed deeper understanding. Patients also learned a lot from each other.

One outcome of my visits, especially from the art therapy, was to go into therapy myself. At one point, I was referred to a male therapist who, when I arrived at the door of his reclaimed garage for my first session, greeted me with: 'My name is Roy, er, er, I mean Roland.' He then told me how he was trying to get in touch with his adolescent self, before he had changed his name to 'Roy'. This was not (as I remember) a helpful experience, though he was a kindly man. With another therapist I came to realise how unkind, even cruel, I could be. Like Homer's sinners, I clearly needed to be slowed down by something akin to 'Prayer'.

It was Elspeth who recommended Marion Milner's *On Not Being Able to Paint*, which included her account of discovering how her hostility combined with her repression of it led to inhibition as a painter. I went on to read much of Milner's work, both before she became an analyst and after. She was the first current analyst whom I encountered in print. I loved her work, and later (in 1976) asked her if she would be my training analyst. Born in 1900, she was, she told me, too old to take on a new patient for training. As I was leaving, she asked a question of me: what is a hat-trick in cricket? Her grandson had just got one, and she hadn't had the heart to tell him she didn't know what it was. (It's dismissing three batters in consecutive deliveries.) Later, I tried to fob off a persistent journalist who pressed me to come to dinner by saying that I'd come if she could get anyone I mentioned to join the dinner party. I proposed Marion, and Marion in her enterprising way agreed. I remember only that the other guest was a man (Robin Knox-Johnston?) who'd sailed single-handed round the world.

In 1982, Mana and I moved with our two young children into our current house, in Chalk Farm, north-west London. It happened to be a few houses from where Milner lived. We became friends until her death in 1998. At the end, I had known for some days that she was dying, but when the news of her death was brought to our house by her carer, I burst into tears. At that very moment, the bell rang again. At the door was a man who had arrived early, and at the wrong door of the house, for a consultation. I had assumed this second ring was to tell me more about Marion. I wondered how the prospective patient experienced me, drying my tears and then trying to recover from that traumatic, though expected, message. The consultation did not lead to his coming for treatment.

* * *

When in 1971 I left Newcastle for London, Karl Britton helped me in more ways than one by introducing me to his sister, Clare, a psychoanalyst who was the recently widowed second wife of the distinguished psychoanalyst, Donald Winnicott. I visited Clare several times over the following years, as she coped bravely with skin cancer and the numerous operations that entailed. She gave me two suggestions that were crucial in how things turned out for me. One was her firm advice that I should give up any idea of embarking on academic psychology as a next step in furthering my idea of becoming a psychoanalyst.

I'd spent enough time in academia, she said – what I needed was more first-hand experience of working with people with emotional difficulties, to get a sense whether this broad field would suit me (and I it). This was without doubt the right approach for me, and as a result I made enquiries and kept my ears open. Through Sue Gray, who had been a psychiatric social worker at Paddington Green Hospital, where Winnicott had been the director, I heard of the Northgate Clinic in Hendon, north London, where I was accepted to work as a nursing assistant. I spent two winters there between cricket seasons.

This was an experience that convinced me to follow up my intuition towards psychoanalytic training.

Her second input had a less intended, but even more consequential, impact. In 1976 when I was about to tour India to play cricket, Clare told me that, if I was going to Ahmedabad, the biggest city in Gujerat, I must meet 'the beautiful Indian psychoanalyst, Kamalini Sarabhai', who had trained in London and then returned to set up a mental health institute for children, families and adults. The institute, still flourishing in 2023, contains on its campus a clinic for a range of treatments, two small schools for young children, a workshop and an occupational therapy centre for adults with other abilities. Kamalini engaged me in a discussion with the staff about the unusual combination of cricket and psychoanalysis. How, she asked, did I get from one to the other? Through her, on that day, I met her beautiful daughter, Mana, who became my second wife.

* * *

Northgate Clinic was an NHS, adolescent in-patient service run on psychoanalytic lines. Each young person living there had individual analytic therapy three times a week; all were in small groups with staff members, and there were twice-weekly community meetings. In addition, the staff had 'sensitivity groups' on Wednesdays to discuss staff tensions and the conflicts that emerged both from our interactions with patients and their projections, and between ourselves.

Working as a nursing assistant at Northgate was for me a formative experience. I was a member of one of the small groups, and went to other meetings. Apart from these formal involvements, our task was to be around patients, to prod them into getting up in the morning, take them on outings, and generally be in contact with them in their everyday lives. I learned a lot about mental difficulties, and about how a therapeutic community worked. There was in effect a set of different systems or nets. Individual and group work, large- and small-scale seminars and meetings, formal and informal interactions – all functioned like interlocking Russian dolls, each containing each. For instance, individual therapy would address (among other things) the problems patients had in the clinic, with their peer group, staff and families. The small groups would discuss acting out that might arise as a result of inevitable disturbances produced by the one-to-one therapy, as well as those arising from the functioning of the group itself; and whole-group meetings would address overall management, including various ways in which disruptive forces threatened mayhem.

I remember one community meeting at which the excellent medical director, psychiatrist Brian O'Connell, raised an issue of repeated leakage from the bathrooms upstairs. His tone and content expressed vividly the fear that perhaps everyone – patients and staff alike – more or less consciously felt, that the whole operation could be flooded by the strength and violence of feelings aroused in this emotional hothouse (or wet-house). On top of the ordinary turmoil of adolescence, the patients had serious problems, such as depression, anger management, delinquency, psychotic episodes. One patient, a seventeen-year-old boy who had been admitted on the same day as I started, committed suicide when away from the unit. Another boy could not bear the tension and left; some months later he wrote from a juvenile prison saying how much he valued the work at Northgate, but it had been harder to face his feelings there than to act them out outside and be punished in prison. He wanted to encourage people to stick it out at Northgate.

One of the most significant experiences for me was the series of seminars for the nursing staff run by deputy director, Donald Bird, an experienced psychoanalyst and psychiatrist. Healing processes start with raw, scarcely articulated, emotional experiences. Dr Bird would begin each meeting by asking for one of us to speak about interactions with a patient or group of patients that had made an impact on us, and for others to comment on how the patient(s) being discussed made them feel. He noted the degree of unanimity or otherwise, and invited us to enquire into these different impacts. He helped us to see, for example, how some patients provoked a split in the staff group; they were inclined to form special relationships with a staff member, who became the idealised carer who 'really understood' them, while other staff members were regarded as rigid and unsympathetic. These excluded carers might become highly critical of the lack of boundaries that ensued. In another seminar, discussing what it was about a particular patient that invited bullying, we came to recognise in his way of being a certain long-suffering arrogance that turned him into an almost willing martyr or victim. He comes back to me now, with his air of self-righteous superiority and an inexorably pained expression. The seminar helped us to convert or expand our initial feelings from simple irritation and impatience into a larger and more articulated empathy.

In the first fifty or so years of psychoanalysis, the analyst's counter-transference was viewed as pathological; it was felt that the therapist was allowing his or her feelings to interfere with the requisite steady neutrality. (Perhaps this view was shared by the psychiatrist at Brent Samaritans.) The appearance of troublesome emotions in the analyst could even be seen as a reason for further analysis. It was not until 1950 that Paula Heimann shifted this view of counter-transference to include situations where feelings in the therapist (like the feelings we nursing staff felt) were not only (up to a point) inevitable, but also, potentially, sources of information about conflict or disturbance in the patient. I came to realise that what Bird did was to introduce us to the helpful potential of thinking about the feelings stirred up in us by the patient. As Clare Winnicott said, self-awareness and awareness of others were two sides of the same coin. I found this insight, along with these discussions, fascinating. They, along with the whole experience in Northgate, clinched my conviction that entering this field was what I really wanted to do.

* * *

In 1976, I applied to train at the Institute of Psychoanalysis (another name for the British Psychoanalytical Society). I had also had an interview for training in child psychotherapy at the Tavistock Clinic; but a friend suggested that I might later wish I had done the arguably deeper training at the institute. I was invited to a preliminary meeting, with Anne-Marie Sandler.

Anxious, I turned up at the institute in New Cavendish Street to discover that I had been misinformed; I was supposed to be at Mrs Sandler's consulting room a few miles away in St John's Wood. I was angry at this error. I felt that an organisation involved in helping people should have taken care to give me the right information for such an important (for me) meeting. I didn't consider fully the possibility that the error might have been mine, but I don't think it was, since no one suggested that to me, and my memory is that the institute paid for a taxi to take me the few miles to St John's Wood. I mentioned earlier a couple of factors that helped me to be myself at interviews. Here was another motivator: I felt entitled to be forceful, even angry, at the start of the meeting. Certainly, I was not on this occasion timid or over-eager to please. And getting my frustration off my chest was the beginning of what I think was a good discussion.

Shortly afterwards I had a letter from Mrs Sandler. The feeling of the committee was that I needed more experience in the field before going ahead with the formal admission process. This made sense to me; I'm not sure if I wrote back; I assume I did. A few weeks later I had a second, even more charming, letter from her. This one said that some of the English members of the committee had informed her that captaining a professional cricket team might have more relevance to the kinds of experience required than she, a Swiss woman, was able to appreciate; I could go ahead with my formal application.

Subsequently interviewed by Pearl King and Eric Brenman, I was accepted. Later in the same year, I was selected to play cricket for England, against West Indies, and then to go on the tour to India, Sri Lanka and Australia, which included the Centenary Test. This late call to Test cricket gave an extra lease of life to my cricketing career. I was at an age when some cricketers are ready to retire, so I was both surprised and of course intensely pleased. I had planned to stop in two or three years. Instead, I played on for six.

I knew I needed analysis. What's more I would have to have a training analysis. I went to see two possible training analysts. My impression of one was that she was physically disabled. While being taught by her later, I realised she wasn't; this must have been my projection based on my conception of her emotional posture as not what I wanted. She knew I was playing cricket professionally, and planned to do so for some time. I did not think it a favourable omen when she told me that she would soon have a vacancy for a regular session. At 11.25 each morning. Not far down the road at Lord's, 11.25 was the precise time the umpires would be walking out to put the bails on the stumps ready for the first ball of the day.

* * *

I began my training analysis in 1978, and the training at the institute in 1981. For my last four years in cricket, I would go to analytic sessions at 9.35 in the morning, and get to Lord's ten minutes after they had finished. Very generously, my analyst would see me on some days at 6.15 in the morning when I was playing away from London (but not too far away).

What was it like combining the two? More often, I think, the calm before the storm rather than the other way round. At a time of being in the public eye (I was captain of England) there was a lot of pressure and demand. It often felt like a welcome retreat, probably in the good sense, from this hectic life. Time for slowing down, a helpful space.

One Monday morning, a fellow trainee whom I didn't then know had just finished his session at 9.30, in which he was, he told me later, basking in some minor success in his own club cricket game the day before. Arriving for mine, I happened to park behind him. Glancing in his mirror, he saw the captain of England drive up, and shortly after go to the analyst's front door and ring the bell. He felt embarrassed, but also amused.

He made me smile. But I didn't find the combination of being at the top of one tree and the bottom of the other easy. I didn't want to be known as 'the cricketer'. On the other hand, I had nothing much to offer yet as 'the therapist'. One difficult aspect of the analytic training, not just for me, is that one feels, at times, infantilised and deskilled, more by the situation than by senior individuals. We have to encounter our own child-selves in analysis, we are more or less lost in this strange new world of the unconscious, and we have this powerful transference to our analyst, and to some degree to other teachers.

Aged forty, I retired from cricket in 1982. I was ready to finish. In my end was my beginning – an on-drive wide of mid-on. My first runs in first class cricket came from a similar stroke, off the bowling of Eric Bedser. This last one, off the bowling of slow left-armer, Richard Illingworth, produced the winning runs in the final match of the season against Worcestershire; three days earlier, on Saturday 11 September, we had gained sufficient bonus points to win our fourth Championship trophy in seven years. I ended on a high note; I was tired, ready to go. We had a new child, Lara, born 9 June; a new home, and I had the makings of a new career. It was not a mid-life crisis. Over the next summers, I rarely missed playing, feeling the lack when Middlesex were about to play arch-rivals like Surrey or Yorkshire on a lovely June morning. But I had much else to look forward to, and to be stimulated by.

I have now been working analytically for exactly half my life. I regard myself as very fortunate to have found this vocation. Age, writing and psychoanalysis itself have all enabled me to work to integrate more fully these very different modes of thinking, living and of earning a living.

CHAPTER 7

HAYDN'S DUCK QUARTET

Private Eye once wrote of me that my favourite piece of music was Haydn's 'Duck Quartet'. Because that was what I usually scored. I sometimes got letters asking for the opus number for this apparently little-known work.

As it happened, it was Haydn who was the first classical composer I knew the name of. When I was ten or eleven, our music teacher, 'Doc' Wray, played the class recorded extracts from two pieces by Haydn. One was the passage in the symphony nicknamed 'The Surprise', in which a quiet, decorous calm is interrupted by an explosive chord; the second was the slow tick-tock of his 'Clock' Symphony. When he asked us what we felt these pieces were about, I was at a loss. But I remember the moment of enlightenment when he named them. *Yes*, I thought, *now I understand, now I can hear them*. (And I've remembered them ever since.) Our teacher went on to play us 'Rose among the heather', Schubert's song, the tune and words of which also come back to me now, almost seventy years on, though their fuller meaning, about desire, cruelty and the pricking of conscience, was way beyond me at the time.

I like it when apt words are found for music. It's similar to what happens when our Gujerati host tells me that her 'green chutney' contains green garlic, coriander and mint. Knowing the ingredients, I can taste more specifically than when, blandly, I found it merely 'tasty'.

In 2020, I was invited to be the interviewee in the Radio 3 programme *Private Passions*. The format is a conversation with composer Michael Berkeley, interspersed with six or seven musical excerpts, usually but not always classical, chosen by the guest. I had been asked before, but declined, for two reasons; one that I was nervous that being personal in public might detract from analytic neutrality, the second that I find I don't often listen to music. But now that, outside sessions (besides of course inside them), patients have many means of forming opinions and learning facts about their analysts, and now that I am more convinced that these impressions do not necessarily obscure or shut down the transference, which is strong enough to survive such peripheral encounters, I feel more relaxed about doing a public interview of this kind. And I'm writing a memoir, something I thought I'd never do! What's more, patients can choose whether or not to bother themselves with a programme or book. As for not listening to music much, that I now see as of interest (to me at least).

Here is something of what I said, or thought of saying, in commenting on four of my selected pieces.

First, Bach's *Goldberg Variations*, with Ralph Kirkpatrick on the harpsichord, the instrument I prefer to the piano for this piece; it sounds less 'smooth', more 'clangy', more rough-edged; one critic called it more 'honest'. The work, book-ended by the initial theme with its relative simplicity, consists of thirty variations of extraordinary range, from brilliance to sadness, stateliness to exuberance, from earthy conviction to open-endedness and otherworldliness. With its ten clusters of three, each cluster starting with a canon, each canon starting at a different tone, the whole piece is governed by a strict mathematical structure. The ending reminds me of T. S. Eliot's 'In my beginning is my end' from *East Coker*; in the *Goldberg*, it is also the case that in the end is my beginning. (One sometimes finds this in psychoanalysis, both in individual sessions, and when towards the end of an analysis themes that were prominent at the beginning recur, brought back more as memories than as simple repetitions. Like the *Goldberg* theme, these repetitions and echoes are now weighted and enriched by what has gone on in between.)

Michael Scholar, a talented amateur pianist and organist, told me that in his dedication Bach describes the *Goldberg Variations* as 'Exercises for the keyboard' – a modest claim, as if this great work were merely a training routine in preparation for the real thing. But Bach adds that they are 'for the delectation of the soul'. Along with humility, he aspires to high-mindedness. And the combination of emotion and intellect is extraordinary.

Second, Mozart's Violin Sonata No. 32 (K. 454), with Jascha Heifetz and Brooks Smith. This is a limpid work, in which the two instruments have an equal conversation rather than being, as in earlier works for this combination, a piano solo with violin decorations. I am struck by the cool intensity of Heifetz's playing. I learned recently about his personal integrity in playing as an encore the Violin Sonata by Richard Strauss in Jerusalem in 1953, thereby breaking a 'ban' or taboo on German music in Israel. Heifetz said, 'There are only two kinds of music, good and bad.' This led to an attack on him by a fanatical youth with an iron bar, which permanently damaged his right arm.

Third, Schubert's D 960 Piano Sonata in B flat. The first movement begins with a beautiful lyrical theme, mainly in the right hand. Soon this is interrupted by a starkly contrasting growl in the bass. Serenity is disturbed, the snake has made its presence felt in the Garden of Eden. It's as if the music is bipolar. As the movement develops, the growl is articulated, so that it is no longer a mere expletive, it becomes a narrative. Beauty and the beast are integrated, part of a whole. The development is psychological as well as musical. The serenity of the first theme becomes more poignant, the pain does not simply invade. (I like the word 'poignant'.)

One potential achievement of analysis occurs when a patient's depression and mania appear closer together, within the same session, not split off from each other. This is one aspect of the process of integration. Then happy, serene times are tinged with melancholy, and when the melancholy mood descends, it is not so absolute or so overwhelming. Analysis may also enable the patient to slow down sufficiently for different moods to be filled out, articulated, and seen to be not merely growls or cries. Analyst and patient together may come to hear and speak the moves of the mind, and the patient becomes less at the mercy of his moods.

Towards the end of her treatment, one patient told me that, whereas to start with she had been simply depressed, now she could 'walk round her depression'. Though this phrase might have indicated a state of being cut off from the feelings (walking round them as opposed to going through them), I thought they were in this moment more a matter of being able to see that the feelings had boundaries, that she could occupy a space from which to look at them. This seemed to me to represent a shift akin to that from grief to mourning.

As for Schubert himself, writing this sonata shortly before his death from syphilis at the age of thirty-one, it is hard not to hear it as his way of bringing together differing feelings about his own impending death.

My last choice was Harrison Birtwistle's opera *Punch and Judy*. I was drawn to this partly by meeting the composer, who became a friend. (Sadly, he died in April 2022.) I liked the arresting, powerful emotion of the music, as of the opera overall. Its stark violence is depicted onstage, in our faces, in Punch's callous murders of his child and wife. Also disturbing is Punch's strutting mockery of human values (an echo, to me, of Shostakovich's depiction in his Fifth Symphony of dictators, whether of the fascist right or of the Stalinist left). Benjamin Britten and Peter Pears are said to have walked out of the Aldeburgh premiere of *Punch and Judy*, muttering about 'intolerable violence'. If so, I think they were wrong; the work is not all violence, and there are elements that make the violence more tolerable, interludes that remind me of mournful, tender, resigned choruses in Sophocles' plays. These passages are slow, quiet, even mystical or mysterious, in which Birtwistle is reflecting upon the violence and cruelty. And there is too Punch's yearning for Pretty Polly, whether we hear it as sentimental or ethereal.

Harry told a story of having been present for the final rehearsal of a piece he had written for a brass band in Derbyshire. During the break before the performance, he was in the toilet when two of the musicians, not realising he was within earshot, came in. 'How do you like it?' said one. 'Not bad,' replied the other, 'it'll be fine when he puts t'tune over t'top.'

For me too, Birtwistle's music is difficult to understand. I chose it partly for this reason. Some months earlier, I had heard Richard Flanagan, author of *The Narrow Road to the Deep North* (about the building by prisoners of war of the notorious Burma railroad), say on *Private Passions* that he wasn't sure he liked one of the pieces he had chosen. Like interviewer Michael Berkeley, I was intrigued. Flanagan elaborated that one purpose of art is to unsettle us (true equally of psychoanalysis, I would add – a student said of American analyst Don Moss that he 'throws a hand-grenade into the water') – and that he needed to be unsettled; perhaps over time he would learn to appreciate the piece and come to feel he has understood it better. Me too. Not all dismantling of cherished ideas is destructive.

For me, words, including by critics, are capable of enhancing the appeal of music. They give indications of what to listen for.

* * *

My mother played the organ at school, and continued to play the piano. She would accompany a local singing group, a keep-fit class and me – she and I played together the slow movements of Mozart's Clarinet Concerto and Quintet.

My father liked to sing. He'd been in the church choir as a boy, and had won a dancing competition (the Charleston) with his sister Lydia when he was thirteen, she sixteen. Soon after the war, he applied for and got a maths-teaching position at Sloane Grammar School in London. Interviewing him, the headmaster asked if there were things besides teaching and sport he'd like to be involved in within the school; my father said he'd like to join the choir. The head said, 'Fine, but you'll have to audition.' My father said, 'I'll sing to you if you sing to me' – which they did; he joined the choir.

When I was about eleven or twelve my parents bought a 'gramophone'. One of our first records was of Heifetz playing Mozart sonatas, including the one I chose for *Private Passions*. While my father was in the kitchen making beer or wine; or making cream by churning in his little machine milk and saltless butter (bought from Sainsbury's in Ealing Broadway, where they cut, weighed and then patted the butter with a wooden paddle that left the blocks neatly furrowed), he would put on the Heifetz (or Kathleen Ferrier, or – his real favourite, whom he referred to as his 'girlfriend' – Joan Sutherland singing *Lucia di Lammermoor*). He took me to my first opera, Janáček's *Jenůfa*. We stood in the gods at Covent Garden, so the stage was a long way off, and we could only see only part of it, but I enjoyed it. He responded that if I enjoyed *that* there's a lot better that we should go to.

When I first arrived at the City of London School aged ten, I joined the choir, as my father had already done. We sang the *Messiah*, some of whose arias come back to me now. As usual in those days, art gave way to sport, and I left the choir soon after. At Cambridge I joined the choir of the women's college, Newnham, which was, understandably, short of basses. We sang *Blest Pair of Sirens* by Hubert Parry.

* * *

When my father had Alzheimer's, music was one of the last pleasures he retained. Tears would come to his eyes. He even enjoyed pieces he might not have appreciated before; he listened intently, intensely even, to Stravinsky's *The Rite of Spring*, especially gripped by its driving rhythms. Finally, even that passion faded away, but he did not appear to be unhappy – in fact, he had been unhappy only early in the process, and some inner grace of character remained almost to the end. He was looked after for the last fourteen years of his life by my sister Jill, in Birmingham. My other sister, Margy, and Mana and I would have him to stay for weekends and for parts of holidays.

My mother had died of Alzheimer's too, more than twenty-five years earlier. She had become more anxious and more angry than he was. But she too kept her sense of music longer than other aspects of herself, and it was touching to know that the high point of his daily hospital visits to her, taking her blended blackberry-and-apple puree or other tasty favourites that he cooked according to her recipes, was their dancing foxtrots and quicksteps together down the linoleum-covered corridor outside the ward.

For some months before her death, her life seemed without any point – no language, no awareness of others, with anxiety and even anguish etched in her face. As winter came on, the four of us in the immediate family agreed that if she got flu she should not be treated. This duly happened, in February 1981; the flu turned to pneumonia, and she was clearly dying. Stubbornly, she, or her body, held on. For three days breathing was laboured, burdensome, grating. We spent hours round her bed, holding her hand, occasionally dabbing her tongue with water. She had not recognised any of us for months. One murky cold day at the end of the month, the rattle of her breathing stopped, she opened her eyes, and breathed quietly. She then looked round at us. It was a real look, we felt she was taking us in, one by one, brown eyes shining, perhaps for half a minute each. I said, 'It's as if she were her old self.' Then she died.

* * *

Of all art forms, music is, I think, the most directly expressive. My friend Jim Cogan once came into our house when I had Mozart's *Così fan Tutte* playing loudly. He screwed up his face as if in agony. When I queried this, he said he couldn't listen to this opera as it moved him too much.

Foetuses respond to music. Mothers speak in a sing-song voice to their infants, humming and murmuring, as well as literally singing lullabies. These musical messages convey emotions, some of them not otherwise expressible: sadness, excitement, turmoil, rage, calm, love, empathy, containment, reassurance. Infants themselves have a sense of rhythm; they move to music; their early 'conversations' include responsive patterns of sound. Music in this broad sense is one of the most basic modes of interaction, a pleasurable form of give-and-take. It is more universal than anything that relies on words alone.

In his memoir, Bob Dylan writes about three performers who, in his journey towards finding his own voice, influenced him powerfully. They had many qualities, high among which were intensity and range of feeling. Woody Guthrie's voice was 'like a stiletto'. His songs 'had the infinite sweep of humanity about them'. The blues singer Bob Johnson 'masked the presence of twenty men . . . [His] words made my nerves quiver like piano wires . . . a screwed-up fishing song with red-blooded lines that's way past metaphor'. And Joan Baez, about whom he writes: 'I'd be scared to meet her. She might bury her fangs in the back of my neck. She had the fire and I felt that I had the same kind of fire. I believed that Joan's mother would kill somebody that she loved. I believed that she'd come from that kind of family.'

Like music, poetry has a different relationship to the ordinary meanings of words than most prose. It is less simply rational, expressing itself more allusively than with orderly logic. It is more condensed and raw, more open-ended. Poets often read their work aloud, to convey mood, feeling and emphasis.

I am capable of being moved by music, as by poetry. But I often feel that taking in either calls for a deeper commitment, a more total availability, than that which words used more prosaically require. I hardly ever use music as background. As I grow older, I find that I listen to music less. When I have time to spare, I am likely to turn to more verbal activities, to stories – novels or documentary writing in one form or another – or to theatre and film. For music, I need to set aside time and space for sustained attention (which, in my case, even then tends to wander disappointingly). I am more able to listen in the sort of way I'd like when physically present, alongside others, in a concert hall. At home, I'm easily distracted or interrupted. I feel I need to be open to music's range of meanings whereas with a story told mainly through words in their ordinary meanings (as in most novels, films and plays) I can first enjoy the surface narrative, as it gives me something to build on in arriving (if I do) at more symbolic and deeper elements.

Like painting and sculpture, music predates or bypasses verbalisation. But verbalisation often enables me to see – or hear – more of what is being played. I like opera best when I can read surtitles (even when the sung language is English).

* * *

In the consulting room, a central aim of the analyst is to register the underlying emotional impact on ourselves while remaining attentive both to the literal story being told and to what it is in the patient that evokes our own emotional, or unemotional, responses. Music, too, evokes feelings, and we sometimes wonder how much is due to it, how much to us. Both activities involve listening at depth. We hear the obvious narrative, that is essential. But behind it or around it is a range of other voices, with echoes and repetitions and variations. It is like noticing a hinterland in oneself or someone else. At moments or periods of flow, there is attunement not only to the surface story, to the prominent 'tune' involved, but also and simultaneously to harmonies, discords and indeed to less obvious and sometimes conflictual polyphonic lines. I may pick up variations to a theme. Silences may be as significant as the words and noises.

Psychoanalyst Roger Kennedy quotes percussionist Evelyn Glennie: 'Listening is about more than just hearing; it is about engaging, empowering, inspiring and creating bonds. True listening is a holistic act.' Really listening is not just factual listening. It is more than registering a practical message, a piece of news. It incorporates bodily impressions.

In 1964, a friend of mine, wedded to the stark brutalism of contemporary designers, told me with a straight, even earnest, face that 'there is no room for the curve in modern furniture'. His enthusiasm and conviction contributed to my buying a daybed of puritanical design, with a Scandinavian air of self-denial, all beechwood, plainness and rectangularity. I still have it, and like it. But it took me some time to wean myself from this austere diet, and to risk a curve (even longer for a curlicue). This was a masculine phase or tendency, perhaps not unconnected, Kennedy suggests, with the then concurrent fashion for serialism in music.

Jazz and other forms of music involve, for those playing it, also improvisation; where there is not only following a score, but also a willingness to go with the offered start, to pick up the baton. The collaboration may develop into a dialogue, even to an argument, but the first requirement is a willingness to run with what your colleague has initiated.

At best, at the top of my form in concentrated listening to a Beethoven quartet, say, my frame of mind is similar to what happens in a session when I feel attuned to the patient. But it's rare.

✳ ✳ ✳

I recently heard on the radio Beethoven's *Grosse Fugue*, originally the last movement of his Quartet No. 13, Op. 130, played by the Talich

Quartet. Years ago, I had felt the truth of a comment by Donald Tovey that in this movement Beethoven comes close to his 'old Adam' of hyper-emotionalism, of an assertiveness run riot. The Talich played it differently. They eschewed overt emotionality; the violins were played without vibrato, almost muted. And accompanying it all, in a more prominent way than I had noticed before, was a metronomic beat, emphasising a firm – even rigid – structure in which the emotion expresses itself by its contrast, without too much stridency. The experience was a little like hearing the same composer's symphonies played on original instruments, with small ensembles, rather than with huge mid-twentieth-century orchestras. My impression of the Talich performance was of the familiar rendered unfamiliar; the impression of massed and strenuous assertiveness had been modified into individual phrases of insecurity and complexity. It was as if the grand surge of a uniform crowd had been resolved into more tentative individual actions.

Music expresses mood and personality rather as people do, via gait, via mode of movement. The music may slouch, or glide, or jump and dodge about. When the tempo changes, the mood changes too. Developing a theme by making it more brilliant, inserting semi-quavers into the prominent notes of a sedate first statement, makes for a different content, more energetic or frenetic; it may become wilder, like the dance of a dervish. A baby expresses excitement with her whole body, 'running' with her legs months before she can walk, and a toddler or older child when excited runs everywhere; my six-year-old granddaughter, Maia, literally jumps for joy. Trills may be more than merely decorative. They change the content of the piece. There is no sharp distinction between form and content.

In music a theme is presented and a journey is embarked on. Themes 'develop' (for example, by moving into the minor key and becoming sadder). Changes of key may be either conventional and expected, or unconventional and shocking; the non-technical listener (me) might pick up the mood and 'meaning' of such shifts without being able to articulate how the transitions were brought about. At the end, the music returns to its 'home key'. A movement in sonata form, for instance, tells a story – the starting situation becomes conflicted or more complex, the journey takes the players and listeners through changes and developments, and then resolves (or doesn't). In content and form, in moves towards complexity or simplicity, music and analysis can mirror each other.

* * *

Music is a field which should be spoken of, or listened to, not only in terms of 'purely musical' categories of expression. It is a human activity, not an esoteric one. A piece may be sad or bright, confident or tentative. Many sorts of descriptions are appropriate, even intrinsic, whether or not the music has words attached.

I was cheered when I heard composer and psychoanalyst Francis Grier speak about feminine and masculine aspects of Beethoven's music. Grier is not afraid that this will seem incongruous or far-fetched. One clue to the emotional message of a piece would be to compare music that has no words with music that is set to words (songs, opera).

Carlos Kleiber, regarded by many as the doyen of conductors, spoke to his orchestra in human terms about the shifting emotional feel of the music: 'A rush of hormones here! . . . Here he dances lightly . . . This next bit must be played commandingly; a gorgeous woman with long legs floats by, the more affecting because of her slight look of contempt.' He might not get away with such references in the current atmosphere of sensitivity to sexism. But my point, and his, remains.

C. L. R. James, the social historian, asked: 'What do they know of cricket who only cricket know?' In Radical Uncertainty, John Kay and Mervyn King write of economists that if they understand only economics, they don't understand economics. The same is true of music. Within any field, human factors are needed. To be a good batter, say, or a good violinist, we need far more than a capable technique; we need also human qualities such as determination, resilience, spontaneity, emotional intelligence. And being in touch as a listener or spectator calls for similar qualities.

On the one side, there is no such thing as 'pure' music, music that carries no hints or suggestions of emotion: of fear, excitement, calm, wonder, despair – whatever. On the other, interpretations that are restricted to these lines alone risk being banal, fanciful or merely subjective. But when this happens, it is an example of second-rate understanding, not a sort of category mistake.

* * *

I joined the school orchestra as one of a bank of clarinet players. There were two teachers who played the instrument reasonably well, and some restless little boys such as me as third or fourth clarinets. We were playing Mendelssohn's *Italian Symphony*. There were long rest bars for us back-desk wind players, resulting in the need to count so as to be ready for our next entries. I remember the terror of my first rehearsals, feeling utterly inept. I was unable to see the music clearly at the shared desk, and helpless at this counting business. I felt like a child lost on a mountain as darkness was drawing in, or like a humiliated outsider who can't get back into a group or a conversation.

During my first summer at St John's, there was a more exposing panic. I had become friendly with two musicians who were contemporaries. Leon Coates, later a conductor whose job therefore was to keep players in step with each other, had been declared unfit for National Service because, as he told me, he couldn't march in step; the other was Tim Salter, now a composer. They persuaded me to play with them a Mozart trio, for clarinet, viola and piano. (It was in fact his Trio in E-flat major, K. 498, called the *Kegelstatt Trio*, named as such as it was supposedly composed while playing skittles.) Each of them was playing his second or third instrument. On the morning of the concert, Leon suggested that I might prefer his sister's clarinet rather than my own, as its tone was better. Without trying it out, I foolishly complied. Starting the first movement, I discovered to my perplexity and horror that some fingerings produced no sound. The rubber bands holding down these keys had loosened. Instead of having the nerve to call a halt and start again, I reattached the bands and continued – in mounting panic. The performance was a disaster. George Guest, the college's choirmaster and organist, left noisily after the first movement (fortunately I was in too much of a state to notice). I vowed never again to play music in public – one vow I've kept.

I later lost my clarinet, stolen when several things disappeared from the house when I was about thirty.

* * *

In *Blink*, Malcolm Gladwell tells a story about a top tennis coach. On the basis of watching on his computer screen recordings of a serving player's build-up to the moment when racquet struck ball, the coach could predict, with remarkable accuracy, whether the outcome would be an ace or a fault. He could see things that others couldn't. Moreover, he could see them instantaneously, in a blink of an eye, so to speak. There was no need for him to work it out, or make conscious inferences. He had arrived at simply seeing.

When in a game park with a guide, I realised how much the guide was able to see that I couldn't. As casual observers, we miss what has become obvious to the expert. We don't know our way around. We haven't learned how to look (or listen). The guide knows how to use his eyes. When a Chinese speaker hears a sentence in Chinese, he and I in one sense hear exactly the same thing. But he can repeat it while I can't.

One advantage of knowing a lot about one particular field of activity or enquiry is that you come to realise, however much there is always to learn, that in most scenes within your own skill area you can see more than other people, and with more immediacy. This should teach us a certain humility with regard to other fields, in relation to which we, however expert somewhere else, are outsiders.

I regard myself as an expert in observing many aspects of technique, skill and distinctiveness on the cricket field, including aspects of captaincy. But with regard to the theatre, when I meet serious actors and hear them talking about their roles and interactions with other characters, I'm aware of how thoroughly and deeply they have a sense of their character and of his or her relationships with others. They are often articulately knowledgeable, but this may not be the main feature. They have their knowledge on their pulses, in their expressions, gait and timing. The same goes for musicians I've met.

These facts about expertise need to be set against facts that are apparently contradictory: experts may also see things narrowly, only according to their own criteria. They – we – may recognise new examples of the already familiar; but that very familiarity may preclude us, at times, from seeing something in a radically new way. Specialist knowledge comes with its own basic assumptions. Specialists tend to experience everything through the traditional lenses.

Expertise, hard-won through attention, experience, discipline, and overcoming pitfalls and failings, is indeed valuable. But you never know in advance where insight will next originate. In Hans Christian Andersen's story, the child sees and asserts what the grown-ups have missed or denied – the emperor is naked. 'Out of the mouths of babes and sucklings you have perfected praise' (or, as later paraphrased, 'cometh forth truth'). But like the young fish, puzzled by the polite greeting from the older fish, 'How's the water?', who says 'What does he mean, "water"?', we may be too close to our element, to our paradigms, to see their distorting or limiting, or indeed enabling, effect.

Experts need to challenge themselves and be challenged. Their models and algorithms, for example on the spread of pandemics and how to respond to them, may turn out to have flaws that lead to disastrous distortions, and thus to faulty decisions. David Sylvester, the great art critic, would listen with profound attention to comments from people without specialist knowledge about works of art that he himself had long studied. In some instances, he had even hung the exhibition he was showing us. Occasionally he would, flatteringly, take out his notebook and jot down one of our observations. He was open to the fresh take of a naive viewer. (And the one whose opinion had been noted glowed with a rare pride.)

On small as well as large matters, paradigm shifts may produce revolutions in thinking. And as Freud said, as analysts we need to set aside conscious expectation and wish in order to be open to the new, to allow our unconscious to be attuned to that of the patient. In everyday life as in recondite science we are all liable to the risk of a blindness that comes from sophistication.

Being a psychoanalyst offers set times and spaces for a certain sort of concentration. I am paid to provide this and to work at what interferes with such attention. A similar kind of attention is called for if one is to get as much as one can out of listening to music or reading poetry.

As I say, I find myself giving priority to activities or arts that rely more on words used in ordinary ways to tell stories – literature, plays, films. The regret about not having listened more to music is different from that which relates to not having played bridge or golf, activities that I avoided because I imagined becoming obsessive about them.

In their case, had I indulged, I might have wondered if I had been failing to use my time as well as I might have, despite the lure. But with music, though I do wish I'd done more, there are so many things to fit in, even to cram in. There are limits.

I'm aware that I make it seem like a lot of hard work, and people who love music, simply or complexly, would find this rather odd. But there it is, that's my take.

* * *

MUSIC FOR *PRIVATE PASSIONS*

Monteverdi: *Coronation of Poppea* – Act III, 'Pur ti miro . . .'
English Baroque Soloists, conductor, John Eliot Gardiner
Singers: Sylvia McNair; Dana Hanchard

Mozart: Violin Sonata No. 32 in B flat, K. 454 – i. Largo-Allegro
Jascha Heifetz, violin; Brooks Smith, piano

J. S. Bach: *Goldberg Variations* – Aria, Var. 15, Var. 29, Aria da Capo
Ralph Kirkpatrick, harpsichord

Beethoven: String Quartet No. 14 in C-sharp minor, Op. 131 – vi. Adagio / vii. Allegro
Endellion Quartet

Schubert: Piano Sonata No. 21 in B flat, D 960 – i. Allegro
Alfred Brendel

Tchaikovsky: *Eugene Onegin* – Act 2: 'Love is no respecter of age . . .'
New Zealand Symphony, conductor, James Judd
Singer: Jonathan Lemalu

Birtwistle: *Punch and Judy* – 'Resolve 1' and 'Passion Chorale 1'
London Sinfonietta, conductor, David Atherton
Singer: Stephen Roberts

CHAPTER 8

'A STRAIGHT BALL, MICHAEL, HAS A CERTAIN LETHAL QUALITY'

Cricket has been part not only of my life but of me for longer than I can remember.

As a boy, and often beyond, I simply loved playing – catching, throwing, bowling and especially batting. I played with other boys (often older than myself), and with my father, or with any other adult I could press-gang. When I was seven or eight I would walk along the beach during our summer holidays at Bognor asking people if I could join their game. In the summer, I couldn't have enough of cricket. (During winter it was football, and at various stages fives, rugby, hockey and also lacrosse. I never got the hang of racquet games, and was never any good at sports without a ball, such as athletics, swimming or boxing.)

For many years I played at Middleton-on-Sea during August, alongside Mike Griffith, who later won caps at hockey for England and captained Sussex at cricket. He once mentioned that he'd had too much of the game; he was at boarding school, where the cricket fields were next to the school and they played every day. At that time, I found it hard to conceive of any sense of overload in this department.

My friend Hugh Brody told me recently that my wife said to him once that there were two Mikes, the cricketer and the psychoanalyst.

'Which one did you like best?' he asked her. 'The cricketer' was apparently the reply.

I'd not heard Mana's opinion in quite those stark terms. She has said I'm more relaxed when in the company of cricketers. And my editor, Andreas, tells me I write with more spontaneity on this topic than on psychoanalysis; in the latter, the words don't tumble out, but are at times squeezed out through a sort of word-wringer, censored, over-edited. I am more aware of potential criticism, of letting down or disappointing those to whom I'm affiliated. The psychoanalytic superego is nowadays more scathing and more wide-ranging, and the inner accusation of being an imposter is more liable to get going, especially in the middle of the night.

But I also know that having been analysed and being a psychoanalyst help me to recover from the panics of ineptitude or fraudulence more quickly than when I was younger. And my recent writing has had a lot to do with bringing the two parts of myself (two selves?) together.

I'm not saying that I am now, or was before, exempt from feelings of mortification at foolish or feeble cricketing failures from long ago, especially at mistakes caused by unworthy or self-sabotaging states of mind. I am also reminded of the dream I had before my first Test as captain of England: *I appeared onstage as a timid creature in a shell, unlike the exuberant and confident Tony Greig, whom I was replacing as captain.*

Despite the shell, I rarely lost that sense of sheer enjoyment from cricket.

I went with my father to many of his games of club cricket. A small, faded-red, primary-school workbook somehow survives from when I was six. The little critic therein opines: 'His hiest scor this-year is 73: that is not-bad.' On Monday 27 September 1948, I wrote: 'I went-to brentham crickit club and watchet daddy [changed laboriously from 'baddy'] play crickit he got 50 runs I scord evrey-man untill he was-out, nobodey got ass-menny run,s ass 50. I did not scor the boling becase I can not do the bowling yet.' (I still over-do – there I go again – the hyphens.)

Watching was good, but primarily what I wanted was to play. When I was fifteen or sixteen, I asked Lawrence Collins, a year ahead of me in the Classical Sixth Form, later a member of the UK Supreme Court, what sort of music he liked; when he said 'Jazz,' I asked him what he played. No, he said; he liked listening. I found this puzzling. I was then ignorant enough to think that jazz was limited to what one improvised at home, with a skiffle board and a strummed guitar. But my response was not merely a matter of ignorance and superiority; I wasn't that interested in being 'merely' a spectator.

I was touched by reading an account of an interview Brendon McCullum gave in 2013 before a Test series against England. He had been New Zealand captain for a year. With coach Mike Hesson, he had set about changing the culture of the team after they had been bowled out for 45 by South Africa. 'Just because there is more at stake now doesn't mean you should lose the innocence of why you played the game in the first place. For a long time I had lost that, and I think our team had lost it . . . We expected the game to owe us something. We almost felt entitled . . . There was no soul about our cricket . . . It sounds a bit corny, but we talk about the playful little boy who fell in love with the game. When you have that mindset you can be positive and aggressive because you're thinking about what can go right rather than what might go wrong.'

Now, almost ten years on, he is England's coach and, along with Ben Stokes as the new captain, has transformed England's Test team with just such an attitude. No doubt there will be hiccups, but the initial impact has been instantaneous and impressive. After winning only one of their previous seventeen Test matches, the team won ten out of their first eleven under this leadership – and lost the twelfth, against New Zealand, by a single run.

My spectating has almost always been of a near-participatory kind. When I retired from professional cricket at the age of forty, I wrote a piece about lounging back in a deckchair on the boundary of a treelined ground, asking someone to top up my glass of white Burgundy, an image of lazy, dreamy detachment. But it hasn't ever been much like that. I can't settle for this for long. I get bored. I prefer watching with intent, and then I can't but think of the game psychologically and tactically. I enter into what I imagine is the mindset of the players, for instance, watching Rishabh Pant, the talented Indian wicketkeeper/ batter; I try to sense how he's feeling. Is he getting impatient? When will he try to break out and, if so, what would most insidiously tempt him? Should we just keep it tight, frustrate him a bit longer, until he launches himself – perhaps unwisely? Who among our bowlers would he least like to face, and with what policy, what field placing? As an observer I'm almost a participant. I can't help it!

* * *

But what do I mean by this strange British game being part of me, rather than merely part of my life?

Cricket, a team game whose every little drama is a contest between two protagonists, has long formed for me a central setting for issues of selfishness and altruism, of loyalty to team but also to the self. For almost eight decades, cricket has made its appearance in my dreams, especially in dreams of *being unprepared or unconfident; the game is taking place in a constrained space, or on a busy street. I score runs but the best bowlers were not being used,* so my success is invalidated. *My bat has turned to rubber in my hands* – a repeated mini-nightmare. (I leave the interpretations to you.)

As a patient in analysis, I came to realise that a hostile bowler in my dream might stand for the analyst, as did a *football-playing priest whose hut I visited in one dream in order to confess my fears.*

Cricket has entered my unconscious, shaping images of nervousness, confidence, restriction, freedom, providing a frame for thinking about my life. It has structured my thinking and feeling. Psychoanalysis has given me a sense of the confluence of general fears and insecurities with their cricketing counterparts.

In waking life too, I enjoy cricket metaphors, like being stumped for an answer, or being on the back foot in life. In 1973, at an MCC game in India, the man on the microphone announced with relish that 'Chris Old's middle stump' – he pronounced the name as one word, with the emphasis on the first vowel – 'has gone for a walk in the fresh air': metaphors can go in either direction.

* * *

There are and were of course many anxieties. When I was ten, I was about to play my first 'proper' game of cricket, for Middleton Colts. As the matchday approached, I was agonised about whether the white, cord, long trousers, which were being sent by post from London to our holiday bungalow in Bognor by my Aunt Norah, would arrive in time. They did – just. How humiliating it would have been to play in grey shorts!

Cricket gear was also a matter of pride, care and hope. I was given my first proper bat, with springs and grain and a rubber grip, at the age of the trouser crisis, or perhaps the year after. My father took me to the sports shop run by legendary England cricketer Jack Hobbs in Fleet Street, near my school. He bought me a bat called, I think, Summer County. We went into the room behind the shop, where the great old man himself (he must have been seventy) was sitting at a desk, in a dark suit and tie. He kindly signed my new bat, in copperplate handwriting, with a fountain pen, J. B. Hobbs. The ink slightly seeped so that the letters had a sort of halo. Having a bat meant oiling it, and 'knocking it in', that is, bouncing a cricket ball on it to temper the surface. The smell of linseed oil has a Proustian effect on me, redolent of that annual April bat-care.

(Recently I was touched to read that Sir Jack Hobbs nursed Ada, his wife of fifty-six years, up to her death, and then himself died later that year.)

As for cricket balls, I was given one by my Uncle Percy, for my eighth birthday (I guess). He came down from Ossett in Yorkshire for a weekend every May to watch the rugby league cup final at Wembley. On this occasion he brought me what was to me more beautiful than any work of art, a nearly-new cricket ball. I got him and my father to come that evening to play with it at the Brentham recreation area, near the river Brent. Disaster struck. I hit the ball into the hedge above the river bank, and we were unable to find it. Perhaps it burst through into the brown water. What a sad, brief possessing!

In the summer following my long-trousered debut (five not out, a cover drive and a hook, one for one and one for four, I can't remember which was which), I was due to play my first match for the school. Two years before, my planned change of school from the local primary school to City of London had been postponed for a year because of my nausea on the Underground. On that Saturday morning, I woke up with a stomach ache. Even then, I think I knew this was an expression of anxiety, a psychological ache. Eventually I decided I wasn't well enough to play. Twenty-four years later, and three days before my second Test match (against West Indies at Lord's), as I walked through the grounds of Shenley psychiatric hospital to a weekly meeting in a series of psychodrama events, stomach gripes were so acute that I was forced to lie down in a ditch beside the narrow road that led up from Radlett station, my knees pressed against my belly. This time I did play.

A great love provides a setting for one's greatest hopes, and therefore the potential for one's greatest fears and disappointments.

* * *

Now, as when I was a professional cricketer, I love seeing shots that I found hard to play, such as full-face straight drives against fast bowling, weight transferred with total balance, the ball placed, preferably between the stumps and mid-on; or forcing back strokes past cover point's right hand (a skill I once saw in the young Geoff Boycott, who played it several times in an innings against Sussex and England fast bowler, John Snow, when representing Yorkshire against MCC).

I love watching hard-fought contests between top bowler and top batter – Jimmy Anderson against Virat Kohli with a new-ish ball, for instance, a period when maiden overs, the ball skilfully left several times, are more dramatic than slogged sixes. Everyone would know that the outcomes of these one-to-one contests were likely to be pivotal to the course of the match.

I loved playing in contests between old and respected rival teams. In county cricket, there was always a special *je ne sais quoi* about matches against Yorkshire, or local rivals Surrey; Kent too, though crowds at Canterbury were too purringly complacent when Colin Cowdrey was batting or when Kent were doing well, too quick to melt away when we were winning.

I like cricket best when the conditions slightly favour the bowling side, so that they are committed to attack while batters have to be skilful to survive, and have to make choices between attack as the best form of defence, and defence as the best form of defence.

Cricket appeals to my aesthetic sense. I remember a ball bowled by Philippe Edmonds at Lord's, on an easy batting pitch, to Keith Fletcher, one of England's best players of spin, who was well-set on sixty or so. Edmonds had a fine high action, with a strong swivel of the body across his front leg. This enabled him to put more rotations on the ball, and also to make it drift in. This particular delivery curved in, dropped a bit shorter than the batter anticipated, landed on off stump, turned, beat the forward defensive shot, and hit the top of off stump. There is beauty in such a combination of perfect action and perfect execution.

There are too the aesthetic and psychological pleasures deriving from the longer arc of a whole spell or innings, and the satisfaction of a player's or team's development over months or years.

Much of the delight for spectators is a matter of 'becoming' the batter or bowler in imagination, however remote from reality that might be. This reminds me of having watched a Pinter play, especially if he himself were acting in it; I would be impelled to 'be' Pinter in tone and presence, even making my voice more rich and full, like the man himself on the stage.

* * *

I have always liked too the companionship of a team on and off the field. The dressing room atmosphere was down-to-earth, usually full of bonhomie and humour; occasionally bad feeling and tension.

Certainly, one has to get used to passages of fatigue and boredom. At the start of a season, the first day spent in the field seemed unending, but soon it became familiar, and less tiring. Cricket matches go on for a long time, and one of the drawbacks of the game is that a cautious approach can be tediously persistent. Baseball followers find it hard to imagine that in cricket there is no such thing as 'three strikes and out'. During my early days as a professional with Middlesex, I would sometimes write parts of Shakespeare sonnets on my hand or wrist before going out to field, and learn them by heart. I still remember, patchily, lines from 'Shall I compare thee to a summer's day', or 'When to the sessions of sweet silent thought' or 'A woman's face with nature's own hand painted, hast thou, the master-mistress of my passion'. So the time was not entirely wasted (as those who find the game completely absurd might concede).

More often than not, cricket was an area or arena where I could be fully involved, fully alive. When a game is played in a positive spirit, often with a balance between bat and ball, I find the tussle absorbing.

* * *

I enjoy the humour of cricket. One locus for this was nicknames (surely many of them more inventive than those of today?). Middlesex off-spinner Don Bick was widely known as 'Narf' from his catchphrase 'it 'ain' 'alf', as in 'Narf 'ot today'. My Middlesex colleague Mike Smith gave our ace fast bowler Wayne Daniel the sobriquet 'Rent and Rates' (which his skill made affordable). Fred Titmus was affectionately known as 'Teddy Fritmus', a tribute to his tendency to spoonerisms. At The Oval, Surrey and England fast bowler Geoff Arnold was named 'Horse' (or 'Orse'), as a result of his initials, GG, and his team-mate Arnold Long was known universally as 'Ob'. I myself was variously 'Egghead', the 'Ayatollah' (when I had a big black beard) and 'Scagglethorpe Singh' ('Scag' for short) referring to my Yorkshire heritage (Scagglethorpe being a village near Scarborough) combined with my passion for India. This name was given to me by Chris Old, known of course as 'Chilly' (C.OLD).

Smith also came up with the nickname for a Glamorgan bowler, Lawrence Williams. He was short for a fast bowler, and not that fast, but had some of the surface attributes of the great Dennis Lillee; at Middlesex, we referred to this good county cricketer as 'the Lily of the Valleys'. I remember an episode involving Williams; running in to bowl against us, he suddenly delivered a ball from about 26 yards. Everyone wondered what he was up to. 'Sorry, skip,' he said, 'but I came to the end of my run-up.' Most bowlers would simply have held on to the ball and reassessed their run-up.

West Indian cricketers produced some of the most engaging
ripostes. When Middlesex played West Indies in 1976, we had them
nine wickets down when off-spinner Albert Padmore came in to bat. I
stood near the batter directing the field with Titmus. Padmore turned
to me: 'Man,' he said, 'all you need is the bowler, the bowler and the
ball' (rhyming with marl or snarl). Next ball he pushed forward along
the line of middle stump, the ball, undeviating, hit the off stump. We
all subsided into laughter, including Albert.

Years before, as captain of Cambridge in 1963, I went to the
University Arms Hotel to welcome the West Indies team on the
afternoon before the game. Some kind supporter had put up in
the pavilion at Fenner's, the university ground, a terrifying picture
of the great fast bowler, Wes Hall, his gold chain swinging wildly,
having just delivered a bouncer. I was to open the batting against
him over the next three days. I was introduced to Wes (or Mr Hall as
I addressed him). Awed and apprehensive, and seeking a neutral topic
of conversation, I asked him if he slept well on tour. He replied in his
hoarsest Louis Armstrong timbre that he didn't. He woke often at 4
a.m. What did he do then?, I asked. 'I tear telephone directories,' he
told me, dramatically.

Even in my state I could see the humour of it. It reminds me
of meeting the equally great Fred Trueman two years earlier, on
the cold early-May first morning of my second match, against
Yorkshire. Fred loved talking to undergraduates, putting the fear of
God (in other words, of himself) into us. Warming his backside in
front of the coal fire in the home dressing room, he told us about a
self-confident amateur who'd fancied his chances against him the
season before, in a match at Leyton in Essex. 'He thought he could
hook, did this jazz-'at,' Fred announced. 'We spent half an hour
searching for his teeth in the footholds.'

(I now think I have mis-remembered the date of this story.
Checking in *Wisden*, I learn that Essex did not play Yorkshire at

Leyton in 1960, but rather in 1965, when a primary school teacher, Roger Wrightson, playing one of his twelve first-class games for Essex, had two front teeth knocked out while batting against Trueman. I came back to play a few games for Cambridge in 1966, one of them against Yorkshire, in May, in which Trueman played. It must have been then that I heard the story from the great man's mouth.)

To return to Wes Hall. Next day, he scored a hurricane century, when West Indies amassed 512. We had to bat for half an hour or so at the end of the day. The light was poor. We appealed against the light (as was then permitted). I overheard the umpires exchanging cynical words about not letting the undergraduates get away with it, before they turned down the appeal; and a couple of balls later I missed an alarmingly fast ball and was clean bowled by Mr Hall for 6.

We had arranged a party for the West Indies team that evening. My one image of that event was that every time Basil Butcher, a man of few words, spoke, Lance Gibbs, his team-mate for Guyana as for the national side, would jump up excitedly, with: 'You know what Butcher mum died of? Butcher mum died of the earache.'

Also at Cambridge I remember a moment in a game we played against the Pakistan Eaglets (a national A-team) in 1963. Their opener, Faqir Aizazuddin, was on 180 or so when the ninth wicket fell. As the young number eleven batter approached the wicket, the opener urged him to: 'Please, play like a gentleman' (in other words, try to stay in while I get to 200). The opener was disappointed, but not in his partner who had been a gentleman so far; he himself was dismissed for 186.

I enjoyed a story told by Clive Radley, my team-mate at Middlesex for many years. The setting was the first three-day match of a D. H. Robins XI tour of South Africa, played at Port Elizabeth, which was captained by the redoubtable, tough, engaging, blunt and always-in-the-right Yorkshireman, Brian Close. Close was never in want of an excuse. Both sides had scored around 300 in their first innings. It was such an easy pitch that only the side batting last would have much chance of winning, so Close, announcing to his team-mates that we can't give them any hope, set a target – ridiculous in those days – of 280 in less than three hours. The great Graeme Pollock flayed and caressed an elegant 160 or so in no time, and his team strolled home with several overs to spare. Close was livid; he slammed the dressing-room door shut before announcing, 'We're not having anybody in here till we've sat down and analysed what happened.' He continued: 'Have any of you youngsters learned anything from that?' A young Lancastrian called John Lyon, reserve wicketkeeper to Farokh Engineer, the Indian Test player, was sitting next to Radley. He hadn't said a word on the trip. But he politely offered his opinion. 'Yes, Mr Close, I've learned something. You declared too fucking early, that's what I've learned.' Close was rendered speechless.

* * *

I suppose this humour had a juvenile tinge, but I enjoy that too. When my family was groaning at a bad joke of mine, my grandson Luka, then aged four, piped up with, 'Well, I think Mike's jokes are really good.'

One element in these jokes and stories has been cricket's broad social range. Through cricket I've met people from all classes, origins and ethnicities. Class has always been the starkest division in top-level cricket in England. I'm worried that school cricket in this country is now becoming increasingly restricted to public schools.

Invited to Lord's on Monday evenings for coaching during my last two summers at school, I learned a lot about the distinction between amateurs and professionals, otherwise known as 'Gentlemen' and 'Players', a formal categorisation that was not officially abolished until January 1963.

My coach, Jim Sims, an ex-Middlesex player who had played four times for England, was a shrewd and kindly man. He told me stories about his time as junior pro during the 1930s, including being responsible for the team's cricket baggage on epic cross-country train journeys, from Brighton to Scarborough for instance. The Sussex match might have ended at 6.30 on a Tuesday evening, the game against Yorkshire beginning at 11.30 the next morning. Jim would be responsible for getting the gear to the ground on time.

I heard about the rough life of the average professional, especially in those days. While the amateurs stayed in fine hotels, he would often be put up in 'digs'. During August, he might find himself left out of the team when schoolmasters (or indeed, for a while, academics like me) became available during their holidays. It was not long since some players, to keep body and soul together during the winter months, relied on maintenance jobs such as painting the benches at Lord's.

For these after-school sessions (which got me out of compulsory Combined Cadet Force training) I changed in a room in the semi-basement of the pavilion. The room's windows, at head level, offered a restricted view of the match on the main ground; one looked out through the legs, backs and seating of members who were watching the match outside. In the old days, this had been the dressing room for professionals who were playing in the current match, while the amateurs would change in grand accommodation upstairs. The two groups would enter the playing area through different gates. Here, I was also initiated into the excellent game of shove-ha'penny.

One day in the early 1950s, Sims told me, Middlesex took the second new ball shortly before stumps. Their young fast-medium bowler Alan Moss was bowling from the Pavilion End. Sims, then near the end of his career, was at wide mid-on and there was no mid-off. The batter straight drove the ball past the bowler. Sims shouted, 'Sorry Al, but you've got to go,' so Moss turned round at the end of his follow-through and chased the ball to the boundary. There was a little slope up to the pavilion railings, which in those days formed the boundary. The ball crawled up this slope and then rolled back. The batters ran four. Moss ran in from the boundary to continue his over.

Jim told me he was certain I'd play for Middlesex, but not sure if I'd quite make it to the England level. You may imagine how amazing a boost this was to the confidence of this seventeen-year-old. As things turned out, it was an accurate assessment, describing well what I became as a batter. He also gave me advice. 'A straight ball, Michael, has a certain lethal quality.' Pause. 'If you miss it you've 'ad it.' (Conspiratorial pause.) 'Do you follow me, Michael?' In a similar vein he told me how he'd 'once taken eight wickets in an innings against Sussex. The *Evening News* reported that six of them wickets were with long-'ops. But what they didn't write, Michael, was that five of them long-'ops were straight long-'ops.'

Jim spoke out of the side of his mouth, as if what he told you could not be risked in other company. He later warned me when I was playing for Cambridge that I would be able to cope with two of the three main aspects of college life – girls, work and cricket – but not all three. And his shrewdness continued into his later life, when as Middlesex's scorer he would arrive for lunch wearing his large, multi-pocketed beige raincoat, into which he stowed a bottle or two of beer to sustain him through the long afternoon in the draughty scorebox.

I sensed that he was looking after me, almost adopting me as a future cricketer. He even confided in me at one of my first Second XI matches that the reason Bob 'Bloodnut' Hurst would not make it in first-class cricket was that 'he was not properly shod'. This was mysterious. But the prediction, if not the basis for it, turned out to be true.

Jim was well aware of the need for compliance to his social superiors while knowing how to get advantages from them, how to work the system. One of his stories concerned being sent as a young cricketer to play for MCC in an 'out-match', that is, against a club or school side. He arrived early, wearing blazer and smart trousers. The captain asked him his name. 'Sims, sir,' he replied, 'Jim Sims.' The captain, quickly registering his low status, replied, 'Good morning, Sims, you will be batting at number ten.' For his next match, there was a different captain. This time, Jim, his accent modified, said, 'I'm James Morton-Sims, sir, with a hyphen.' 'Ah,' came the response, 'James, would you care to bat at number three?'

I think this mixture of wiliness with apparent simplicity and deference was one way that the class system was subverted, or at least managed. The same was true of the college servants at Cambridge. Outwardly subservient, they knew exactly how to put us 'young gentlemen' in our place. 'Sir' conveyed outer respect, but also information about our true status. Cyril Coote, the legendary groundsman at Fenner's, used 'sir' in just that way. Speaking to us about batting on a soft wicket he would say, 'Get on the back foot, sir, and play it with a broomstick, sir.'

The snobbery and arrogance also had less humorous outcomes. I remember a fast bowler at Middlesex called Mike Mitchell, who looked like Elvis Presley and bowled genuinely quickly. He was young and raw. As I saw it, no one seemed to value or encourage him. The attitude was one of a near-sneering superiority; as if all he had was a lot to learn. He dropped out of cricket far too early. And at a more personal, more trivial but also salutary level, in another of my schoolboy games for Middlesex second team, at Hove, I was sent to change in an upstairs room furnished with sofas and carpets with the amateur captain, Charles Robins, while the other ten players (all professionals) changed in a tiny room that was almost an extension of the showers and toilets. The lesson arrived on the pitch: I was run out in each innings.

Assumptions of superiority and inferiority, of knowing your place, were in those days mostly oriented and expressed in class terms. And cricket provided a cultural locus for a whole range of these complex interactions. I suppose it's not entirely a matter of chance that P. G. Wodehouse, the creator of Jeeves and Wooster, was so keen on cricket.

These interactions remind me of the apparent humility of the civil servant Sir Humphrey to his 'boss' Jim Hacker in the TV series, *Yes Minister*. England was class conscious at every level; in *The Frost Report* of 1966, the tall John Cleese sneered at the middle-height Ronnie Barker, 'I look down on him because I am upper class'; this Ronnie looked up at Cleese, 'I look up to him because he is upper class,' and then, turning his eye onto the shorter Ronnie Corbett, 'but I look down on him because he is lower class.' Perhaps the missing final scene that would have completed the circle would have had Corbett looking down on Cleese by his mode of looking up to him.

* * *

Another older cricketer I got to know was the famous Len Hutton, England's first professional captain. I met Len in 1962 through his son Richard, who had arrived in Cambridge as a student a year after me. Len had already been a legend in my life, not only publicly, as England's greatest opener. In his one game for Yorkshire, against Middlesex at Sheffield in 1937, my father had batted with Hutton in the second innings (and had complained that Hutton stole the bowling). Sims himself also played in that match along with two other Test leg spinners, Walter Robins and Tuppy Owen-Smith. The match had a cast of great names including, for Middlesex, Patsy Hendren, Bill Edrich and Denis Compton; and for Yorkshire, besides Hutton, Herbert Sutcliffe, Bill Bowes and Hedley Verity.

Like Sims, Len was a fascinating mixture of naivety and shrewdness. He had striking, light-blue eyes through which he would gaze wide-eyed, with apparent innocence. Often inscrutable, he nevertheless conveyed a shy warmth. I came to feel warmth and affection towards him. Coming to watch Richard's first game for Cambridge, he invited captain Tony Lewis and me for dinner at what was said to be the best hotel in Cambridge, the Garden House. Hutton must have stayed in many such during the later part of his career and afterwards (no doubt there had been dingy digs earlier on). But looking through the menu, Len asked with vague interest for several main dishes, as if he had no idea how to order a meal. The waiter said, 'Sir, you have to decide *between* the main courses.' 'Ah,' said Len. After these puzzling negotiations, and indeed after the first course, at what I imagine was a prearranged signal, Richard left for the loo. Leaning forward, Len got to the main point of the dinner. 'You haven't seen the best of our Richard yet.' Pause. (Richard had not been picked for the earlier matches.) 'It's this Economics he's studying. It's not easy. I've looked at his books.'

Colin Cowdrey, in his autobiography *M.C.C.*, describes beautifully his impressions of Hutton as the successful captain in Australia in 1954–5. Cowdrey was a young player, who, when docking in Colombo en route for Perth, received the shocking news that his father had unexpectedly died. He describes how in his quiet way Len looked after him on tour.

Cowdrey conveys Hutton's mixture of understatement, humility, opacity and cunning. When asked at his first press conference about England's prospects, he was 'pointed and drily witty . . . It was all underplayed. We 'aven't got mooch boolin'. Got a chap called Tyson but you won't 'ave 'eard of him because he's 'ardly ever played . . . We 'aven't got any batsmen really. We've got these youngsters, May and Cowdrey, but we haven't really got any batsmen. What it comes to is that we're startin' out all over again. We're 'ere to learn a lot from you.'

A few weeks later, MCC played New South Wales at Sydney. Frank Tyson hit Neil Harvey on the front shin. Len's comment was: 'He had to take his pad off to rub his leg.' Pause. 'Then I knew we 'ad a chance.'

At the end of a dinner at Lord's on the night before MCC's tour of India in 1976, several of us players gathered round the great man. Tony Greig, the captain, who had notoriously announced, before the recent summer series against West Indies, that 'we would make them grovel', asked Hutton if he had any advice for him on the upcoming tour. As usual, Len took his time before speaking. We hung on his words. At last he said, succinctly, 'Don't say too much.'

In 1966, I played part of a season for the Minor County, Cambridgeshire. Our key bowler was Johnny Wardle, the former Yorkshire and England left-arm spinner. It was a great pleasure to keep wicket to him, especially when I could persuade him to bowl his 'chinamen' and googlies (the mirror image of the right-arm leg spinner), with which he brought the game alive with his flair and inscrutability. He was a minor genius in this mode. Wardle told me that years before, in a pre-season practice game at Headingley, he had bowled in this style as well as he ever had to Hutton. 'Not to boast,' he said, he 'had never seen a great player so bamboozled.' But despite that, Hutton didn't trust wrist spinners in general, and Wardle in particular, not to give runs away; the contortions of wrist and fingers is almost bound to produce the odd loose ball. Especially in Test matches, Hutton required Wardle to bowl defensively, in his orthodox slow left-arm style, to keep runs down and enable the fast bowlers to rest. Len's respect for sheer pace, rooted in his own tussles with Ray Lindwall and Keith Miller, was well known.

Hutton was cautious and could be pessimistic. In the Fourth Test in Adelaide in 1955, England needed only 94 to win the match and the Ashes. When our fourth wicket fell at 40, Hutton could not restrain himself. 'The boogers 'ave done us.' Denis Compton, about to go in, was at his side, and heard it. 'But I haven't gone in yet,' he said. 'I know, I know,' said Len. Compton finished on 34 not out, and England won by five wickets.

He once said to me about one of my sisters: 'You've got a nice sister. You've got a very nice sister. By God you've got a nice sister.'

* * *

I realise that I've gone on about the conversations, the characters, the atmosphere of professional cricket. What about the cricket itself? When I was fifteen or so, my father, who was in charge of cricket at my school, must have persuaded the City of London Corporation to do two things: one was to put down artificial nets in the playground, the second to employ a part-time coach, Reg Routledge, who had recently retired from playing as an all-rounder for Middlesex. The pitch was quick and true, and Reg taught me to throw my hands after the ball in order to drive 'on the up', that is, when the ball was short of a half-volley length. This freed up my batting no end. Years later, my friend as player and coach, Tom Cartwright, used a similar phrase, 'Let your hands flow through the ball.' In my last three years at school, I scored several centuries and in 1960 was selected for the Public Schools team to play the Combined Services at Lord's.

A year after leaving school, I had a dream start for Cambridge. The first match was against the best county side – Surrey. As wicketkeeper I came in to bat with the score 107 for 6. Eric Bedser bowled me a full-toss that got me off the mark. I was last out, run out trying to farm the strike, for 76. In the second innings I learned a lesson. I was batting when it started to rain. The umpires were about to take us off, when Surrey captain Peter May suggested we stay for a few balls. Next ball, as the squally rain came down harder, I played an airy shot off Peter Loader and was caught in the gulley for 13. Everyone then left the field.

My second match was against the next best team, Yorkshire (the setting, as I was convinced, for the jazz-hat's teeth story). This time I came in with the score 29 for 6, and ended up 33 not out. I did hook Trueman, for four. He grunted, 'Good shot, son, but tha won't do it again.' Two balls later, a much faster ball arrived.

I pulled out of the hook. Fred generously announced, 'You got out of the way well, kept your eye on the ball.'

A few weeks later we played the Australians on a placid pitch. Their first four batters all scored hundreds: Bill Lawry, Colin McDonald, Brian Booth and Ken Mackay. Next day, still batting at number eight, I arrived with the score 107 for 6, and was again last out in my seventies. Since one of our opening batters was injured, I was asked to open the batting in the second innings. I scored 89 before I managed to snick a full toss from slow left armer, Ian Quick, into Barry Jarman's gloves. I had been pegged back by defensive bowling by Mackay. A lesson 'not to lose concentration when getting a ball that makes one's eyes light up,' as one of the Australian stars said to me consolingly.

Despite these early successes, I had a vast amount to learn, especially about batting in more competitive cricket and on less placid pitches than Fenner's. In 1964, my last year, I had another good season, and then played the remainder of the season, after the University match in July, for Middlesex. County Championship cricket was a different kettle of fish – batting on less easy-paced pitches against bowlers who were fully in earnest. In 1961, I had played twice for Middlesex, first against Derbyshire's Harold Rhodes and Les Jackson at Lord's, second against Butch White and Derek Shackleton on a green pitch at Portsmouth. In 1964, there were similar challenges. In August, I was out for the only pair of my career, against John Dye of Kent; the first 'duck' on Saturday, the second on Monday. On the Sunday the MCC team to tour South Africa was announced. I was included.

I thought I could come and go from cricket in those semi-attached years as an undergraduate, and between 1966 and 1971. During one summer vacation I went on holiday to Greece for six weeks, driving with two friends in a Mini; in another I went off to Denmark to coach cricketers for a week, following this with a trip to Norway. In 1968, returning from a holiday in Provence and Florence, I came back on a Monday to find a letter inviting me to play against Lancashire at Lord's on the Wednesday. Their opening bowlers were Ken Shuttleworth and Peter Lever, both future England bowlers, and I was out second ball. I thought I could have everything, perhaps even that I could do anything.

Despite my real and assumed attitude of enquiry and modesty, there was a sort of arrogance; a more or less secret assumption that I knew better. I would welcome offers of help, but didn't completely trust them or follow through with what I was told. I never found a regular coach or mentor whom I could rely on for informed, honest and supportive advice. On that South Africa tour, selected as a young hopeful aged twenty-two, I did well until the First Test, averaging 45, but then lost form completely. I wasn't properly serious, nor seriously committed, though I thought I was. Many well-intentioned people gave me their advice, the variety of which was bewildering rather than useful.

I was a late developer. I was first selected for a Test match at the late age of thirty-four, an age at which many international cricketers retire. I had by then developed a technique organised around a fairly sound defence, a somewhat limited range of strokes, and a rather tight kind of courage against fast bowling.

The small creature hiding in the shell was too often the more appropriate image, especially when it came to Test cricket. For many of the best players, playing at the highest level felt to them like performing on the stage they have been born to, the setting made for them to strut their skills. I think particularly of Viv Richards and Shane Warne: both conveyed, with conviction and justification, that they were entitled to be there, this was their appropriate home, here they could bring their whole selves to each contest, including a proper pride, aggression and resilience. They could harness emotion without losing a sense of fair play. They could live the game, exuberant with love and passion, but also with all the benefits of experience, discipline and learning. Towards the end of my time as a player, I could feel 'right to be present' in county cricket; never, fully, in the international game.

The other side of the coin was that, including in my years away from regular professional cricket, between the ages of twenty-four and twenty-nine – key years for the development of a batter – I did a lot of other interesting things, particularly teaching philosophy at the University of Newcastle-upon-Tyne. These activities, holidays and struggles enlarged my view of life. In relation to cricket, the five years constituted a long dalliance rather than a committed marriage.

* * *

Becoming once again a contracted professional cricketer in 1971, leads me into the other main strand of my cricketing career: captaincy. I was interested in aspects of this role for almost as long as in the playing with bat and ball itself.

My first lessons in captaincy came informally from my father. Yorkshiremen and women are often practical, opinionated and questioning. They have a healthy belief in the rights of all to a view. They can be stubborn and cantankerous with each other, though they often close ranks against outsiders. Within the Yorkshire team there have often been fierce rivalries and division but, as in families, Arthur is 'our' Arthur, Elizabeth 'our' Lizzie. Youngsters are kept in their (lowly) place, but also spoken of highly to outsiders. There was a clear-cut social division. The solidarity of the working class was strong, but it didn't preclude vigorous disagreements within the group. There was a great pride in the county and its traditions of hard work and loyalty. I came to see that many of these qualities applied to Australians.

I like the sketch in which a Yorkshire Airlines plane takes off from Leeds airport. The passengers are told to get out their newspapers as plates onto which the heavily battered lumps of fish and thick chips are dumped. Soon after, the plane lands – back at Leeds. The pilot announces that there was after all nowhere worth going to outside the county.

Until 1992, you had to have been born in Yorkshire to play for Yorkshire. I believe there had been occasional intruders, including Lord Hawke, born in Lincolnshire. And there was a story, probably false, of one Yorkshire cricketer who had been born on a plane over the Red Sea. As the journey was risked in order to return the mother to the promised land, he was given exceptional right of qualification. But these cases were kept under the carpet. The innovations were, first, that men who had been educated in Yorkshire, though not born there, including Michael Vaughan, became eligible to play for the county; second, that Sachin Tendulkar was signed as Yorkshire's first overseas player.

Yorkshire was one of the last counties to appoint a professional captain (Vic Wilson in 1960). In 1925, Lord Hawke, by then more or less running the county's cricket, pronounced: 'Pray God that no professional shall ever captain England. I love and admire them all . . . But . . . when the day comes that we shall have no more amateurs captaining England, it will be a thousand pities.'

This attitude did not preclude powerful inputs from influential senior pros. 'Call them in, skip,' was said to be what Arthur Mitchell, later a much feared but also respected coach, would throw over his shoulder while playing cards in the dressing room, and the figurehead amateur captain would publicly clap his hands to declare.

This was the world of cricket in which my father grew up, and it didn't prevent him from having his opinions on fancy batting, silly field placing and aimless bowling. I was brought up with certain values: don't show off, don't draw attention to yourself, don't think too highly of yourself. (As a man in the crowd at Headingley shouted as Middlesex took the field: 'Don't think yourself so clever, Brearley, just because you wear socks.')

I was also brought up on a cricketing diet of forthright views on tactics. Arguments and debates about such things, as well as about players' characters, were part and parcel of the life of most cricketers from the Midlands or north of England, especially from urban, working-class backgrounds. Tom Cartwright moved from Warwickshire, who played most of their matches in Birmingham, to Somerset. When playing against him in Taunton, I asked him how he liked it in the West Country. He didn't. 'Too much forelock-touching,' he said. He missed the trenchancy and argument of the shopfloor, whether in the car industry or the cricket team.

* * *

Towards the end of my career, I used to be asked if my interest in psychology helped my captaincy. I think that, if anything, it was the other way round. Playing cricket, and captaining, taught me a lot about what makes players tick, both those on the same side and opponents, and it stimulated my interest in what others and I myself feel, how we respond to pressure, how we impinge on each other, and so on.

There are of course two main features of the job of captaincy – one to do with tactics and strategy, the other to do with human relations. The latter calls for personal qualities of empathy, truthfulness and courage.

Being captain was almost never boring. It could be frustrating, emotionally difficult and anxiety-producing. But it has been unfailingly interesting to me. There is in the role always something that can be done better or worse, there are always choices to be made, usually without grounds for certainty. One has to combine intuition with disciplined knowledge.

Field placing, for instance, includes both elements. There are ordinary tactical reasons for putting people in places where catches are likely, or to save runs. But there are also psychological reasons, such as bluff and double bluff, unsettling the batter with implicit comments on what he can't do well, inviting him into tense caution or rash risk-taking. Or one might want to reassure a nervous young bowler with a more cautious field setting at the start of his spell.

There are considerations that captains, and I think pundits, too frequently ignore, such as: 'What would the opposition *least* like from us, and can we afford to deliver it?' and 'What do my team, and/or each individual player, most need from the captain at this point?' 'What do I have to do in advance to prepare bowlers for a range of possible approaches?' I remember talking at length to Derek Underwood, an already brilliant and experienced left-arm spin bowler, about an option that he had not seriously considered or favoured. This was to bowl over the wicket to a right-hand batter, aiming to pitch the ball on or just outside the leg stump. I drew pictures on the back of an envelope of possible field placings. He felt confident to try it out against Australia at Old Trafford in 1977, with success.

I became captain of Middlesex after being on the fringe of top-level cricket for those five years. This meant that I was captaining several senior players older than myself, with long experience, including at Test level, people who were likely to be contributing more through their first-order skills of batting, bowling and wicketkeeping than I would through my batting. My appointment also meant that one of them was being ousted as captain, and at least one other, who might well have expected the role, may have been disappointed. What's more, the person who was being put in charge was younger, and had unsettling ideas about levelling up (the prevailing context had as one of its unspoken rules that young players should be seen but not heard). I tried to bring in ideas of team consultations about how things were going. I was also, in those early days, sometimes foolish and inappropriately 'rational'. Overall, I found it much easier to captain younger players, being more able both to encourage and confront them. I was flattered to be told by the chair of cricket at

Middlesex (Mike Murray) that one senior player, complaining about my putting fielders in unorthodox positions, had added: 'But oddly enough the ball keeps going there.'

These first few years were hard for me, and there were times when I almost resigned and gave up; I needed the support from a range of people to stay on. And after about three or four years, I had more grounds for self-respect as a batter, and our recognition of the need for new players, especially bowlers, had born fruit with Mike Selvey and John Emburey joining from Surrey, and Edmonds, deciding to join Middlesex after university. In 1976 we also signed fast bowler Allan Jones (who was about to move to New Zealand, having fallen out with both Sussex and Somerset). Our most important signing of all was Wayne Daniel, the Barbadian fast bowler, who transformed our attack from 1977.

* * *

My cricket career had many highlights, as well as some regrets and disappointments. There was, too, the ongoing element of luck, especially good luck. Middlesex might never have invited me to captain the side in 1971. Without the dry hot summer of 1976, we probably would not have won the Championship. Had I not batted resolutely when brought in as a late replacement for Richard Lumb to open the batting for MCC against the West Indies at Lord's in 1976, I would probably never have had the chance to play Test cricket. My Test career would have been much shorter if Tony Greig had not been de-throned as England captain after he was instrumental in setting up Packer's World Series Cricket.

And luck played a huge part in the most exciting period of cricket in my life – the Ashes series in 1981 – when I came back to replace Ian Botham as captain; and largely thanks to him we won three consecutive Test matches after being in disastrous or precarious situations in each. That extraordinary summer catapulted me to a realm of minor legend in some people's eyes. But the experience of it, with the excitement and satisfaction of the team as a whole, was extraordinary.

In 1975, Middlesex reached (also by the skin of our teeth) the finals of two one-day competitions. That paved the way for the last seven years of my captaincy there, in which time we won the Championship three times outright, and once jointly with Kent. We also won two Gillette Cups (one-day competitions). Again, there was a terrific team spirit, and an eagerness for every challenge. As I've implied, it was during that period, and in that context (of county cricket), that I felt most sure of my standing as a professional player, and most satisfied with my often-vigorous interchanges with the team as a whole and with individual players. I was able to be myself.

I once told a cricketer from another county that their captain must have done a good job in that team's success. He responded, 'Yes, he did. But we felt that, playing against Middlesex once a year, we knew you better than we knew him.'

As for regrets, there have been many, too. Some of these troughs derived from overflows of emotion on my part, including unkindness and lack of consideration for others. Disappointments with myself concerned also my batting in Test matches, opportunities missed due to ineptness, inhibition and, of course, on occasion, bad luck.

The innings I most regret was in the 1979 World Cup Final against West Indies. We needed 287 to win, a huge target in those days, especially against what was a great bowling attack, and at a time when there were no fielding restrictions. In twenty-five overs before tea, Boycott and I reached seventy-nine for no wicket. This was not bad. I think we lost the match in the next few overs. We allowed Richards, the one non-specialist bowler, to get through his ten overs conceding only thirty-five runs. The run-rate mounted, and the innings subsided as Joel Garner took five wickets as the light got worse. I should have made sure in that period after tea (at least) that I (and Boycott) either scored at six or seven runs an over, or got out and let in our powerful stroke players – Graham Gooch, David Gower, Derek Randall, Ian Botham and Wayne Larkins.

It's also true that, however we had batted, we would probably have lost. But we would have given ourselves a better chance if my mind had been sharper and my intentions and instructions more whole-heartedly attacking.

Each leader has to make personal decisions about how to balance caution and risk. Overall as a captain I was, I think, usually positive and willing to take risks. I was happy to try unconventional strategies, without underestimating the value of orthodox wisdom.

Overall, once again, I was also fortunate. Contrast Botham: he captained England in twelve Tests, of which nine were against this powerful West Indies side; the other three against the next best team, Australia. When his team were struggling in the Caribbean in 1981, I sent him a letter of advice. 'Try captaining against someone else', I wrote. I imagine he smiled, ruefully.

CHAPTER 9

THE CRACKED VASE

By the summer of 1981, I had already been in analysis as a patient for three years, and was about to start the training proper in September. I would rountinely take my son Mischa to school, drive on to my analyst in Child's Hill, and get to Lord's at about half past ten in time for the start an hour later. It was a strange transition, but one that I found helpful. Fifty minutes of saying whatever came to my mind, being relatively unrushed and detached (at least from the immediate pressures of playing cricket), felt like a relief. The car journeys – perhaps fifteen minutes for each journey – were just long enough to make a transition from the inner, private world to the inter-personal intensities of the dressing room and pitch.

Despite a rain-affected season so far, I had by mid-June scored four centuries for Middlesex in nine matches. I was in good form. One morning, as I arrived, fellow-batter Graham Barlow said to me, 'Maybe we should all lie down on your analyst's couch before a day's play.' I took this not only as a compliment, but also as an expression of curiosity about this strange process of psychoanalysis.

The most touching suggestion along these lines was made by six-year-old Mischa. 'One day, Mike,' he said, 'why don't you drop me off at your analyst's so I can lie on her couch, and you sit at my desk at school?' (He has had an almost-lifelong idea of making a film about an analyst's child, who looks through a keyhole of the closed door to the consulting room – which he did once, I discovered, having observed a striking young man in leathers arrive at our flat for sessions.)

It's not surprising that psychoanalysis is a topic for curiosity. For the participant, curiosity about the self and how we 'tick' is central. For others, there is a couch, or bed; and there is the intense privacy of this intimate, two-person activity. Later, after we had moved to our house, Mischa had it impressed on him that he couldn't go into the room above my consulting room when I was seeing patients, and there was of course no social mixing. The process naturally arouses fantasies. There is this exciting idea of intimacies of the body, called sex. What is there *not* to be curious about – and then worried about because of our intrusive wishes. Mischa was open about his passing thoughts – aged seven, he wanted me to watch the (now disgraced) Miss World programme with him, adding, 'I'd really like to have one of those ladies for my mum, just for the weekend'.

* * *

'You do psychoanalysis?', people ask, incredulously. 'Five days a week? For years? Isn't that as dead as a dodo; like Marxism!' Others say, 'Isn't it terribly boring? Or depressing? How can you bear it?'

Or at social gatherings, people shy away, with a look of mock retreat, as if to say, 'Is it safe to talk to you? Are you about to meddle in my mind? Are you already meddling in it?'

These represent two main lines of alarm about and criticism of psychoanalysis: first – what on earth do patients, and what do we psychoanalysts, get out of it? Second – what are we up to? If we take away people's neuroses will we remove their creativity? Are we in the business of brainwashing, of conversion therapy?

The first of these suspicions and anxieties is that psychoanalysis is ineffectual, a waste of time, that the process is mere chatter or navel gazing. There is in this view no room for its seriousness or for the intransigence of patterns of thought, feeling and action that have built up from early in life, perhaps as character armour, the kind of habit we all find hard to recognise as such and even harder to change. As Freud says, the patient has to come to see his or her 'illness' – the rigidities and defensive organisations – as powerful, as an 'enemy worthy of our respect'. And though we don't get rid of our neurotic thoughts and feelings, we may modify them, make them more articulate, become more able to tolerate what we defend ourselves against, and be enriched by access to more of ourselves.

I've mentioned Wilfred Bion's remark: 'It's fascinating how boring this patient is.' He implies that we psychoanalysts have to take seriously our own responses to the boring patient. Our boredom may be more to do with us than the patient. But suppose the patient really *is* being boring; this may be one outcome of the loss or suppression of his or her creativity and liveliness. Sometimes the question we need to ask ourselves is: 'Why does this patient *not* arouse any erotic fantasies in me? What has happened to her/his sexuality and capacity to seduce?'

In the second scenario, in which we're cast as snooping brain-washers, analysis is not tame, it's all too effectual, even dangerous. The analyst is far from being a mere listening post, a cipher who achieves nothing; he or she is a threat to the patient. In response to the cocktail-party suspicion that we are about to meddle with the questioner's mind – one older colleague would reply, 'Don't worry, you have to cross my palm with silver before I'll start on you.' (I did, though, think of her as a bit of a witch.)

Alongside the scoffing provocation, there is also a wish to understand and sometimes real worry. And it has to be said, being a psychoanalyst is a rum job. We need to explain ourselves.

Similar cynicism came my way when I was doing philosophy. In my early days playing cricket for Middlesex, Fred Titmus, the senior player (whose first game for Middlesex in 1949 coincided with the first of my father's two games, so that after Fred played in my last game at Lord's in 1982 he was able to say he 'saw the father in and the son out'), would prod me with questions like: 'This philosophy that we're all paying for, what's it all about?' He was being sarcastic, goading, but he was also genuinely curious. I took his curiosity seriously, and tried to give some sort of answer. In other lives, with different backgrounds, Fred might have been doing philosophy and I might have been born and brought up in King's Cross, and have left school at fourteen, and learned cricket, football and boxing at a local boys' club. (I once had a spare ticket for Benjamin Britten's *Peter Grimes*, and asked him if he'd like to go. We sat in the gods, and Fred was taken with it.)

Certainly, I was an odd fish in the dressing room. Geoff Boycott once snapped at me, 'I don't want any of your egghead intellectual stuff.' (Hence one nickname for me.)

I think a central element in the suspicion of psychoanalysis lies in the nature of the curiosity. At one level it's gossipy and intrusive, trivial or colonial: at another, there is a wish to know that arises from a wonder and puzzlement about life, a vital element in broadening our sense of the world and expanding our horizons. Both kinds of curiosity are present, in different proportions in every individual, in the analyst, the patient, as indeed in the dressing-room cynic or the cocktail-party alarmist. Curiosity killed the cat; but without curiosity, the cat would have been dead already.

I see a link in all this with espionage. There is a continuum between empathically seeing things from another person's point of view, and on the other hand 'entering' them to spy on or exploit them. Sometimes stepping into someone's shoes is more like surreptitiously treading on their toes.

For the psychoanalyst, being invited by patients to see and hear what goes on inside their heads, to be a fly on their internal walls, is also a privilege, even if the invitation is repeatedly withdrawn.

We have not only erotic, aggressive and infantile fantasies (that may or may not in time be sublimated); we also have an instinctual drive towards making sense of the world. Melanie Klein coined a term for it, from the Greek words for understanding and love: the 'epistemophilic instinct'. And despite the narrow line between intrusion and empathy, despite the tendency towards short attention spans and the wish for quick fixes, neither that drive, nor this profession, is dead.

Whether or not traditional, five-times-weekly psychoanalytic treatment will have a major role over the next decades, intensive individual therapy is only one of the contributions of our discipline to the world at large. We must consolidate other kinds of input. Psychoanalysis also provides a philosophy of life, a certain picture of human and social thinking and emotion, a set of implicit and explicit values. We should aim to have a larger role in public discussions on issues such as autocracy, democracy, the arts and sciences, and religion. We should expand our inter-disciplinary participation.

We should develop our contributions to psychiatry and to many other fields, both in practical ways (by becoming consultants, for example, as many do, to people who are struggling on the front line with forms of behaviour and states of mind that are puzzling and frustrating). We need to publicise what we do and think.

People may not always agree with the sense a psychoanalyst makes of disturbing behaviour, but the openness to such thinking may enable a health professional to see patients not as black boxes awaiting medication, but as persons whose madness has a method.

The incredulous person at the cocktail party wishes not only to tease or mock, but to know more. Fools who come to scoff remain to pray – but only if we can convey something of the experience, for patients and analysts alike, to people who have never been near a psychoanalyst's consulting room.

* * *

Becoming a psychoanalyst is to become a patient as well as a practitioner. Central to the training is having a training analysis throughout. For this work, we need to be as much in touch as we can be with our own patient-selves, so as to know our way round from the inside, and to increase our empathy with, and understanding of, the people we have in treatment.

The two processes are closely connected. There is a tension in the qualities required to be a psychoanalyst. We need to be in touch with our own emotional difficulties, our psychotic and neurotic tendencies, if we are to understand on our pulses those of our patients. At the same time, we won't help our patients much if we're in exactly the same boat as them. There is a narrow line between a solid common sense, which risks a blanking out of deeper emotions, and flair, which may lead to wildness or breakdown.

What, then, did I get into, half my lifetime ago? Has it been worth it? Might I have contributed more, and been more relaxed and enlivened, by becoming a civil servant, or a teacher, or continuing as an academic philosopher; or for that matter working in cricket in media roles, or as an administrator, commentator, coach or umpire?

What, then, are the pleasures and satisfactions of the analytic couch, whether one lies on it or is sitting behind it?

* * *

First, as patient. For me, the process of being in analysis was often enjoyable. Within the profession, this is not a fashionable thing to say. It may smack of superficiality and denial. And if the experience remains at a level of self-satisfaction for either party, it is bound to be indulgent and avoidant. But for me, and for many, to be invited to say whatever came into my mind was freeing. And there was this person listening quietly, intently, behind my head, commenting from time to time.

Psychoanalyst Sándor Ferenczi said, 'You have to catch your hare before you cook him'; free association is essential for catching hares (including 'mad March hares', who alternate between racing around and standing stock still). This offer of a listening ear opened me up to a fuller sense of how I experience the world. I began to feel less grey, more alive.

As the analytic process deepened, and the honeymoon period segued into a more complicated 'marriage', periods of hurt, outrage and unease, not to mention guilt and shame, became more palpable. Gradually, the process helped me to take more seriously, and to accommodate with more awareness, less admirable aspects of myself.

This enlargement of a sense of self and other does not develop smoothly, nor is its outcome simply benign. The shameful perverse, tricky, selfish, ruthless, possessive thoughts don't evaporate. Anxiety enters in, one source of which is: can the analyst possibly like me? What does (s)he think of me? Is the silence from behind me a silence of love, disapproval or boredom? Are interpretations in fact condemnations?

We cannot disown or get rid of such states of mind, though we hope we will understand better where they come from, get less stuck in them, and sometimes transform their energy in less selfish or narrow directions. As Harrison Birtwistle suggests in a different context: 'you may stretch your intuitions by analysis and thought'. One development is that the destructive elements come to take up a less dominating place. Certainly, I can now interrogate them in myself. Night-time self-laceration occasionally recurs for me, disrupting sleep. But I have the resource of a better capacity for self-analysis, for looking at such attitudes and behaviours more steadily, less indulgently, and also in less, or less long-lasting, persecuting ways.

There were periods of time in analysis when I was convinced I was being told to shut down these 'bad' desires. I sometimes defiantly repudiated what I was told; sometimes, I did so secretly. Links could seem to me far-fetched; was I really thinking of the analyst when speaking of a man in a white suit who thought too much of himself? Had I turned a benign parent-figure into this haughty know-all?

Other interpretations, however, even to this paranoid me, came across as dismally plain; for example, the realisation that when someone got between me and my desires, I hated them more than I knew, and became murderous (I had been talking about my seat in a theatre, where my view of the stage was blocked by a huge man in front, and I had muttered imprecations against him, which he heard). And then doubts crept in again as this idea ramified: do such powerful resentments lie behind my irritation at my access to a scene being interrupted? And then again: how furious I can still get when efforts I think of as my trying to help are interpreted as striving to get back into the other's good books, as 'help' that is more trouble than it's worth, or even as instances of patronising superiority.

One aspect of (orthodox) psychoanalysis that is both difficult and enabling is its frequency. Five lots of fifty minutes to fill! I have nothing to say today. The time drags. Someone demands that I speak (or is that impression my invention?). So much of my life is taken up dealing with demands on my time, and here I am, having to come to yet another session, another burden of expectation. No dreams to resort to, either: at least with a dream there is something specific to go on, something that comes from my unconscious but can be regarded dismissively as not really belonging to me. Am I wasting my time and money?

At other times, by contrast, I would feel that the frequency and regularity of sessions made me feel held, supported, my reactions recognised; loved – toughly loved – a loving form of attention.

For me, and for others, there was a taboo against looking round at the analyst. I would occasionally sit up, whether from cramp or feeling unwell. But only once do I remember explicitly breaking the unspoken rule. Feeling intensely curious, I looked round to check on my analyst. This felt like reading a lover's diary to see what she really thinks of me, or listening in to a conversation about me between two authority figures. (One evening at Newcastle the famous philosopher, A. J. Ayer, came to give a lecture. On the way to the lecture hall, I found myself a few yards behind him and Karl Britton, the head of department, in a narrow outdoor passage. Suddenly I heard my name; 'How is this Brearley doing?', Ayer asked. In consternation, I turned round and fled, consumed with curiosity and guilt. I heard nothing of the reply.)

And yet that moment of looking round at the analyst, that look, was consoling. My analyst was totally attentive, deep in thought. Unlike one analyst I heard of, he was not asleep, unlike another, he was not doing a crossword. There was no trace of condemnation, only thought. I felt I was in the presence of a person with a serious take on life and on me, a take that included compassion and detachment – it was as if I got a glimpse into my analyst's inner orientation, and found him kindly as well as just, a loving not a jealous or judgemental God.

As I write, I'm reminded of Tolstoy's description of the way the Russian general Mikhail Kutuzov listened to couriers bringing dispatches during the battle of Borodino; he knew that the crucial element in war was 'that intangible force, the spirit of the army', so 'he kept his eye on that force and guided it as far as lay within his power'. His 'general expression' was one of 'concentrated quiet attention'.

I still feel a trace of guilt about breaking the rule, but I don't regret it. In retrospect, I think of it as a turning point. My impression is that I became less touchy, less paranoid. Had the working through of these features been sidestepped by my peccadillo? Difficult to say, but I don't think so. There were other opportunities for analysing the rule-breaker me.

There is something akin to joy in seeing things more fully, including knowing oneself better, more as a whole. Being a psychoanalytic patient involves the discomfort, denial and later at least a degree of acceptance, of seeing what's on the underside of the pebbles – both muck and beauty. Truth really can be nourishing food for the mind.

We also have to come to terms with the limits of analysis, of the process and of our own capacity to use it fully. No analyst can analyse everything. Failings have to be mourned, as does the loss of the analyst. But the process carries on long after the sessions themselves have ended.

I hate the ambivalent (or is it simply hostile?) term for an analyst – 'shrink'. Analysis does not, except as a defensive response to the process, shrink the patient; it does the diametric opposite. It expands the self, opening us up to more of ourselves, to a richer experience of the world.

* * *

'The wounded surgeon plies the steel / That questions the distempered part. / Beneath the bleeding hands we feel / The sharp compassion of the healer's art.' T. S. Eliot could have been describing the psychoanalyst at work.

Being a psychoanalyst has something of the discipline of a monk. Like monks with their fixed times for prayer and meditation, we aim to ready ourselves for whatever comes our way (while allowing disturbed feelings of all sorts to affect us), attempting to provide a setting of quietness inside and outside ourselves, aware of the lure of various kinds of temptation. Our days of work come to have a steady rhythm, a mindset that is both continuous with how we are in ordinary life, and also more reflective and detached.

Monks and psychoanalysts have their loneliness and their dark nights of the soul, too. The monk who lives in a monastery and not in a cave has people who share this difficult path of renunciation and discipline, while we psychoanalysts have a largely virtual community. In my early days in the work, when I was more anxious than I am nowadays about the day's prospect stretching ahead, I would find a degree of support in the thought of other colleagues doing likewise; a degree of reassurance – I was not utterly on my own. Like others, at times I also need the input of real-life supervisors or members of regular CPD groups (Continuing Professional Development), as non-virtual partners.

Our ethics, like the monk's, require us to work to find a stance that includes both a proper warmth and a necessary abstinence. This latter quality has its obvious behavioural aspects – no sleeping with patients, no social contact, no financial dealings with them beyond payment for sessions – but its more subtle and ongoing aspect is a matter of our analytic stance.

As in all human relationships, patients may seduce, pull, lasso or lure us into playing certain roles. In ordinary social life, we respond more or less spontaneously or automatically to each individual. In friendships as in more superficial contacts, we respond to subtle hints and messages from each other; we are on the whole skilled at creating and maintaining unique relationships with each person we encounter, without losing our own selves.

As psychoanalysts, by contrast, we are centrally concerned not to enact such exchanges but to notice what each patient characteristically, and more or less unconsciously, evokes in us, putting pressure on us to conform to their demands or pulls. Or, failing that, we hope to recognise some of these tendencies sooner rather than later. One patient may provoke us into a quick playfulness of interchange; another is comfortable only when he has a prearranged set of topics to lay out before us and thereby invites us to be a sort of teacher; another requires us to treat her with kid gloves as a child.

These patterns have evolved over years, sometimes even from pre-verbal days in the patient's life. I find useful the notion of 'memories in feelings', a phrase used by Klein in her *Narrative of a Child Analysis* and based on Freud's notion of 'memory traces'. Freud wrote, 'No mortal can keep a secret. If his lips are silent, he chatters with his fingertips; betrayal oozes out of him at every pore.'

As for patterns, Joseph Sandler and Anne-Marie Sandler describe a patient who had had infantile eczema. His mother would come to him in the night when he cried and put a soothing lotion on his itchy back. This developed into a personality style, in which much of his character was based on his need to have constant itches of one sort or another. The analyst was being tempted to play the role of the comforting mother. The analyst's seeing of the pattern led to the patient's awareness of its ramifications in his life. Gradually, he become freer, less compelled to repeat it.

Apt analytic abstinence gives us the mental space to observe, and then in due course the opportunity to introduce the patient to, important aspects of themselves. It also lessens the likelihood of our imposing our own patterns and expectations on the patient.

There are patients who for various reasons sit face-to-face with me, but my feeling is that generally my sitting behind them, out of their view, helps this process. I feel more able to allow myself to notice my crude or instantaneous responses, and even to let them be expressed in my face or posture. I hope I'm not cut off from the person on the couch, or from these patterns, just more able to notice them as they arise. This is one reason I find working on Zoom or Skype (as was necessary through the pandemic), with the picture turned off after the patient and I have said hello, helpful in facilitating my awareness of these pulls and pressures. Whatever its limitations, this arrangement has for me advantages over face-to-face sessions, whether on screen or in the room. I am encouraged by the way we have become converted at least to the possibility of good work via the internet. Necessity may be the mother of invention and discovery.

One patient irritates me. Once I've noticed this, I'm able to see that it arises especially when he minimises what I say; his responses, I realise, often take the form of 'Yes, but . . .' He persistently resists my comments, preferring not to run with what (I think) I've just noticed. For instance, if I comment on his feeling of helplessness, he gives me an example where he made something happen. If I talk about his having the capacity to do this, he says, 'Yes, but really I can't do anything, look at how impossible my circumstances are.' I point out how with his 'yes buts' he jumps away from me when I take up any aspect of him. He renders me helpless. With him or other patients I may at times recognise that a hint of sadism or impatience has entered into my tone of voice, perhaps responding to the patient's masochism. Further thoughts now come to my mind, of how his parents never fully listened to him, how he had to look after himself and not rely on anyone. All this may lead to my becoming less judgemental, more empathic, yet willing and able to take up with him these ingrained ways of being.

So, part of our job is to learn to give attention also to the moves of our own minds.

Another overarching aim is to be alert to whatever might be the hotspot of intensity or anxiety in any given session, phase within a session, or moment, an aim that is central to both the efficacy and the satisfaction of the work. We are always attempting to get closer to the emotional truth. We may detect such hotspots by sudden awkwardness or hesitation in the patient's demeanour and speech, which often hint at a sudden eruption of feeling – anxious, hostile, erotic – towards ourselves.

All analysts have patients with whom there are periods of stasis, of distrust and incomprehension, even of impasse, which elicit a deeper challenge, that of trying to find what animates such atmospheres.

We have to tolerate and live through frustration, anger, self-doubt and even despair. If we look calm, we may be like swans appearing to glide upstream, while their legs are paddling hard under the water. Our job then may be to attend to the overall attitudes of the patient and ourselves more than the specific details of whatever is brought. We might have to refrain from turning over a particular pebble, and broaden our focus to the whole beach.

* * *

The analyst or other interpreter may speak with apparent paradox. I'm reminded of two particularly analytic remarks, one by Tom Main, the other by Wilfred Bion.

First, Main. As director of the Cassel Hospital in Richmond, near London, Main was confronted by a young psychiatrist, who, troubled by a difficult patient, demanded anxiously, 'What should I do, what should I say?' He replied: 'Don't just *do* something, *stand* there.'

The phrase 'Don't just stand there, do something' is directed at people who are indecisive, who avoid committing themselves. Clearly Main is commenting on a reverse failing: he is addressing someone who thinks he *must* act, and quickly.

The patient makes the young doctor anxious. 'Is he going to kill himself? Or attack someone? The patient keeps on and on at me for a solution. What should I say or do?'

Main's point is that sometimes the most important thing one can do for a person who is desperate and demanding is to *be with them*. Being with, 'standing there', may include really listening, attending to what they feel. And also noticing what they make us feel. This patient is perhaps handing his own problem over to the psychiatrist, pressing him to feel he has to do something instantaneously.

I had a patient who was clever and intellectual. He used to feel panicky at times, especially when threatened by, or in the throes of, separation. One defensive resource he had was to rush to use his intellect, inviting me to use (or overuse) mine. During a session he could become extremely anxious, perhaps fearing that I didn't like him, or that I wished he wasn't there. At such times, I felt a powerful pressure to say something to reassure him, and/or to make a (clever) interpretation. If I did either, the panic might be assuaged; we entered a different world, one in which rationality had quickly been restored. But then, I came to believe, the force of the panic had been too quickly dissolved. The pain had been sidestepped, not understood. Even if my words were true, offering them at that time and in that way had not been the most helpful response. They provided a superficial comfort, a pseudo-solution. In his early life, his family of origin had required him to be cheerful all the time. They couldn't stay with him in depressed or anxious moods.

In education, it is important to balance security with challenge. The skilful teacher knows when and how far to push an individual or group. One form of challenge is to leave them to ponder a problem for a while. Similarly, a skilful interviewer stays silent for longer than the other expects, leaving room for the interviewee to go beyond their 'official' story, their first reaction, and this may lead to a fuller, more informative and honest response.

A colleague once told me: 'One of the most important things my analyst gave me was: she allowed me to be depressed in peace.' Depression may need to be experienced, by both parties, before the analyst gets going with interpretations.

The psychoanalyst Nina Coltart wrote: '*Precipitate control of the material* may lead to a sense of satisfaction in the analyst, and often appeal to conscious layers in the patient, whose resistance to exposing his or her true unknown reality will have been served by it.'

If by contrast I am able to *stand there*, the patient may begin to think further about the situation. Like the man in the Aarhus taxi, he or she may feel held by my steady presence. Think of the etymology of the word 'understand': emotional understanding involves bearing the load, standing under and supporting the patient. Understanding is not only an intellectual matter.

So: what Main advocates is not actually 'doing nothing': it is doing what is needed, but this may well not be a busy '*doing*' of something.

Second, Bion. His remark, allegedly made to a patient, was: 'I don't know why you're angry, I wasn't trying to help.' The conventional, expected response to a patient might be: 'I don't know why you're angry, I *am* trying to help,' which assumes that patients – people, we ourselves – always *want* help. Part of Bion's point is: we don't, and he recognises that.

So, what is he saying? In the first place that not all offers of help are welcome. The child has a natural wish to 'do it myself'. Some parents take over too quickly, leaving no room for the child to solve the problem for himself, with all the satisfaction and sense of agency achieved.

Moreover, 'helping' may be, or be felt to be, scornful, superior, belittling – 'you mean you can't do *that?*' It may be patronising, implying that 'I the helper can of course do this, but you, poor thing, can't!'

Or again, the patient may feel resentful at anyone else being able to do what he can't do, and thus rubbish helpful suggestions rather than give them house-room. While I was still training, one patient of mine would quickly dismiss virtually everything I said. At first, on each occasion, I thought I must have got it wrong. But gradually I came to realise that this was not necessarily so; it dawned on me that she hated it if she was not the one who had had the idea first, and her immediate reaction was to say no to whatever I suggested. I managed, laboriously, to work out in my mind that this was envy. I made a policy decision: I determined to be more courageous with her; I faced the fact that I would have to be ready for opposition, even hatred, if I voiced how much she resented such a challenge to her need to possess the truth. I had to 'gird my loins', as it were, against the inevitable onslaught.

A supervisee told me of how a breakthrough was made when she realised that the reason her patient resisted help was that for him it always was disappointing, that the whole problem was not thereby resolved once and for all. Like a small child, the patient insisted that mother magically extinguish his headache or his frustration, taking away, perhaps even taking on, the child's discomfort. Now adult, this patient felt disillusioned, and without hope of help. His characteristic reaction was that the only way to avoid disappointment was to give up wanting.

More generally, we are all more or less torn between wanting to know about ourselves, including things that make us feel ashamed or guilty or feeble, and not wanting to know (or, more actively, wanting to not know). Bion's patient may have wanted not to know, and Bion ironically reassures him: 'I wasn't trying to help, don't worry.'

* * *

Main has a paper called 'Psychoanalysis as a Cross-bearing'. He was referring to what psychoanalysts may offer psychiatrists and others. As in navigation at sea, one needs cross-bearings to know where one is, where one is heading, and how to get to our destination without hitting rocks; an analyst may help by offering another set of bearings alongside the more formal, more instrumental ones in the doctor's kitbag.

I am struck by another potential meaning of the phrase 'cross-bearing'. It seems hyperbolical to compare our work to the horrors of a crucifixion, or even to someone bearing the sins of the world on his shoulders, and I do so cautiously. But psychoanalysts not only share (however partially) our patients' conscious grief and pain, we also have to take on some of the pain that they disown and project.

Arthur Hyatt Williams, a senior colleague, worked with prisoners. He had just spent an hour with a murderer who was in an extremely disturbed state. On his way home, he almost had an accident with a lorry. The driver looked at him, then said, 'If you don't want to get into a fight, you'd better not look like that.' Hyatt realised that he was carrying with him some of the violence, whether murderous violence or suicidal guilt, from the man in prison. He decided there and then never to drive after sessions of this kind until he had managed to digest and mitigate such projections.

Here is a less dramatic example of mine. One patient was superior and quick to find fault with me. After weekend breaks, she would come back full of the importance of the people she'd visited or had to do with. They lauded and flattered her like deferential servants. She was treated like a queen. There was no sense at all that she missed the sessions with me. In fact, not only was any such feeling obliterated, the situation was stage-managed so that I was the one to feel disparaged, of no value or competence. I took it that I was reduced to the status and feeling of a dispensable servant. I came to regard this feeling as something that belonged to her in the first place, but which she skilfully loaded on to me. I had to feel, and register the feeling, of loss and inferiority in order to begin to find ways of handing it back to her in a non-toxic way.

Here is another vignette. In one Zoom session, a patient is disturbed by rubbish from building work on the roof rushing through a funnel next to his window and being dumped into a skip below – loud noises, which I also hear. He describes envious attacks by others on himself, including expecting him to function at levels that he can't live up to. He takes this expectation on in his own mind, feeling that he really is rubbish. He expresses this in a particularly forceful way, speaking hurriedly and repetitively. I feel assaulted by this tirade; his words are hammered into my ears and my mind in ways that resemble the dumping of rubbish into the skip. As his analyst, I too feel helpless, not unlike Main's young psychiatrist. I find myself inclined to become a supervisor rather than an analyst, speaking as if my patient was a colleague rather than a patient. Noticing this, and feeling uncomfortable with it, I manage to give more space to my feeling of being assaulted. Gradually I become clearer that something really is being forced into me along with a parallel, resultant sense of having to 'do something'. With these thoughts, I am beginning to be able to 'stand there', rather than rush after a solution. I become able to say something about the live interaction between us that is happening right now in the session.

There are, then, demands on the analyst, both to feel and enact something that the patient is evacuating, but also a deeper demand, sometimes a test: will we be able to take on board the projected pain and discomfort? If we are able to do so, besides finding ways to put what is going on into words, we are giving an example to the patient. Patients probe us to see what we're capable of tolerating, perhaps provoking an un-analytic response, or for that matter a merely routine and banal one.

In our relatively small ways, we do carry some of the sins of the world on our shoulders.

* * *

Pianist Jonathan Biss, who has recently recorded all Beethoven's piano sonatas, said on radio that, as long as he is a musician, as long as he lives, he will 'play and work on' Beethoven's piano sonatas. 'Play and work', that is part of the extraordinary job/vocation of being a psychoanalyst. There are times of course when the task feels burdensome, more like enforced labour than play. And times when it feels trivial, and degenerates into game-playing or manipulation or avoidance. At its best, it seems to be seamlessly, even simultaneously, playful work and serious play. I think we tend to minimise the satisfaction, even joy, in our work. I notice a tendency to speak with pride of how exacting the task is. We boast about our tiredness, implying that we are not among those superficial therapists who steer clear of the darkness and destructiveness.

* * *

Salman Akhtar, a psychoanalyst who works in Philadelphia, once gave a lecture on patients with severe character disorder. A questioner asked whether, after the successful completion of an intensive psychoanalytic treatment, 'an individual with severe character disorder would be indistinguishable from a person who has always been well-adjusted and healthy?'

My first thought on reading this was that no one is perfectly normal. It's hard to know what sort of state this might be!

Akhtar spontaneously came up with a much better response, involving an image of two vases. 'Both are of comparable value elegance and beauty. Then a wind blows and one of them falls and is broken into pieces. An expert painstakingly glues the pieces back together again. Soon the vase is intact again, can hold water without leaking, is unblemished to all who see it. Yet this vase is now different from the other one. The lines along which it has broken, a subtle reminder of yesterday, will always remain discernible to an experienced eye. However, it will have a certain wisdom since it knows something that the vase that has never been broken does not. It knows what it is to break and what it is to come together.'

The tightrope walker with perfect balance stands on one foot on the rope with ease. The wobbly tightrope apprentice has to adjust. He has to strengthen the weight-bearing leg in order to hold himself through the wobble. The apprentice who wobbles thus strengthens other muscles in order to maintain a balance. He may as a result have strengths that the person who hasn't wobbled or fallen hasn't developed. Like the vase, a patient who has gained resilience from her breakdown has capacities for understanding herself and others that those who have had smoother journeys may lack.

The singer-songwriter Leonard Cohen employed a similar metaphor in his song 'Anthem': 'There is a crack, a crack in everything / That's how the light gets in.'

The Japanese art of *kintsugi* (golden repair) involves repairing broken pottery by filling the cracks with lacquer dusted with powdered gold. The cracks are thus highlighted as part of the history of the piece. Imperfection may enhance beauty. Cracks lovingly repaired may be expensive but come to have a value and strength lacking in the person who never cracks up. In fact, it is not only the patient who is broken, repaired with gold; it may also be the analyst.

There is no such thing as a perfect analyst. We fail and fail; hopefully we fail better. Some failings are mended.

* * *

Shakespeare understood the conflict between disturbing the fragile ecosystem of the mind, and on the other hand letting it be, allowing it to remain in delusion. In the second half of *King Lear*, Lear is frankly mad. He has rejected his loving daughter, Cordelia, and has then himself been rejected by his unkind daughters, Goneril and Regan, whom he foolishly trusted. He also imposed on them in his old tyrannical way, taking for granted that he could bring a hundred knights to carouse and create chaos in their castles. In the parallel subplot, the Duke of Gloucester has naively trusted Edmund (his illegitimate son), who twisted his father's mind against the loving (legitimate) son, Edgar. Towards the end of the play, Gloucester, who has been cruelly blinded by Lear's daughter Regan and her husband, comes across the mad Lear near Dover. Appalled and also challenged by what he encounters, he reflects:

> The King is mad: how stiff is my vile sense
> That I stand up, and have ingenious feeling
> Of my huge sorrows! Better I were distract:
> So should my thoughts be severed from my griefs,
> And woes by wrong imaginations lose
> The knowledge of themselves.

This dense speech captures much of what psychoanalysis claims. Gloucester contrasts his own 'standing up' with the collapse of the king. He wonders to himself if it might be better to be 'distract' (that is, mad, but also distracted from, oblivious to, the reality of his actual states of mind. His own sanity ('sense') is 'vile' – horrific – in its 'ingenious', in other words torturous, feeling and knowledge of his own pain ('huge sorrows'). Distracting oneself from such pain (as the king has done) means that one's knowledge, 'thoughts', of one's woes is 'severed', by 'wrong imaginations', that is, by self-deception. We cut ourselves off from intolerable pain, from our own woes, thus becoming distracted – neurotic or even mad and deluded.

This speech does not, though, tell the whole story. We know that Lear has in some ways moved on from the childish tyrant that he was at the start of the play. His breakdown was also the beginning of a breakthrough. We are moved by the newer, more vulnerable man who has emerged in the emotional and physical storm on the heath. His 'imaginations' are not totally severed from reality. Indeed, we probably sense that he is less mad than at the start of the play, when one might say that he had been in a borderline rather than a psychotic state. We have no reason to disbelieve the verdicts of his 'bad' daughters, that he 'has but slenderly known himself'. He has been capable of praying for 'noble anger' one moment and in the next breath building up to cursing them with the hideous but childish imprecation: 'I shall have such revenges on you both . . . / What they are yet, I know not; but they shall be / The terrors of the earth.' His imaginations have been 'wrong' or perhaps wrong-headed, from the start, and his frank madness is in some sense closer to sanity than his earlier states.

But still, if one knew the consequences, one might have held back from exposing him to the passage into 'distraction'. One might at least have been troubled by Gloucester's question – is it better to risk knowing oneself, or not?

As in psychoanalysis, Shakespeare shows how relief from pain, from unbearable pain, is often bought at the cost of one's sense of reality, at the cost of 'wrong imaginations'. Psychoanalysts and others are at times faced with ethical questions in our practice: how far should we go in pressing unwelcome, perhaps extremely disturbing, knowledge on to the patient, and how far on the other hand should we let sleeping dogs lie? We have to ask ourselves whether the patient has the resources, internal and in terms of support from others, to go through a 'withdrawal' from his addiction? Might a deep analysis lead to a breakdown that he can't bear?

Michael de Montaigne quotes a figure from antiquity called Lykos, who went to a doctor because he had the mad idea that everything he did occurred on a stage (an occupational hazard, perhaps, for novelists and directors?) The doctors cured him of his 'wrong imagining', but were rewarded by being sued by their patient for taking away the only pleasures he had in life.

Becoming a psychoanalyst, with its struggle to understand, to go deeper, has suited me. Its rewards for me are ongoing, as is the process of continuing to learn more. And one lesson is: the learning is never complete. It always involves work on ourselves. The work and play of development is like climbing mountains; behind almost every peak or valley there are others. New troughs and climbs face us as we travel on, but the view is enlarged, and we are changed. As are at least some of our patients.

CHAPTER 10

A PICTURE HELD US CAPTIVE

Disputes are, in many spheres and walks of life, repetitive and interminable. This happens at home, in politics, in philosophy and in psychoanalysis. We go round the same circles. We 'commit the oldest sins the newest kind of ways'. Why so? Why can't more or less rational people come to agreement?

Fixed, subliminal ideas are often involved. Our presuppositions are like glasses or frames through which we 'see', or distort, reality. As captain of the MCC cricket team that toured Australia in 1978/9, I was a selector. We chose Mike Hendrick as one of our pace attack. He was at the top of his form, though I (and others) also saw him as someone more suited to English conditions than likely Australian ones. He was not chosen for the first Test, which we won by seven wickets. We then travelled from Brisbane to Perth, with a game against Western Australia immediately before the second Test on the same ground. The pitch for this game offered variable bounce and movement for the quicker bowlers, and we won the match easily, bowling the State side out for 52 and 78. Hendrick took eight wickets for 34, Ian Botham eight for 53. Despite the evidence of my own eyes (from first slip) I was not convinced that Hendrick should replace Chris Old for the Test match (to play alongside Bob Willis and Botham). My 'glasses' reduced the quality of his bowling: he remained 'more suited to English conditions'. It was only when talking about the match with Western Australia captain John Inverarity, who stated unequivocally 'Hendrick is of course your best bowler', that the scales dropped from my eyes. Subsequently, Hendrick played a key role in our winning four of the remaining five Tests. It took Inverarity to jolt me into a more realistic, less hide-bound assumption for him to have the chance to do so.

Here the conflict was between two voices in my own mind. In many cases conflicts are fought out between different people. Here is an ongoing domestic tension. A wife, Sarah, likes to keep the house tidy. Having a big family party to host, she plans to cook the food weeks ahead, and stow it away in the freezer. Her husband Joe is more easy-going, even casual. He characteristically leaves his discarded clothes lying around; he puts things off. Confronted by his attitude, she becomes anxious and irritated. Joe hates to be nagged and withdraws. Sarah complains and pursues. A vicious circle gets going, each seeing the other as provocative. His underlying belief is (and has long been) 'here is another bossy woman. I will protect myself from her by avoiding her, by staying away, by keeping silent'. Hers is 'here is this typical man, selfishly refusing to help and leaving it all to me'.

The nub of the conflict lies in the assumptions of the couple, each seeing these familiar intransigent patterns of thinking and behaviour, and, without conscious intent, eliciting such patterns. The outcome is a dance routine that's been choreographed long ago.

In all walks of life we have strong, opposed presuppositions, which are often hard to shift. Behind the differences there may be a shared false picture of how things must be.

* * *

Wittgenstein's posthumous *Philosophical Investigations* (1953) begins with a quotation from St Augustine, which offers 'a particular picture of the essence of human language. It is this: the individual words in language name objects – sentences are combinations of such names. In this picture of language, we find the roots of the following idea: every word has a meaning. This meaning is correlated with the word. It is the object for which the word stands.'

The account is a picture not only in the metaphorical sense (such that one might as appropriately use the word 'account'), but also in that the elements of language correspond to, or match, or are isomorphic with, elements of the world. (Psychoanalyst Wilfred Bion spoke of that which is invariant between a wheat-field and a picture of that wheat-field.)

Philosophers have long argued about what kind of thing or object a word stands for. One answer is Plato's theory of Forms: a metaphysical 'thing', an essence abstracted from all actual things; the word 'good' stands for not any specific act or kind of goodness, but for what is essential to all cases, goodness itself; as is the case with the concepts of a table, a game, or a wheat-field, etc. The Form is a picture of a wheat-field but without specific configuration. Knowing what is meant by 'wheat-field' is being acquainted with this Form.

Or is what a word stands for a psychological entity, what John Locke referred to by the term 'abstract idea'? This account implies that there must be 'ideas' abstracted of all detail. Locke's idea of a chair, for example, like Plato's Form, has no particular shape, colour or material.

Or again, what the word stands for may be that which underlies all definitions; we might define 'kingdom' as 'rule by one male person', and we might go on to define 'rule' as 'having the right to command' and so on; but at the end of our definitions all we can do is point and hope the other person is pointing at the same thing, at what Wittgenstein in his earlier theory (in his *Tractatus Logico-Philosophicus* of 1921) referred to as the ultimate, that is, not further analysable, meaning a kind of logically simple object or atom, the ostensive endpoint in this process of definition.

In all these proposals, the underlying notion of understanding the meaning of a word is a matter of acquaintance; one is or is not acquainted with the Platonic Idea, the psychological abstract idea, or the object to which a simple sign corresponds. The Form or Idea is a kind of sample.

The later work of Wittgenstein is a brilliant working through of the inadequacies of this basic assumption, an assumption that leads us astray when doing philosophy into either insoluble arguments, absurdities and pseudo-sense; to metaphysical exaltation, or to scepticism and reductionism.

Referring to an Augustine-type of view, that 'the meaning of a word is a thing', Wittgenstein uses the phrase: 'A picture held us captive.' The picture that we are held captive by restricts our thinking, imprisons us. The quotation continues: 'And we could not get outside it, for it lay in our language and our language seemed to repeat it to us inexorably.'

Wittgenstein's method is not extended logical argument; rather, he challenges the reader in a variety of ways. For instance, he asks us to reflect on what actually happens when we speak or think; he famously says, 'Don't think, look' – a suggestion not unlike Bion's proposal to forgo memory and desire. He prods us first to look at what does or doesn't happen when people say what they mean and others understand them.

He decentres us by highlighting in detail many ways in which language is liable to mislead us, especially when doing philosophy. He is like a person doing self-analysis in our company. He interprets the temptations to make meaning into something sublime or meta-physical, as he had done in his early work, forcing it into a 'crystalline purity', according to which only statements of fact based on observation and induction, or mathematical or logical analyses, have meaning. The last words of the *Tractatus* are: 'whereof one cannot speak, thereof one should remain silent'.

Sometimes we do indeed apply a word or a name to a thing by pointing and using a name. But Wittgenstein shows how this phenomenon, when generalised as a theory of meaning, is confused, and he does this by getting us to look at our everyday uses of language. In the *Investigations* he opposes his own earlier views: 'What we do is to bring the words back from their metaphysical to their everyday uses.' He makes us realise with a shock how much we take for granted when we are drawn to offer an Augustine-like account (that words name things).

One form of confusion arises because we fail to take account of the fact that the activity of naming requires that we already know the role played in the pointing by the kind of word-use that is in question. He shows that Augustine, like the early Wittgenstein, leaves out the complex activities into which language is woven. One of his most illuminating parallels is between language and a game like chess. Pointing to a chess piece and saying 'this is the king' may have different meanings; but for the listener to understand such pointing, he has to know already something about boardgames, and perhaps even about chess itself. 'The ostensive definition explains the use – the meaning – of the word when [i.e. *only* when] *the overall role of the word in the language is clear*' (my emphasis). Meaning, then, is a matter of how a word is used, the role it has in the language activity as embedded in shared ways of behaving. The philosophical theories that Wittgenstein in his later work opposes, including his own earlier ideas, occur when people get stuck, not knowing their way around.

Philosophers had been inclined to focus on the moment of saying something and meaning it, as if that moment contained the essence of the meaning, if only we could isolate and describe it. Whereas the later Wittgenstein insists that we can only understand the meaning by looking at the whole context of such moments of intuition, even assuming these moments exist – but 'Don't assume they must!'

He writes: 'In order to get clear about the meaning of the word "think" we watch ourselves while we think; what we observe will be what the word means! But this concept (i.e. thinking) is not used like that. It would be as if, without knowing how to play chess, I were to try and make out what the word "checkmate" meant by close observation of the last move of some game of chess.' There is a wonderful simplicity of insight in this analogy.

Meaning, Wittgenstein says, is to be found in the use of words within the whole language or 'form of life' – a notion of a shared set of ways of being, thinking and acting, an informal system which one normally joins as a child entering her social groups, learning to share in the activities and experiences that root our language.

He suggests that we are 'bewitched by language', by the fact that words look as though they all function in the same way. Rather, he says, they are more like handles in a locomotive, some working in one way, some in another. 'Philosophical problems arise when language goes on holiday' – a kind of interpretation.

After reading the *Philosophical Investigations*, understanding the meaning of a word or sentence looks different; many philosophical theories or ideas begin to seem odd, artificial, the result of underlying logical confusion. We may no longer feel the same puzzlement, the same need or inclination to argue in these ways, or to posit these 'solutions'.

Wittgenstein reminds us, then, that meaning arises out of our participation in a system of rules and practices, just as we most naturally learn the meaning of 'king' in chess by participating in boardgames, and in chess itself. As children we join a language activity as we join a game; both are linked to interaction and to bodily expression. (I'm reminded of Freud's saying the original ego is a body ego.) Language is a social activity, bound by rules, related ultimately to man's physical and emotional nature.

* * *

In every aspect of our lives, we have pictures or stories or ideas that animate and organise the way we read the world and other people. In some cases, they restrict us, or hold us captive, but they also enable us to think, to link, to make sense (or non-sense) of the world. We say of people that they are sincere according to their lights – these underlying pictures are the inner lights or glasses through which we see the world, the illumination whose source casts shadows accordingly. (This way of putting things suggests one interpretation of Plato's cave; we always see things according to lights of various kinds. We may modify particular lights, even grow out of them, but we cannot see the world without lighting.)

Domestic arguments, too, hinge on the couple's competing underlying assumptions. These are often hard to sort out.

＊　＊　＊

In psychoanalysis we are similarly concerned with pictures that hold us captive in ways summed up by Freud in terms of templates perpetuated in the repetition compulsion – a form of captivity. (As German psychoanalyst, Helmut Thoma, put it: 'The common denominator for all neurotic and psychosomatic suffering is the vicious and self-perpetuating circle of repetition.') And such circles or cycles of interaction are inevitably repeated and re-experienced in the relationship with the analyst, the understanding and working through of which has become a, if not the, key element in the process of psychic change through psychoanalysis.

Psychoanalysts use the spelling 'phantasy' to make a differentiation from 'fantasy'; the latter being something like wishing, or daydreaming, whereas phantasy extends beyond that limited area to include imagination, though it is also broader than that.

I smuggled into my elaboration of 'a picture that held us captive' a phrase that has resonances in psychoanalysis – 'basic assumption'.

This term is central to Bion's account of group functioning. Groups are liable to certain kinds of basic assumption thinking, in which a picture holds the group captive. The picture may be: we can only function as and in a group if we have someone on whom we can totally depend. Or: if we have an enemy we can fight or run from; or: if we can find a couple who will answer all our problems by creating a new idea – a baby – that will transform our lives.

Such ideas, Bion has shown us, drive the group to function in ways that may well be unsuited to the task in hand. If the demand is for a leader on whom the group can depend absolutely, the group interpret the group leader's interpretations, his or her invitations to them to think, as saying more about *him* and his refusal of their (as they see them) perfectly rational demands than about *them*, the group. Bound together in an emotional solidarity (what Bion called 'valency'), the group members cannot (easily) think about what is happening. Their behaviour is predicated on and organised around the basic assumption. Everything is seen in the light of this idea, and the group attempts to make reality fit it, by for example getting angry with the so-called leader of the group if he or she doesn't quickly and powerfully take charge and give solutions. Or the group may sponsor a rival leader (or pair) from within its ranks, or create an enemy within or without. In such states of mind, it is difficult if not impossible for the group to be able to learn from experience, since any contribution of a potentially helpful kind is instantly experienced by the group as a failure or refusal to offer what they believe they really need.

Basic assumption tendencies are inevitable; what varies is how fundamental, how realistic, and how dominant they are. In some florid versions of basic assumption malfunction, a group is so cut off from reality as to resemble individuals in psychotic states. (After the 2020 US election, 'Stop the steal' placards abounded at rallies supporting Donald Trump. Contrary to the evidence, millions believed that he had won by a wide margin. A number of them went even further, believing he was the country's saviour in a crusade against a paedophile conspiracy led by the Clintons.)

All is not, or not always, lost, however. Alongside this basic assumption mentality, a parallel working capacity operates, with varying degrees of prevalence. In this state, the task of the group is likely to be carried out efficiently, there is discipline along with space for independent thinking, and the group as a whole is capable of learning from experience. What binds this group, or this mode, is not glue but respect, including respect for differences and for individuality within the group.

The basic assumption may also be to some extent suited to the task. Bion gives examples of this: the army's function in wartime is fuelled by fight–flight states of mind, which may contribute to its efficiency (though there is a risk that this attitude may become excessive or misguided; it may also infect parts of the task that go beyond fighting or withdrawing). The Church, he suggests, is particularly suited to the valency of dependence.

Similar situations occur in the psychoanalytic consulting room. The patient experiences the analyst as refusing to help in the way he or she (the patient) feels is natural and necessary. The analyst is felt to be subject to prejudices that make him captive.

One patient's conviction that therapeutic provision is niggardly took the form of hating the limitation of the fifty-minute hour; this could leave her with her insides hanging out, when, as the minute (and second) hand on the analytic Swiss clock came to the mark, I would throw her out. Would anyone go to a surgeon, she asked rhetorically, who told her he would allow exactly fifty minutes for her operation, and even if the operation wasn't finished, would move on to the next patient? My patient saw this practice as a self-serving device of the psychotherapy profession (a limiting form of life, she might have added, or a picture that holds us captive). As a group, she added, we psychoanalysts delude ourselves into the idea that this is a good enough system. My – our – strictness about time feels like a repetition of her childhood when, she believed, she was unwanted, bent out of shape, boxed in, to fit into her parents' priorities.

Well – does she have a point? She may indeed have felt as a child, as she does again now, that her needs are always ignored, that she is being eviscerated and abandoned. But it might be equally accurate to suggest that, if she were a surgical patient, she wouldn't tell the surgeon which scalpel to use; and/or she is ignoring both the differences from actual surgery and the care with which I try to spare her unbearable last-minute shocks.

Is the patient demanding to be the special, omnipotent child, telling her grandmother how to suck eggs; or is the analyst failing to be aware of how sensitive and painful a topic this is? Am I callous if I don't, for some patients and at some times, offer more flexible timings? Both views have plausibility; and it may be hard to be sure which is closer to the truth in a given case.

Certainly, our offer of fixed times and limits is partly practical, in that it enables us to run a practice and be reliably available to several people. It also enables us to establish boundaries, and protects us from having to make omniscient moment-to-moment decisions about when something important is or is not about to happen, or on which occasions disappointment is, or will be, unbearable. It helps make clear to both parties that we are not able to protect the patient from all suffering, nor do we insist that we are perfect providers, 'better' than the patient's internal parental representatives or than their actual parents. It also offers us the opportunity to focus on what patients do with frustrations and jealousy, and helps provide a rhythmic framework that can be supportive partly by being so clear-cut, even if (in respect of timings) sometimes experienced as rigid. The analogy to surgery is only partial.

As psychoanalysts, we may do our best to consider the force of the kinds of arguments (re timekeeping) expressed and marshalled by my patient, without being paralysed by them. While being open to self-scrutiny we also need to keep in mind the possibility of an underlying belief in some patients that, if and because we fail to offer unconditional, perfectly attuned love of one or other kind (maternal, erotic, intellectual or friendship love, for example), we offer nothing.

In George Eliot's *Middlemarch*, Dorothea has to bear disillusionment in order to free herself from her idealisation of her husband Edward Casaubon, to begin to see him for what he is, and to 'emerge from that stupidity in which the world is an udder to feed our supreme selves'. Eliot conveys vividly the demand for the perfect breast to satisfy Her Majesty the Baby. 'Yet,' the novel continues, 'it had been easier to her to imagine how she would become wise and strong in his strength and wisdom, than to conceive with that distinctness which is no longer reflection but feeling that he had an equivalent centre of self, whence the lights and shadows must always fall with a certain difference.' Compare with this, Freud's: 'We recognize the phase of incorporating or devouring, a type of love which is compatible with abolition of any separate existence on the part of the object.' More simply, as the Jamaican servant in Lolita Chakrabarti's play *Red Velvet*, set in London in the 1830s, says about racists: 'I'm jus' sayin' people see what them a look fo'.'

I hope it is now clear that basic assumptions, unconscious phantasies, both in terms of content and in terms of the closed-mindedness that they are likely to engender, are common to philosophers, patients, analysts and to all of us in our personal lives, and that they may inhibit productive, creative thinking, and interfere with getting things clear and facing facts of life.

They also create further problems, as we patch over the gaps, embellishing the stories with crazy ideas, or deal with our disappointments by throwing the baby out with the bathwater. For example, philosophers create fantastic worlds and ways of knowing in order to deny uncertainty, and to accommodate within their 'pictures' the possibility of knowledge. In our personal lives, we are liable to conceive grandiose fantasies (like those of Freud's Judge Schreber, who tried to deal with his terrors by identifying himself with God).

Or, in more ordinary ways, the disappointment with the other (for not being the perfect udder) can lead to the nurturing of grievances rather than grieving. We may all at times rid ourselves of feelings of insignificance, projecting them into the person who it seems makes us feel unwanted (the analyst over the weekend, or at the end of fifty minutes, for example). We are outraged at our servant the analyst for not doing just what we want, when we want it, and thus cut ourselves off from loving feelings. We may self-righteously embrace power instead.

A nine-year-old patient (described by David Bell) renders her analyst momentarily unsettled and at a loss when he goes to collect her from the waiting room for the first session after a break; she is demurely reading a newspaper, and he has to wait to catch her attention. She thus creates a tremor of insecurity in him rather than in herself. She makes him experience the feeling dismissed by an unconcerned analyst busy reading his newspaper over the break. She gives him a small dose of his own medicine. Such mental and emotional moves provide magical solutions to one's unease or to one's sense of loss or hurt; when extreme, they may result in a more or less devastated inner world, in which any helpful generosity of the other is first denied and then generalised as non-existent.

Pleasure may be found in something easily attainable, in substitutes or addictions of one sort or another, as in the child whose unconscious thought when his mother is away too long is: 'I shall bring her back by stroking myself', and who thereby finds comfort in masturbation. The pleasure-giving addiction then spreads and takes on a life of its own, no longer necessarily depending on a feeling of current abandonment.

* * *

Basic assumptions, pictures, at times hold us captive. They may alternatively help to release us. The philosopher is not only, or inevitably, the person imprisoned, he is also the one who can show us how to get out: 'What is your aim in philosophy?' Wittgenstein imagines an interlocutor asking him, and replies: 'To show the fly the way out of the fly-bottle.' Wikipedia says of fly-bottles: 'Flies enter the bottle in search of food and are then unable to escape because their phototaxia leads them anywhere in the bottle except to the darker top where the entry hole is.' An equivalent of human phototaxia keeps us from seeing how to get out of the internal fly-bottles in which we have become trapped: in addition, it blinds us to knowing how we got in. Wittgenstein vividly reminds us how such fixed ideas contribute to our buzzing imprisonment. He loosens our shackles.

He also suggests that, while the philosopher's anxiety has a kinship with that of the neurotic or even psychotic parts of ourselves, healing is akin to psychoanalytic work. This suggestion was taken further by John Wisdom.

This image of the fly-bottle is not totally satisfactory, I think, for Wittgenstein's purposes. It sounds as though it might all be done once and for all, instantaneously. Reality is more complex; our reasons for being trapped are more deep-seated, and the ways in which resistance to insight and to change occurs are multiple. Neither the Wittgensteinian philosopher nor the psychoanalyst can be sure whether his or her words will, at least in the short run, extricate or further entangle. Rather, the process of getting free is more like the laborious business of 'working through' in psychoanalytic treatment – a second psychoanalytic term I used earlier in relation to Wittgenstein. The fly-bottle story may imply a belief that there is a simple solution, that a single interpretation will free the patient for ever from whatever trap he is in. Frustration or fury that this is not so only makes the problem worse.

We all wish that the arduous and halting process of psychoanalysis could be magically sidestepped or minimalised; for example by revelation. A faith healer's acolyte told me once that her guru could do in an hour what it would take psychoanalysts such as me years to achieve. I had a patient who lived this out, announcing out of the blue on a Friday that this was our last session; the previous night he had had a mystical, religious experience. He parted from me with a kindly pity, grateful to me for my help, which he felt to have been real and sincerely motivated. It was clear that his view was that we had been struggling in the darkness of Plato's cave – whereas now reality was lit by Divine light. Sadly for me, but perhaps not for him, that was the last I saw of him.

The processes of learning and re-learning that we call working through are close to, and indeed participate in, grieving. When someone close to us dies, we have, as Freud said, to let the lost person go, not just once for all, but in all sorts of different situations; the face we see in a passing crowd is not theirs; they will not come in through the front door of an evening as they have done for forty years. We go through similar processes in giving up or reducing the impact of powerful unconscious ideas, whether on the cognitive front (in philosophy) or on the personal front (in everyday life, or in psychoanalysis, or in the course of other attempts at psychological change). We have to suffer the pain and emptiness of the loss of our old 'solutions', and of the loss of the security and/or excitement provided by them. Giving up long-term conflicts means among other things facing life without regular built-in dramas of fights or flights, without a parent figure relied on to provide a never-failing udder of kindness for us to feed on, without a couple who will produce a baby that will cure all our ills.

We all revert to default positions, especially at times of stress, falling back into our various traps. Re-configuring our world is painstaking, never-ending work.

Nevertheless, both the philosopher and the psychoanalyst, who have themselves been, and no doubt are still to some extent stuck in worlds created as a result of outdated or over-compensatory unconscious pictures of how things must be, are also capable of helping current sufferers.

They offer pictures that help to free us, that convey a sense of needed security. I have already mentioned a patient who previously knew little of psychoanalysis but in her first session said that she felt that this was something she had been waiting for all her life. She used the couch from the beginning, which for her clearly represented the lap or mind of a potentially attentive and loving mother. There would no doubt be complications and ambivalences when she became aware of more hostile feelings; but from the start she had a helpful phantasy of a safe home for herself and her feelings.

Contrast the patient whose first association on moving from the chair to the couch was a memory of an attempted rape. The frightening picture that had held her back from using the couch had been that I might force myself on her in a domineering, sexual way. Experiencing and understanding this was useful to the patient in enabling her to come to recognise and gradually modify her fears about allowing herself to be close, especially to a man.

When after much agonising, another patient, equally frightened of the couch, lay down for the first time, he immediately 'remembered' being in a tin bath, and his terror that his mother was about to strangle him in a fit of fury. I put 'remembered' in inverted commas because it was unclear to us both whether this was a memory of something that had actually taken place or was, at least in the literal version, a construction of his own. Whichever it was, it brought to the surface this horrific image: if he allowed himself to be undefended, he would become a helpless victim of someone sitting behind him who wanted him dead.

One of psychoanalyst Antonino Ferro's vignettes is about sessions with a patient called Clara, who came to recognise, both in her sleeping and in her waking dreams, some of the thoughts and pictures about her analyst's state of mind in the previous day's session. In that preceding session, Ferro had been somewhat distracted by a disturbing phone message from someone else, which he had listened to just before Clara's session. Clara ended that session with the remark that 'suggestions she had made in a group at her work had not been accepted'.

In the next day's session, she spoke of a 'freak wave' – 'she had been involved in a dispute that had nothing to do with her . . .' She had dreamt: *there was a skyscraper with glittering lights, but then she was in some underground caves, in the dark. She was a little girl, unable to find her daddy and mummy . . . and when she did find them, they were preoccupied.* In a second dream: *she was teaching in a school; the children were not listening to her and she got angry; she realised that this (not listening) was not out of any disregard for her, but because they had to say hello to a disabled girl who was passing. Even so she decided to break off the lesson and leave.*

Ferro writes that these dreams made him aware that she felt she had not been listened to by him (she could not find her parents, and when she did, they were preoccupied). He interprets that she might have felt that the previous day he had not been able to give her the attention she wanted. The patient was able to say that 'the main thing was not to give up; if only one kept trying, the door would surely be opened.' Thus one feature of the session was the patient's ability not to leave in anger (or not to leave definitively), not to 'break up the lesson and leave', but to keep at the problem, holding on to the idea that the analyst's not-listening was only a 'freak wave', 'not out of disregard for her'. Ferro later considers the possibility that the distracting element – the disabled girl passing by, to whom the children in the dream had to say hello – had also something to do with a psychotic part of Clara herself.

These 'pictures' – the dream of a session plunging into darkness, the memories of suggestions not being accepted at work and of children who don't listen to her, her anger at this and the temptation to walk out but not doing so as the dispute didn't concern her – all these coalesce in the analyst's mind to create a (to me) convincing story of how she experienced him in the previous session and of her going over it subsequently in her mind.

In passing, I should like to mention that this approach by Ferro represents a tendency that I think is more common in current psychoanalysis. This is the recognition that associations within the session to external or past events, or to fictions or dreams, which are insightfully linked to recent actions or attitudes of the analyst, may well express unconscious phantasies that are importantly perceptive and accurate. In this account, for example, Ferro is able to accept that the patient *correctly* intuited his preoccupation with someone else in the previous session. It is therefore important for the analyst not to speak as if the patient's imagining is misguided or mistaken; overt analyst-centred interpretations, such as 'you experience me as having been preoccupied', may easily become superior and dismissive in tone, conveying the covert additional message: 'which shows just how deluded you are'. Instead, we may learn, or be reminded by the patient, of something about our own attitudes and states of mind.

So: psychoanalysis is an attempt (among other things) to locate and articulate the unconscious phantasies that hold one captive, as well as those that are freeing, in their detail and in their ramifications through a person's thought, emotion and life. Both forms may be found and traced in the relations between the patient and the analyst.

* * *

I now want to say something about the *activities* involved in or resulting from phantasying as opposed to the *content* of what is imagined.

Psychoanalyst and philosopher Jonathan Lear notes that unconscious phantasy is a unifier of the self, or of part-selves. He reminds us how activities make sense when seen under the rubric of their 'telos' or aim; thus, the otherwise random actions of a man who breeds cows, feeds them with special food to condition their skins, pays special attention to curing the skin of the slaughtered cow, and then punches holes in the treated skin, make sense when one knows that he is a shoemaker. Similarly, many different activities, thoughts, images, ways of interacting make sense, are unified, once one understands the unconscious phantasy that links them by giving them sense. Dorothea Casaubon's high-minded exaltation, her attempts to be a humble assistant to her husband, her superiority in relation to her sister's apparently more prosaic marriage, all this and more makes sense in the light of her unconscious compulsion to place her husband as the ideal provider of answers to all her needs, as the 'udder for her supreme self'. What follows is an account of a case in which the patient has a mental picture of the other as selfish, uncaring, and rejecting. She is stuck in a timeless state of fusion with this maternal figure, a situation that is repeated in the transference. There are too glimmers of trust in a more loving, more separate analyst-mother.

This negative picture is like an image in a dream, in that it is a condensation of a story or narrative. It involves impressions of events, actions, emotions. It is like a snapshot or cartoon of the mother, encapsulating what the patient feels to be the essence of her mother's attitude to her. The presence of this internal figure is felt by the patient to be repeated in the attitude of the analyst towards her; it forms part of the frame through which she sees and distorts the world. Her conviction is that the analyst's care and concern for her is a sham. She thus feels compelled to respond and react to events on the basis of this unconscious assumption.

To say that it is a picture that held her captive would be only partly true. It is more like a story that holds her captive, along with her own active structuring of the world in accordance with it.

Much of her behaviour makes sense in the light of the story. She has agency in all this, both living out and creating that which the story represents.

Rachel has been in three-times weekly analytic therapy with my supervisee, whom I'll call Gerald. From the very beginning of her life, when she was adopted, she had a troubled history. There had been, it seems, a deficit in the provision of parental care. The adoptive father had disappeared soon after her first birthday, so there was no second parent around to help with her care or with emotional separation from mother. Around the same time, she was placed in a full-time day-nursery. When she was six, mother took her to a seaside hotel for a week, where she locked the child in their room while she went out until late at night. When the girl showed her terror and loneliness, mother was furious at what struck her as an intrusive complaint. There has always been a risk for Rachel that, if she expresses anger and upset, further rejection will be inevitable.

After a long illness, her mother had died shortly before she came to therapy. At the age of thirty-nine, Rachel still lives, now on her own, in mother's house. Wanting to train as a therapist, she had put off applying, ostensibly because of mother's illness and death.

Eight years previously, she had had a breakdown, in which she had cut her legs and arms. She had been hospitalised, first because of infections, later from a worry that she was too depressed to look after herself.

In the consultation with Gerald, Rachel reported a dream: *She is in hospital, looking for a bed. She couldn't find her bed.* Gerald and I understood this as a regressive wish to park or bring her ill part. There was acknowledgement of her own sickness, and both hope and doubt about whether she would find the help she needs. There was also a suggestion of passivity.

Arriving at the consultation sessions, as later during the treatment itself, Rachel would spread her belongings all over the waiting room, and would take a long time to gather them up before leaving. The analyst was nervous that Rachel might occupy his space for ever, certainly beyond the time when he himself would be ready to retire. These counter-transference feelings were matched by reality, in that Rachel was, he felt, far from ready to start a training; if she became a patient, her attachment would become adhesive or fusional, and the idea of having to leave before she was ready (if she would ever be ready) might feel to her catastrophic.

The analyst decided, with misgivings, to take her on.

Early in the treatment, Rachel brought a dream: *She is in a closed-up bus with her mother. The bus doesn't stop or arrive anywhere. No one gets in or out. She doesn't know where they're going.* It seemed that she is stuck in an endless journey, that goes on and on in a pointless, unchanging way, with an analyst who is identical with her mother. Time itself has become rigid and repetitive, she lives in a perpetual present within her mother's orbit and mind.

Rachel wants to take up residence as the sole patient of her analyst. She is disturbed and resentful at any signs of other patients.

Four years on, the analyst's apprehensions are being borne out, as are some of his hopes. Rachel is often dependent and demanding. She complains that the analyst, like her mother, puts his own interests ahead of hers. When the patient sobs uncontrollably, Gerald often finds himself feeling little sympathy for her. On one hand he feels that he has an incontinent baby on the couch; on the other that he is with someone who is using tears to control him.

There have also been more promising developments, including physical ones. For instance, Rachel got out her bike, unused for twenty years. Encouraged by a friend, she rode, wobblingly, down an empty lane. Trying to turn round, she fell off, hurting her hip and fingers. But she got back on, and managed to feel more confident.

This and other stories seemed also to be transference messages – with the help of her friendly analyst, she is able to move, risk failure, and recover from setbacks. She is more resilient, getting back on her bike.

Rachel has started her training. She is able to tell her dreams and sometimes to think about what the analyst says to her. She trusts him enough to bring hostile thoughts. More frequent too are passages in which the two are able to have 'conversations', with give and take, before the sense of disillusion sets in and Rachel is back to her paranoid state of being with someone who doesn't care for her at all.

This feeling of rejection has become even more intense since the analyst has recently (and reluctantly, with full anticipation of the enormity of the decision for this patient) told her that he will retire in fifteen months. The patient has been able to convey her belief that the analyst, having inveigled her into trusting him, has then betrayed her; she has never trusted anyone before; if the analyst understood the patient at all, how could he abandon her? She complains further that she had read about a therapist who retired but continued to see one patient for four years after. Why would Gerald not do the same? Her analyst, she says, is interested only in himself, is unprofessional, and his professed care is a a hypocritical pretence.

Gerald feels guilty about his decision and wonders whether to change his stance and comply with the patients as the other therapist had done. But he also knows that this might be damaging to the patient, especially as he himself would no doubt feel resentful at this intrusion into his life. The decision to retire had not been made lightly.

I remind Gerald that he is aware of the manipulative and guilt-inducing aspect of his patient, whose dramatic tears are expressions not only of sadness and hurt, but also of a tendency to project her pain, hurting her analyst by making him feel guilty. Rachel often introduces hostile feelings hesitantly and slowly; the recipient is kept on tenterhooks, uneasy about whatever precise accusation is imminent. The analyst is thus exposed to long-drawn-out punishment for not being exclusively devoted to Rachel as a mother to her new baby. The process is a kind of torture.

Rachel has indeed found in her analyst a new object, one who can and does care for her. But the other side of her is touchily sceptical about this belief, dealing with her felt lack by means of a sado-masochistic grievance. I suggest to Gerald that, if he were to give way to these demands and, like the other therapist, allow Rachel to be the uniquely special patient, she would never be satisfied. The unconditional love that she has been so desperately seeking would have been revealed as a mere semblance. She would sense that his change of mind had been driven by compulsion, not by love. And she would continue to be tied to this parent-figure, and the parent-figure tied to her; she would continue to carry her parent around with her like a ball and chain.

I suggest that the analyst find ways of articulating with the patient that, alongside her suffering self, there is this powerful controlling self, which entails that the love and attention she craves from him cannot be experienced as genuine.

As analysts, we need two kinds of hands to hold the patient: kindly ones to share their suffering and vulnerability; firm ones to hold the tricky, sadistic, destructive and controlling parts of, or split-off other selves in, our patients. (I learned this from Irma Brenman Pick.)

The idea that Rachel has been and at times is fused or merged with her unkind mother/analyst seems at first sight to be hard to reconcile with what I have also been saying, that she feels hatred of him. Is not hatred the opposite of fusion? Does it not mean standing over against, a paradigm of separateness?

I think this apparent paradox can be resolved along two lines. One is that Rachel projects hatred and complaint into the analyst. She evokes maternal resentment. She is at one level testing her analyst to see if he will repeat the impatience that amounted, she felt, to resentment at her very existence, that she encountered, or believes she encountered, in her mother. Phantasies often create that which they represent. So, the repetition is actually fostered by the patient. She is tied into this mutually sadistic dance. One may be in hate with someone rather as one is in love with them, obsessed, preoccupied, prone to interpret their every move in the light of the overriding emotion (whether hate or love).

Second, she is also identified with her mother. She treats Gerald as she feels her mother treated her. She has become her mother. She has taken the mother inside herself, her identity is at one with hers.

In both ways, unless the analyst, with help from more constructive parts of the patient, can shift this pattern, the result may be an unending merger of patient and mother. In extreme states of this kind, there is no separate other. The two are timelessly bound together, like Pozzo and his slave Lucky in Beckett's *Waiting for Godot*.

The main point I want to make here is that the patient (and potentially the analyst) are held in captivity not so much by the 'picture' – the cartoon – of this mother as by the way Rachel *acts* in relation to the analyst, action driven by her 'framing' of him, by her phantasy-ing. All this has an impact on him that might elicit from him retaliatory, rejecting behaviour. The captivity is fostered not only by her picture but also by emotional activity.

There is also an element of negative therapeutic reaction in Rachel's pattern of response to sessions. Good sessions, movements towards a more truthful and more generous response to the analyst, are often followed by negative reactions which have several sources. First, she looks for familiarity (half wanting to create it). Second, she feels unconsciously that she does not deserve a better relationship. Third, she may envy the analyst's capacity to take this negativity from her and not react punitively. Fourth, jibbing at the possibility of being more separate from Gerald (and her imagined mother), she is frightened to risk the disappointments that a more hopeful, a more trusting, relationship might result in (the analyst's 'betrayal' in announcing his decision to retire is an example).

She is torn about whether she is willing to move out of her mother's house, literally and metaphorically.

Pictures hold us captive; pictures free us from captivity. Picturing holds us captive, and picturing can free us from captivity. And the content of the pictures, combined with the activity involved in her use of them, also leads to ways of acting that become unconscious creators of her dissatisfaction with herself and Gerald. She is a script-writer herself, as well as the receiver of scripts from others.

In our work as analysts, I think we focus largely on the *activities* involved in thinking and in playing scenes out on the stage of analysis.

* * *

I think Wittgenstein too understood this, though he might not have put it in so many words. As we have seen, he focuses throughout the *Philosophical Investigations* on how our language works in practice, as contrasted with how it often 'goes on holiday' when we do philosophy. As another philosopher Bishop Berkeley put it, 'We [i.e. philosophers] first raise a dust and then complain we cannot see.'

CHAPTER 11

'THAT AIN'T GOING NOWHERE'

In 1966 I applied for and was given a position at the recently opened branch of the University of California at Irvine, fifty or so miles south of Los Angeles. It was on the site of a ranch, not far from the small seaside resort, Laguna Beach, a centre for surfboarders, hippies and meerkats. Whereas the undergraduate population was being built up gradually and locally, year by year, talented teachers and graduate students from the East Coast and from Europe, including some doing philosophy, were already in place.

I decided to make an adventure of the journey there, going by ship to Montreal, by train – the Canadian Pacific – to Vancouver, and then by Greyhound bus to LA. I was keen to break the train journey in the Rockies. Somehow, I was put in touch with a sheep farmer and his family not far from Banff, who kindly offered to have me stay for a few days. He met me off the train, and took me to his farm in the hills. He had just come down from the high pasture, where he lived for several weeks each summer with his sheep. Autumn was approaching, when many of them were to be slaughtered. He would go with them to the abattoir, and accompany them right up to their deaths, calming them.

Years later, I came to know another hill-sheep farmer, Ivor Griffith, in Wales. Both men were philosophical in their orientation to life.

For much of the time, they were isolated, except from the company of sheep, and they spent time reflecting on life and what made it worth living.

Ivor was a lifelong bachelor, who, except for war service in North Africa and for a few years at the end of his life when he was the happy cock of the roost in a Home in Crickhowell, lived all his life in the house where he was born, the last building for twenty miles beside a footpath into the Black Mountains. His mother, a midwife who would ride side-saddle through deep snow to deliver babies, had thirteen children, five of whom died by the age of five. Ivor mended stone walls, told us the date the cuckoo arrived each year (16 April), and knew where the best mushrooms grew – they shot up from the spot where a wild pony had died years before. Some of Ivor's views on femininity and motherhood were constructed on the basis of his knowledge of the physiology and psychology of sheep. He was curious about different forms of life. I was reminded of him when I heard on *Desert Island Discs* James Rebanks, 'shepherd and writer', who left school at fifteen with two O levels, was admitted to Oxford in his twenties and then achieved a double first in History.

I loved my few days in the Rockies, in glorious September weather and magnificent surroundings. One day, my host gave me a job. A large field needed mowing for hay. It curved round a steep hill, with big views of a valley beneath and mountains beyond. He took me round in the tractor for the first couple of circuits, then left the field, and the tractor, to me. Full of the joys of youth, fresh air and independence, I went at it with zest. After several circuits, I was admiring the wide swathes I'd made, not quite as neat as at Lord's cricket ground, but even more pleasing, and indeed in more taxing terrain. At some point, the engine coughed and stopped. I got out and began to crank the starting handle at the front. Maybe I left the gear engaged or the gear sprang into place of its own volition; for one reason or another, the tractor leaped forward. Somehow, I avoided both breaking my wrist and being run over by my own tractor. But relief turned instantly to terror. The tractor was moving at pace. Running after it, I couldn't catch it, not that I would have fancied my chances of climbing back on board if I had. The tractor was going across and potentially down the slope. I had visions of it bounding over the edge, falling a thousand feet, crushing villagers below. Fortunately for them (and me), the steering wheel was turned slightly to the left and after twenty yards or so the huge vehicle went up the incline, rather than further down, and came to a halt. Chastened, I went about the remainder of my task with more sobriety.

My friend Hugh Brody told me about his frequent successes with regard to these clunking dinosaurs of motion. The technique fifty years ago was, he explained, to leave your tractor facing downhill, with wedges under the wheels, set the engine going, get off, remove the wedges; then run after the tractor, jump onboard and jam the lever into gear.

Another near-contemporary, Anton Obholzer, was run over by one of his own tractors, a very large one, which he'd left on a patch of land he thought was flat but sloped. The monster ran over him and nearly killed him. This was far from a laughing matter.

The moral of the story seems to be: don't tamper with big engines. Don't in fact go near them. It's also a bit like having a bad back; mention having been (nearly or actually) run over by a tractor, and it turns out that everyone you know has a similar story.

(Wilfred Bion wrote about a panic of his at the front line in the First World War. He had been ordered to advance against the enemy in his tank. As shells dropped more and more closely, it became clear that enemy artillery had its sights on them. Bion ordered his men to get out of the tank. No point in losing the whole crew if and when the tank got hit. They too ran after the tank, but couldn't keep up with it. Bion's nightmare was of the enemy gaining possession of his tank, and of himself being court-martialled for cowardice and dereliction of duty. Fortunately from his point of view, the tank was indeed hit, and blown up without anyone in it.)

I bring up tractors as evidence of my lack of practicality, but perhaps its being almost commonplace makes me less of an extreme case. I'm not unpractical when it comes to sport, to tactics, discipline and a willingness to take risks, though as John Arlott implied with his 'Physician heal thyself' comment, I could perhaps help others more than myself. (I once heard a comment about a distinguished barrister who did himself no favours in committee, that 'he'd do better if he had a good QC to represent him'). Nor am I unrealistic with regard to life choices, though I agonised over many of them. I recognise and accept the need for hard work.

But when it comes to making or mending, to mechanics or crafts, to buildings, engines and computers, I am unpractical. One element in this was my lop-sided education, which as I've said stressed the intellect over the body, and the superiority of the abstract over the concrete. My final lessons in art at school occurred when I was eleven ('fair, with occasional flashes of brilliance', the end-of-year report stated). In all my years of being taught, there was not a single lesson in woodwork, craft, design or technology. I never learned about electricity or engines, or only in a perfunctory, abstract way. I don't remember being shown how to persevere with practical problems as I do in my work as an analyst or in writing. And my father and I never made the pinhole camera together.

The near-disaster in the Rockies was not the only time I've been liable to get excited and then fail to think carefully. I twice broke a bone in my body on the last day of a holiday, once my leg while skiing, the second time my collarbone as a result of being dumped by a wave in Sri Lanka; I realised afterwards that I had wanted to show off with something special on the last ski-run and last body-surf.

A more damaging quality than this short-term rushing in order to end with a bang rather than a whimper – I ended with both – has been a settled disposition, first to the idea that I *can't* do practical things, second to a feeling that any time trying to work such problems out is time wasted. Both ideas have led to my prematurely giving up. I tell myself, *I can't, so what's the point of setting aside time to try when it's bound to be wasted?* I'm like a child who has convinced himself that he can't do maths, gets into a panic about it, and then deals with the panic by adopting the view of Aesop's fox, that he never wanted to do it in the first place, that it's not worth the effort (the grapes are sour). I can see that self-doubt is self-fulfilling, but that doesn't solve the problem.

(Writing a note earlier about my neglect of woodworking, I mistyped this as 'word-working' – something I am willing to spend time and effort on, both in the original word-spinning, and in editing and working over what I've done with a critical but not too self-destructive eye.)

When I was at North Ealing Primary School, we were evacuated for a year or so to what had been a military establishment known as the Gun-Site. We were bussed to this place, which was further from home. Perhaps the move was for repairs or building works; I don't recall or, more likely, I never knew. There was a dinner lady there who would slap the back of your thigh if you misbehaved; with her, to save the world's poor, we had to sit with our disgusting pink blancmange until we ate it up.

After my class returned to the school site in Pitshanger Lane, my sisters, younger than me by three and four years, went to a different primary school, in Greenford. There the headmistress was Barbara McIntosh, an independent-minded Quaker. My sisters were enchanted by the school's goat. Like the goat, they were allowed a longer rein than others of their species. Mac, as she encouraged us to call her, became a family friend. Noticing my light-footedness, she named me 'Baby Elephant', and became my honorary godmother.

She once took me in her Morris Minor for a couple of nights camping at Rhossili, an 'area of outstanding beauty' on the Gower Peninsula near Swansea. From there, one can walk at low tide to Worm's Head. On the way to Rhossili, in those pre-Severn Bridge days, we arrived just too late for the ferry that was to take us across the wide river, seeing it chugging away, and had to wait eight or ten long hours for the tide to allow enough water for the next crossing.

Mac influenced our family in many ways. My mother learned calligraphic writing from her and I followed suit. We got special fountain pens, with square-ended nibs. My mother was already an extremely neat handwriter, as I see from the one or two books of hers that I inherited, books she got at school and had inscribed with her name at the front; she'd also written alongside the text dictionary definitions of words she didn't know.

Possibly also influenced by Mac, my mother took up, or became more engaged in, birdwatching. She bought some binoculars, and this was an important element in our summer holiday walks on the South Downs, inland from Bognor. She and I would study the little *Observer's Book of Birds*. My father would make jokes about lesser-spotted park benches. It was as a result of Mac's initiative that Midge made a rare excursion of her own away from the family, going skiing with her in Obergurgl, Austria.

Mac later moved to Fowey in Cornwall where, for several years in a row, she generously invited us all to stay for a week in the Easter holidays. I remember the first morning in her flat in the grand 'Point Neptune House', next to Readymoney Cove; a wren, then not to be seen in London, woke me at 6 a.m. with the wonderful clarity and intensity of song that belied its tiny size.

We would walk along the cliffs, and take the Polruan ferry or occasionally the Bodinnick ferry across the river. We swam in freezing seas and streams, my sisters braver than me. We would walk along the rarely used railway line between Fowey and Lostwithiel, picking up wet clay that had fallen between the rails from trains delivering china clay to the harbour in Fowey, and would shape little sculptures with it, baking them in the oven. We also visited the Leach Pottery at St Ives, where I bought a bowl. It was a second, flawed but beautiful, with its rough reddish-brown outside and smoother, speckled white inside. I still enjoy using this bowl. I like it and that rare bit of authentic aesthetic taste exercised by me as a teenager.

I mention all this to indicate sources of my love of nature, to recognise Mac's part in its growth, and to make a link between these activities and ordinary bits of practicality and of connection to the environment. Years later, I bought myself some really good binoculars for watching cricket, especially when writing on matches, as well as for birdwatching. I also love using them to look closely at plants, flowers, decorations on cathedrals, details of buildings. The binoculars not only bring things nearer, they put a frame round them. I think it has been partly through this mode of looking, as well as through my wife's and son's architectural knowledge and skills, that I have become more interested in both the massing and the detailing of buildings and gardens.

I have come to enjoy architecture that works on a human scale. One example is the cluster of four or five buildings with old facades, designed and put up by Mana's father, Gautam, in Ahmedabad. They form a sort of prelude to the Calico Museum of Textiles. These fronts had originally been in the old city, and had been rescued by him from demolition (for 'modernisation') not long after Indian independence in 1947. They are richly decorated with ornate wooden carvings dating from the fourteenth to the nineteenth centuries, and are no higher than two or three storeys. I'm reminded of the scale of buildings in the centre of Rome, or those along Amsterdam's canals. This impression of friendliness to the viewer contrasts with the feeling of intimidation and impersonality evoked by fascist architecture, with its inherent assertion of power and superiority.

Our own house in London, built in 1833, is on the cusp between Georgian classicism, with its simplicity and generous windows, and Victorian Gothic, suggested by the steep slate roof, by beige cement disguised as stone, and by the castellated little balcony above the front door – all the latter creating a gaunt atmosphere that contributed, along with other associations, to one patient's calling it an ogre's castle. I love it.

Gardening has become a pleasure and, until we started to get occasional help recently, hands on, at least at a rough-and-ready level. When I retired from cricket and we moved into this house not far from Lord's, one of the assistant groundsmen, Mick Lashley, and I made a new lawn from venerated seed from the cricket ground. The job involved digging up the old, ragged lawn, preparing the ground, adding and spreading topsoil, seeding by hand, protecting the seeds from birds with milk-bottle tops on strings, and so on. Recently we have also employed a company that applies weedkiller and fertiliser, scarifies and treats the lawn, which I still take pleasure in mowing.

The whole garden had been neglected. We dug up a lot of old plants and things we regarded as weeds, and took time planning and planting a new garden. Planting, shaping and maintaining the garden have been a longstanding hobby and task. We have been given rambling and climbing roses by the Scholars, which are now rampant and glorious for three weeks every summer; and we put in honeysuckle and clematis in the back, as well as many other shrubs and flowers.

Since I see patients in the basement with an entrance in the front, the north side, we planted winter-scented shrubs along the side of the patients' route – wintersweet, viburnum, daphne, mahonia, witch hazel – all except daphne still flourishing forty years on. I was privately hurt when, after a busy weekend buying and planting, one patient scornfully referred to people who buy in readymade new gardens. (As I write this, I wonder for the first time if she might also have been referring to what she thought I was doing as her analyst, picking up readymade theories and then thinking I could mechanically plant them in her?)

Gardening is a practical interest, involving planning, evaluation and discussion of what will work and what we'll like; we have a modicum of knowledge, besides the physical energy. It also allows for serendipity, the pleasure of the unexpected, like the inadvertent arrival of foxgloves and bluebells, and the spread of lily-of-the-valley.

Another venture that involved the garden, and plants, was our building two benders, the first in the early 2000s. A bender is not only a drunken rampage. It is also the name for a domed, rustic shelter used until recently by Romany people in Europe. The enterprise involved the noted writer, filmmaker and environmentalist, Roger Deakin.

The idea started, I think, from my seeing works of outdoor art by an artist whose name I can't remember, nor have I been able to find it on the internet. He made curved and interlocking structures of bent wood, living and dead. They were neat, elegant and sat comfortably in the landscape. They were like frames for tents. I loved these works.

We were invited by Roger and our mutual friend Margot Waddell to his old timber-framed farmhouse, Walnut Tree Farm, at Mellis, near Diss in Suffolk, where he lived for forty years. Roger, who sadly died young from a brain tumour in 2006, showed us his spring-fed moat, where he swam regularly, and the furniture he made from steam-bent wood. This led on to talk about benders, rough versions of the works of art I'd enjoyed. In 2000, Mana and I had bought into a cooperative that owns an island opposite Walton-on-Thames Rowing Club. The cooperative started in the 1890s, when swimmers in the Thames wanted a place to stay and, rumour has it, bring their girlfriends. We thought our strip would be just the place for a bender.

Roger bought into our idea with enthusiasm. He told me about the use of hazel saplings that were gathered each spring in Suffolk.

We learned of a settlement in Somerset, near Yeovil, where a group of people lived in benders covered by tarpaulins. Roger, Mischa and I went with Dudley Doust, who lived near Glastonbury, to see this off-grid woodland community, called 'Tinker's Bubble', at East Norton.

In one way, the settlement was disappointing. I liked the porches of the bender-type dwellings, workshops and communal constructions, little add-ons to the domed main room. But the need for shelter and warmth meant that the structure of the homes was hardly visible. I was also aware that the hazel, being dead wood, would last only a few years. I got the idea of making such a frame, and then planting willow round it that would outlive the hazel and create a living dome. We imagined sleeping underneath it on the ground in fine weather, or putting up a tent inside.

We did it! Roger collected and drove the coppiced hazel to Walton from his farm and from two other farms in Suffolk and Essex. The pieces were up to twenty feet in length, and in early April, 2002, just before my sixtieth birthday, we rowed them across the river in the island's tin tub. We had a lovely day constructing the frame with Roger, Dudley, other friends and family. The bender had sixteen main hoop points, and one entrance. It was nine feet high at the centre, and about ten feet across. It was elegant, handsome, appropriate.

Soon we found the best willow that would eventually supplant the hazel – *salix viminalis*, with its shiny brown bark. We bought little cuttings from Stoke St Gregory, Taunton. All we had to do was stick them in the ground just outside the hazel. The island water table was high at that time of the year, so they simply grew. Then we had to train them over to meet, and twine together with, incoming willow from the opposite side.

The outcome was a huge pleasure. Maintaining it was not easy; growth was uneven, more prolific on the south side. Trimming near the top, especially as the matt of growth thickened and spread, was an awkward task. Wind threatened to undo strands, and further tip the structure. Then a few years later, I broke my collarbone and was out of action for a couple of months. The unevenness became heavier and harder to manage. Eventually, regretfully, we cut it down, at first leaving a circle at about chest level, then lower, at knee height. Children from the island continued to treat it as a magic circle. Eventually, we cut it down altogether. One can now trace it by the more impacted, slightly flatter level established by the roots of the willow, themselves now rotted. It's a small-scale version of seeing the traces of an Iron Age fort in the sweeping landscape of Salisbury Plain.

Another installation on the island was a Rajasthani tent brought back from India. It became our shelter at the island during the summer. It looked like a scout or army tent from the Victorian era, with elephants imprinted on the inside of the canvas. It was not well-suited to the rain and damp, getting dark patches of mould.

We also built a small, suburban version of the bender in our back garden in London, using only live willow, without the hazel saplings. Now five of its eight limbs have died, so it has a quaint air as an odd three-legged feature in the middle of the lawn. But for years it was 'Luka's special house', planted for our grandson to play in as a toddler (he was born in 2004).

*　*　*

I've gone on about the bender partly because building something has not been what I do. I can play with grandchildren, both physically and with journeys of the imagination, but making things with them is usually beyond me. I even treasure rare moments of having a practical idea, as when Mana was making a stuffed cat for Maia and couldn't get the tail to stand out, and I suggested undoing a paper clip to stiffen it. 'You're a genius, Michael' was a bit over the top, but to me a treasured compliment.

Harold Pinter once wrote about rare praise from old cricket pro, Arthur Wellard, a man not given to effusion; Harold had saved the day by some dogged batting in a crisis, and Wellard told him he was proud of him. Harold maintained it was the most gratifying praise in the whole of his life. My parallel example comes from Ray, who made a small shed for garden tools on the Thames cooperative. It had to be on stilts to avoid being flooded, which would have resulted in damage to the lawn mower. It needed to have a slope for the mower, with a bend in it to retain a clear passage along the edge of our strip, and I made it, under Ray's supervision. After I'd finished, he came over to inspect. Standing on it, walking on it, jumping up and down; he pronounced: 'That ain't going nowhere.' (I also like the sentence. It reminds me of a pronouncement by a corporal, quoted to us by Stanley Ward to reveal its grammatical incorrectness: 'Them what's keen gets fell in previous.' The only words a pedant would retain are 'keen' and 'in'.)

* * *

While still at school, I got a three-week job as a carpenter's mate at the grand Marlborough House in St James's, central London, where Queen Mary had lived and (in 1953) died; the house was being converted and renovated so as to be leased by the Queen to the Commonwealth Secretariat. My stint there led to little learning about carpentry; I picked up more about class and race relations.

Two types of carpenter worked in the house; the older, white, trade-union craftsmen did delicate work on lead weights used in raising and lowering the large sash windows in the grand reception room. They worked slowly, steadily and no doubt skilfully. They were conscious of hard-won rights and requirements – apprenticeships, tea breaks, lunch breaks, pay rates that recognised seniority. They moaned as steadily as they worked, in drab London accents, much of it sotto voce. The other group were young black men from Barbados, animated, energetic, patois-speaking, possibly not over-skilled. Predictably, the trade unionists had little time for them, contemptuous of their having 'arrived off a boat with a paper bag and a saw', without proper training. The Bajans were given routine jobs to do. I remember standing around 'helping' them put up a false ceiling in a modest side-room; they swarmed over the ceiling, animatedly talking in what was to me an incomprehensible accent. They were fun. Both sets of carpenters were in their own ways kind to, or at least tolerant of, me.

Besides the lessons in racial and social differences, I also had a literary education in Marlborough House. I would take my sandwiches off to a side of the garden for my lunch, sit on a low wall among the inscriptions and memorials to royal dogs buried there, and read *Anna Karenina*.

* * *

I did – and even more rarely, do – make small efforts at making or repairing things, but usually retreat or fail to follow through. Sport was a different matter, though there were limits here too. Friends introduced us to sailing, mainly in the Aegean. We would hire a boat that slept eight (or occasionally two such). Then there was the victualling, the cooking on board, plotting courses, handling the anchor, pulling on halyards to set sail, steering, surviving seasickness. There were occasional sublime all-night sails. One regular delight was swimming from the back of the boat in isolated coves. Later, I did a weekend course with Mischa in Southampton that qualified us as 'day-captains in tidal waters'. But I relied on him for the nitty gritty of knots and clamps and reducing the sail in high wind, and never took the plunge of captaining a boat myself. (When we were about to win the 1981 Test match at Edgbaston, the crowd sang 'Michael, row the boat ashore', with its pleasingly nautical or at least aquatic metaphor.)

I think there are at least two factors in my retreat from practicality. One is the fear of failure, combined with nervousness about being the 'tall poppy' which would be cut down if it stuck up too far. I tell myself I'll never be any good at something, if I do it I'll be mocked, so I don't start. There is no point in trying if you know in advance that you can't do it. I'm far from the Japanese businessman I heard on radio years ago saying, 'I like problems, because problems give chance of solutions.' (As a cricket captain, I had a more practical attitude: I didn't usually give up.)

Second, I have often been stingy with time, compelled to rank activities too sharply into worthwhile and not worthwhile. Stopping work to try to deal with a minor glitch on the computer is time wasted, whereas tolerating and trying to think about an impasse with an aggrieved patient, or thinking of ways to dislodge an obdurate batter, or indeed dotting i's and crossing t's in this book, feel to me worthwhile, time worth spending. I sometimes remind myself how small children are open to everything – the opposite of the tendency I'm talking about. A two-year-old is more interested in sweet wrappers found in a Paris gutter than in the entire contents of the Louvre. Donkeys prefer straw to gold. I divide things too much into straw and gold, so that electricity and plumbing become for me what gold is for a donkey.

I'm in favour of not wasting life on trivia, on doing what matters to myself and to others. One of the most satisfying things about working as a psychoanalyst is that we always aim at getting in touch with what is most concerning to the patient at any moment or over longer periods. But in other areas of life, judgement veers off into the judgemental.

I admire a couple whom I met in India, in their fifties and sixties. They each have or have had good jobs, he occupying high positions in the police and in national counter-intelligence. When he retired two years ago, he was given a detachment of five servants – gardener, driver, cook, cleaner and security person. He and his wife soon decided to make an experiment of doing without any help of this kind. They speak now of the dignity of labour and of their satisfaction at cleaning, cooking, gardening, shopping and so on. They have no intention of going back to their old style of living. I asked if this had anything to do with Gandhi's example and values. They demurred, not sharing his spiritual beliefs. But I do think there was an overlap. George Herbert's poem 'The Elixir' ends:

> A servant with this clause
>   Makes drudgery divine:
> Who sweeps a room as for Thy laws,
>   Makes that and th' action fine.
>
> This is the famous stone
>   That turneth all to gold;
> For that which God doth touch and own
>   Cannot for less be told.

I think this attitude to making 'drudgery divine' is valid, even, if as by my Indian friend, divorced from its religious backing.

* * *

To go back to nature: I love both gardens and wildernesses, the domestic and the less tamed. This love preceded the terrifying longer-term worries about global warming. Now the greening of the planet is doubly precious. We are losing, damaging, that which sustains us. Our politicians bang on about growth and productivity, without any sense of possible conflict with the need to address the crisis of global warming. At times, like many others, I feel despair. This itself can lead to indifference and a sense of doom. Yet we still – just – can prevent catastrophe.

I am torn about climate change. On one hand Mana and I have long been believers that drastic steps need to be taken. On the other, we have continued to drive our car (now an electric one), fly in planes for holidays or work, eat a lot of dairy food, buy food that has been transported and not grown locally. We have been soft environmentalists. I admire my colleague Sally Weintrobe, who has gone much further and has written an important book on climate denial. Overall, our generation has, and will have, a lot to answer for.

CHAPTER 12

PROPHET TO A PROFESSION

When I started my training at the Institute of Psychoanalysis in London in 1981, the remarkable analyst, Wilfred Bion, had died only two years before. Like Freud (and Wittgenstein), he was already becoming, as W. H. Auden wrote of Freud: 'No more a person now but a whole climate of opinion.' But unlike these pioneers, Bion's climate was more local: he was not and is not a familiar figure in the wider intellectual or cultural world.

It took me a while to get into Bion's ideas. I was initially nurtured in the Independent tradition; Bion was clearly Kleinian. I first read *Experiences in Groups*, written in the 1940s but not published until 1961. This was less obscure than his papers of the 1950s, which grew out of his work with individual patients and focused largely on psychotic processes. I was struck by my first training case supervisor, Nina Coltart, telling me that she was going to read all Bion's work on her summer holiday.

Bion used many of Klein's ideas, of course. But he was also a bridge between her group and the other groups at the Institute, in particular in bringing the mother as container into the centre of his work and his ideas. Donald Winnicott had said that there is no baby without a mother; the nature of parental, primarily maternal, holding, was essential to development.

This was one important line of thought that appealed to me. Freud's starting point was a one-person account of human psychology and development. Klein gave greater centrality to the importance of the mother as a figure in the mind of the child. Winnicott and Bion both developed the idea of a mutual role for mother and baby in the baby's growing up.

I began to appreciate too some qualities Bion shared with Wittgenstein, especially in their utter seriousness and individuality, in their almost religious attitude to the work and to the need for honesty and authenticity. I felt I lacked something of that, lacked the courage and willingness to follow through ideas that both had so strongly. They gave me the sense that there are more things in heaven and earth than were dreamed of in my philosophy.

As with Freud and Wittgenstein, the question of what was the core or most lasting of his ideas has been disputed. Wittgenstein intimidated many, and puzzled more, while becoming, for adherents, the creator of radically new approaches in the field. As for Freud, he had had favourite sons who rebelled (as he saw it) or found their own paths, notably Alfred Adler and Carl Gustav Jung. And soon after his death in London in 1939, the 'Controversial Discussions' took place in the British Society, attempts by different followers to champion their own group's entitlement to be the true inheritors of the master's voice.

Towards Bion, too, other members of the profession and field have been ambivalent, while often praising him. His writing is not easy to read. He formulated a language for categorising thoughts and states of mind, his 'Grid', that has an abstract quality that many find off-putting, as I do. Tolerating to a profound degree the tension of not knowing, he advocated for psychoanalysts the cultivation of what John Keats called 'negative capability': 'that is, when a man is capable of being in uncertainties, mysteries, doubts, without any irritable reaching after fact and reason'. Like Socrates, Bion might have said that if he was wiser than others it was largely a matter of his knowing how little he knew.

In later life, Bion took this stance further, suggesting that analysts give up memory and desire in the consulting room, and that it was only through uncertainty and a thoroughgoing relinquishing of presuppositions that an analyst (and presumably others) might become open to that which is not already known or familiar to him. This approach was a shock to many conventional colleagues, who regarded theories, a good memory for the past of the patient and of the analysis, and the desire to heal, as vital parts of what we bring to our work. One Los Angeles analyst described the paper in which Bion first presented this idea as 'provocatively nihilistic of all that we have learned as analysts'. And it is true that silence may also be an intimidating expression of power. In my small way, I felt threatened by John Wisdom's refusal to pour his knowledge into our minds.

In fact, as early as 1912, Freud had encouraged analysts to avoid 'expectations and inclinations', and for similar reasons. But memory is broader than expectation, so that repudiating it is perhaps, also, more provocative. And desire is deeper than inclination.

While we are all tempted to evade the pain of not understanding and to respond to the pressures of the patient's demands for an immediate answer, Bion emphasised that new understanding is precluded if the thinking or complying are driven by fear of emptiness and of not knowing. When these dark features threaten, we are, he said, inclined to shed light via theory or past experience to illuminate the darkness quickly; but doing this is often to sidestep the painful process of being utterly open to the emotional reality of the moment. Hans Loewald, a German-American analyst, contemporary with Bion, once said, 'I hope to shed some darkness on the situation.' Bion speaks of a 'piercing shaft of darkness that can be directed on the dark features of the analytic situation.' Echoing another idea of Freud's, he also wrote that 'he [the analyst] must turn his own unconscious like a receptive organ towards the transmitting unconscious of the patient'. Nicola Abel-Hirsch, in her book on Bion, refers to 'silences which turn the preceding sounds and the succeeding sounds into a valuable communication'.

Bion tried to hold before his mind, and the minds of his readers and patients, the extent and intensity of our resistance to the new, as well as to the deeper regions of the mind. He saw the struggle towards truth as a moral, perhaps religious, journey, a pilgrimage towards redemption.

This kind of aspiration is both humble (I don't know anything unless I give up desire, etc.) and confident, if not even arrogant (I ask you to give up some of your certainties and trust me and the dim light of your unconscious capacity for truthfulness). It is, and needs to be, hard won, by dint, among other things, of having taken in central theories of psychoanalysis and made them one's own, and of having learned to discriminate some of our own unconscious prejudices and assumptions though personal analysis, supervision and reflection. Only through this kind of disciplined digestion of theory and a more or less consistent technique, along with a developed capacity to face emotional reality, will the active avoidance of memory and desire be creative rather than wild, conducive to truthfulness rather than to the conjectural or esoteric.

In many areas of psychoanalytic thinking, one of Bion's strongest characteristics is to give room to states of mind and attitude that are in tension. For example, he notes the necessary ubiquity of the alternation and concurrence of persecutory states of mind with ones that allow for responsibility, concern and guilt. He was clear that both parties to an analysis are bound to be ambivalent towards the process, with all its uncertainty and fearfulness – we tolerate it, even give it welcome, and at the same time resist it. Another life conflict that cannot be sidestepped is between putting oneself first while also being able, or liable, to submerse oneself in the group, sometimes to the extent of risking our lives and wellbeing for it (he speaks of 'narcissism' as being opposed to 'social-ism'). The same openness to tension is required in thinking abstractly and systematically while also laying oneself open to the uniqueness of the present moment; he was always clear that we need to respect the need for both receptivity and discipline.

More generally, the central conflict is between growing towards maturity and denial. The last lines of Bion's novel, A *Memoir of the Future*, read: 'Wisdom or oblivion – take your choice. From that warfare there is no release.'

* * *

One apparently peripheral topic touched on by Bion was his belief in the possibility of sublimity.

The first twenty-one years of his life were overshadowed if not dominated by deprivation, loneliness and the horrors of the First World War. He was born in India in 1897, then sent at eight to boarding school in England, spending holidays as a guest in the houses of school friends. It was three years before he saw his mother again. After leaving school just before his eighteenth birthday in 1915, he joined the 5th Royal Tank Regiment as an officer. He served in France until the end of the war, fighting in the battles of Ypres, Passchendaele, Cambrai and Amiens. Recommended for a Victoria Cross, he was awarded the Distinguished Service Order (DSO) for exemplary courage under extreme fire, about which his comment was: 'I thought I might with equal relevance have been recommended for a court-martial. It all depended on the direction which one took when one ran away.'

One redeeming feature of life at school was his love of and skill in sport, which related to the 'sublime': a form of art or expression that combines intensity, danger and beauty, and of the willingness to engage with the sublime and recognise it, without easy consolations, without too much editing or flattening of the rugosities (rough surfaces), without settling for the peripheral. In Bion's late-life memoirs, he writes in a condensed way about the possibility of 'sublime' games, and indeed sublime religion:

> 'Sublimation', not yet a Freudian term, was used by some for what in fact was a substitution. Games were substituted for sex; even religion was thought of by the more advanced as if it were a harmless substitute. No one thought that sublimation could mean the reaching for, yearning for games which were sublime, a religion that was sublime and not a stopper that could dam back the noxious matter until it stank, or bury the growth of personality till it turned cancerous.
>
> When I reached the Main School I had become proficient at games. Games were in themselves enjoyable; I was fortunate not to have had them buried under a mass of subsidiary irrelevancies – such as winning matches, keeping my ghastly sexual impulses from obtruding, and preserving a fit body for the habitation of a supposedly healthy mind. I liked swimming; I enjoyed water polo; I could be indifferent to the rivalry with others for a place in the team. I was equally fortunate in rugger. It was soon obvious that I was good; I was first class at every game but cricket – at which I was so bad that it presented no problem. I could, therefore, come nearer to playing the game for the sake of the game than I ever came to working for the sake of work. My excellence meant that the prospects of captainship began to appear over the horizon. That would mean that games for the sake of games would no longer be a feasible aim. In fact I became a very bad captain, but by that time war had come and captainship – but not leadership – had become irrelevant. My failure, in so far as it was noted at all, was excused in the prevailing disaster, the war.

So, games (sport) could be (or could aspire to be) sublime, as could religion. And presumably psychoanalysis, too. What, beyond these brief hints, might Bion have had in mind? What do I have in mind, reading him?

Games and religion may, as he says, be mere substitutes; sport presumably for sex, for aggression and fighting, or for triumph (winning); religion for wish-fulfilment and obsessionality. These 'stoppers' are like corks keeping effervescent, fermenting liquids from bursting out; they are defences, barriers, keeping in stuff that becomes even more noxious by its repression or suppression, 'until it stinks' or 'turns cancerous'. The kind of game-playing that Bion 'reached for', whose sublimity he got a taste of, might either be simply, naturally, sublime, that is, enjoyed for itself; or it might be *sublimated*, that is raised from the 'noxious' to the elevated, to the sublime – the Latin root refers to an upward slope towards a house that has steps up to its threshold. If sport or games *are* mere substitutes, the (unconscious) aim is to hide or suppress the baser and more basic motives. They are not only defensive but one might say *deforming* of the personality; whereas when any such motives are sublimated, they are *transformed*, that is, the noxious matter is changed in its nature for the better, like water into wine. (Two simple examples: one developmental task is to modify envy towards admiration, another is to turn narrow-minded, possessive love into love that considers the other.)

And clearly something similar could happen to religion. Did Bion also have such an attitude to psychoanalysis? He confesses that 'I could come nearer to playing the game for the sake of the game than I ever came to working for the sake of work.' He wrote this in his seventies, and since his main work had been as a psychoanalyst, often with psychotic patients, it is clear that for him there was at least the tantalising possibility of sublime psychoanalytic work. I think the whole tone of his writing indicates a passionate aspiration to sublimity in this arena of life, too.

✳ ✳ ✳

Bion's attitude to play is consonant with the account given in 1938 by Dutch historian Johan Huizinga, in his book *Homo Ludens – A Study of the Play-Element of Culture*. Huizinga believes the essence of play to be epitomised by that of young animals. For them, it is physical, enjoyable for its own sake and for no ulterior motive; there are rules restricting aggression – lion cubs may nip each other with their teeth, but don't do actual harm. He adds that there is a certain ceremoniousness about the play. All this applies equally to young human animals.

Like Bion, Huizinga sees play as easily contaminated. For him, professionalism, or perhaps more broadly an attitude that smacks of a strong will to win, especially if it also involves calculation and financial motives, is the major drawback.

Bion's quote continues: 'Excellence meant that the prospect of captainship began to appear over the horizon. That would mean that games for the sake of games would no longer be a feasible aim.' At least for himself, then, captaincy interfered with this purity. Presumably he felt that, as captain, extraneous motives and tasks intruded on the playing of the game – perhaps he had become obliged to think about others, and their wellbeing and contribution to the team. Despite his puzzling differentiation of leadership from captaincy, giving thought to others is what he did in the war as a senior tank officer, responsible for many men (and tanks), and indeed what he did in his work with groups and as a psychoanalyst. But perhaps the parallel between sport and war is inexact. Although, like sport, the risks of war may heighten the intensity of one's existence in the moment, and stir a sense of self, enjoyment of war for itself might be a psychopathic trait. We may more naturally and healthily love sport for itself than war.

Bion and Huizinga are purists, even puritans, when it comes to play, games and sport. Elements other than what we might call serious playfulness are, they claim, foreign to its essence and distract the individual from that endeavour. Both writers are strenuous, even severe in their ideals. There must be nothing trivial, kitsch or second-rate in our attitude. True satisfaction has nothing to do with the rewards of winning, prestige or material success.

Moreover, the concept of 'endeavour' is itself likely to mislead; we may try too hard, or in the wrong way. I'm reminded of Bion's remark that 'it is necessary to disencumber consciousness of the burden of thought by learning a skill', a striking phrase that reminds me of a comment by the fine Australian cricketer and coach, Greg Chappell, that 'premeditation is the graveyard of batting'. The playing of sport may degenerate into a version of work dominated by duty, calculation and a stiff upper lip. Whole-heartedness may be inhibited by self-consciousness. It may degenerate into the desire to win *at all costs*. We should remember, though, that play may also degenerate in the opposite direction, into frivolity or superficiality.

I don't agree with the Huizinga/Bion attitude to winning. It does matter, both to players and supporters. A young tennis player summed up my attitude when she said, 'I know I need to learn to lose better, and I like the game even if I lose; but I do like winning too!' If we really don't care about it, we turn sport into exhibition. It removes the blood and guts of sport. 'Fast bowling keeps you honest,' Yorkshire and England cricketer, Maurice Leyland, said. Winning is conceptually involved too, as it is embodied in the notion of sport and in the rules of each game.

Bion's stance reminds me of seventeenth-century English Puritans, who focused on what they saw as central to the truly religious life, that is, on the individual's relationship with and faith in God. They regarded ritual, aesthetic beauty, and adornments of the church and of episcopal costume as distractions at best, a sort of blasphemy at worst. They cut the heads off church sculptures. To them, priestly intermediaries or, even worse, the practice of 'indulgences' that one could reduce the time spent in Purgatory by monetary payments to priests for them to intercede on behalf of one's soul, were anathema.

In his psychoanalytical work, Bion cultivated in himself and advocated for other practitioners a similarly strenuous attitude, of focusing attention and interpretations on what is available as here-and-now evidence in the consulting room – in other words, on the unconscious, unknown feelings and thoughts originating from the patient towards the analyst, which are often projected into the analyst for him or her to bear and to digest. I think this is a small-scale version of taking on the sins of the world. He thought constructions about the past, or about relationships in external life, take both parties away from that which is present, whether in verbal communication or enactment, in the 'here and now' of the session. John Steiner, an eminent current analyst, has recommended that the psychoanalyst, like Odysseus, tie himself to the mast (of this kind of focus) if he is to resist the allure of the Siren voices that will otherwise seduce him into the inessential, into that which is merely hearsay or second-hand.

The essence of psychoanalytic treatment becomes, in Bion's work and reporting, 'to introduce the patient to that person with whom he has most dealings in the course of his life, namely himself'. It frequently takes courage as well as tact to make these 'introductions'. For that which is disowned and evacuated is that which has been impossible for the patient to tolerate. The analyst's job is often to give back to the patient in a palatable form what the latter has thrown out (or up), and is actively throwing out.

* * *

In *Mountains of the Mind,* the writer and academic Robert Macfarlane explores the growth of the notion of the sublime as part of the Romantic movement in Europe, starting in the seventeenth century but reaching its apogee in the nineteenth, during which period it was liable to become decadent, turning at times into the sentimental, the mawkish and the kitsch.

Mountains featured large in the overall shift in aesthetic and personal values. A sixteenth-century tract, pacifist and puritanical, had referred to a God who will 'make the Stony-Rocks and Vallyes playne' – the rough places plain. Two or more centuries later, instead of being obstacles that had to be crossed or bypassed in order to get to the ordered beauties of Rome (and other civilised features of the Grand Tour), mountains – rough places – became features to visit for themselves, whether to be journeyed in, painted or written about. The canons of the aesthetic shifted. Nature was not at its most moving and intense in the tamed and domesticated, in formal gardens or in parklands laid out by 'Capability' Brown. There were different pinnacles of beauty and meaning. Increasingly, people became fascinated by wildness, wilderness, by untamed nature. People came to require a frisson of danger, often imagined from a safe vantage point, but, as time went by, adventurously sought out despite, or perhaps because of, real risk to climbers and mountaineers themselves. They ventured out on to narrow paths with steep falls on either side. They climbed Mont Blanc.

Certainly, life becomes more raw, more intensely precious, when a slip will result in certain death. Is the primary allure the thrill of danger itself, or is it a matter of the mastery of such fears, especially the mastery of the dangerous places themselves? One fantasy behind the fear of heights is of falling (sometimes also a cover for jumping), while another, contained in the same sequence of thoughts and images, is of being miraculously saved. In 2019, I was fascinated by a news item from Paris: a sixteen-month-old boy had fallen from a seventh-floor balcony; he landed on a café awning below, off which he bounced unharmed into the hands of a passing doctor, Philippe Benseniot, whose wife and son had spotted the toddler falling. 'I was there at the right time,' the doctor commented laconically. The café was closed at the time, and the awning would have been wound in had not the mechanical device for closing it been broken.

Macfarlane dissects the thrill of vertigo, an experience that may be achieved by risking oneself or by observing the high-wire acts of others.

I am both afraid of heights and fascinated by watching tree surgeons. They are like acrobats or dancers in the trees, and in India they work without nets or safety ropes. Clammy hands express my own terror. When I practise balance on my bathroom floor while exercising, I imagine I'm Philippe Petit, walking a tightrope from one New York skyscraper to another.

Francesca Bion, Wilfred's second wife, wrote the following in her introduction to his anthology of poems: it has the flavour of Bion's own writing – perhaps she was quoting him:

> It is easy in this age of the plague – not of poverty and hunger, but of plenty, surfeit and gluttony – to lose our capacity for awe. It is as well to be reminded by the poet Herman Melville that there are many ways of reading books, but very few of reading them properly – that is, with awe. How much the more is it true of reading people. Someone asked, 'Why climb mountains?' 'Because they are there' was the reply. I would add that there are some who would prefer to postpone the exercise till their rugosities, heights, depths and declivities [downslopes] have been worn to a uniform flatness. The Grand Canyon will be tamed, Everest, Kanchenjunga neon-lit . . . William Blake, in *Gnomic Verses*, said, 'Great things are done when men and mountains meet.'

Risk-taking, or risk-imagining, may have dubious motives. When it involves heights, it may be an expression of superiority, elevating oneself over others. It may be masochistic, even suicidal. Macfarlane quotes and then comments on Samuel Taylor Coleridge advising us to: '"Pick a mountain . . . Climb to the top of it and then, instead of looking for the easy way down wander on, and where it is first possible to descend, descend, and rely upon fortune for how far down this possibility will continue". It was Russian Roulette.' Macfarlane goes on to describe an episode in August 1802 on Scafell in the Lake District, when Coleridge followed his own advice. After some time stepping down from ledge to ledge, he came to a gap between ledges. Faced with a sheer wall of seven feet he let himself hang by his arms before dropping blindly to the next ledge. Soon he could go neither up nor down. He was stuck. 'His limbs were all in a tremble' – but what Coleridge did was to lie on his back and laugh, congratulating himself on his powers of reason and will, on being so calm, so blessed. 'He thought himself out of his panic, as he put it to himself.'

He was wrong about this, Macfarlane comments; it was not reason or thought that saved him, but luck. A few feet further along the ledge he was on, he discovered he could lower himself down a narrow chimney in the rockface (now known as 'Fat Man's Peril'), and survived to tell the tale.

We should approach the task of 'reading people' with 'awe'. Awe is closely linked to the sublime.

*   *   *

The only difference between court-martial for cowardice and medal for courage is the direction in which one runs away. *Running*, in either direction, indicates the inevitability of fear.

By the 1960s, Bion had modified, perhaps even transformed, psychoanalytic theory. Instead of sexuality, he placed attitudes to knowledge at its heart. He had long concluded that Freud, in his emphasis on libido as the fundamental motivating factor in life and growth, was mistaking a part for the whole. Bion put at the centre his theory of 'thinking'. He used the terms 'K' and 'minus-K' to indicate opposed attitudes towards knowledge; K is a desire to come to understand, to face reality, while minus-K means a denial or refusal of coming to know, of thinking. The basic issue in analysis is the degree to which patient and analyst seek to evade reality, and how far they are willing to bear it, face it, and try to modify it; whether, in short, they run towards or away from the danger. These are Bion's terms for what Freud referred to as the reality principle.

For Bion, an even more basic question was: how do we come to think at all? He developed a persuasive theory of thinking, claiming that thinking begins when the panicky baby, screaming, is getting rid of what he calls 'proto-thoughts'. If things go well, the carer, thinking, experimenting and intuiting her way into what the baby is upset about, enables this scream – this 'thought without a thinker' – to be transformed into (the beginnings of) thought proper. (His word for the carer's receptivity was 'reverie'.) Thus, the unthinkable becomes, bit by bit, thinkable; a thinking self comes gradually into being. Dreaming, which in Bion's broad sense means something like reverie about experience – he does not confine it to what happens when we're asleep – becomes possible. The containing mother initiates a self that eventually becomes self-aware.

Containment is another metaphor for the analyst's work. (S)he receives the hotchpotch of emotions and thoughts of the patient, does her own 'dreaming', contains them, and hands them back in a detoxified form. Bion used the term 'K' for this desire to understand, this willingness of analyst or patient to work towards a more articulated, fuller self. The analyst brings to the job also his capacity for love (L) and his feelings of hate (H). These terms, K, L and H – purified (I think he meant) of some of the associational and sensuous baggage of the ordinary words 'love', 'hate' and 'knowledge' – indicate some of the essential qualities and aims of psychoanalysts. They provide the basis for descriptions, in abstract ways, of analyst–patient relations.

Over time, however, he felt that even this challenging and risk-involving orientation does not do justice to the analytic task. He began to speak of the need to go beyond understanding, beyond K. Just as we can act without thought, so we can 'think' as a substitute for action; one can 'think' in order to avoid contact with the other.

I think Bion wanted to get beyond the limitations of knowledge, of K, even when it is, or appears to be, alive in the session. He became aware of the limitations of K, and started to speak and write about 'transformations in "O"'. O stood for the 'thing in itself', the unknowable, a Kantian absolute: 'Being itself'.

* * *

I suspect that Bion was all too well aware of his own tendency to sit back as an observer and not act, to be detached rather than make full emotional contact.

He tells a painful story of an occasion in 1945. Earlier in that year, his wife Betty had tragically died giving birth to their daughter, Parthenope. Of this event, he writes that he 'felt as never before numbed and insensitive'. One weekend, having been busy with his work, he was sitting on the lawn, while Parthenope, at the other end of the lawn, clearly wanted him to come to her. He sat and watched, while she crawled painfully towards him, becoming more and more distressed. The nurse twice asked if she should pick the baby up, but he told her not to. 'Let her crawl, it won't do her any harm,' Bion reports. He continues: '"Why is she doing this to me?", I asked myself. Not quite audible was the question: "Why do you do this to her?"' He felt he was in a vice.

Eventually, the spell was broken by the nurse, who went against his orders that she should let things be. 'The baby was being comforted in maternal arms. But I had lost my child.' His next words are: 'I hope there is no future life.'

Bion had begged his wife to have a baby. 'Her agreement to do so had cost her her life'. Unconsciously at least, he must have blamed the baby. But as he says, 'It was a shock to find such depth of cruelty in myself.' Bion had to face the fact that he could be so detached, so cruel.

One ex-patient of his, when asked shortly before her own death about her analysis with Bion, described it (to me) in one word: 'Frosty.' He could be hard, perhaps cold, in his watching, in his not-acting. 'After much painful experience, I learned how to curl myself into a tight ball of snowy innocence and launch myself, with a small sharp piece of ice in the middle, at my foe,' he writes. He speaks also of his climbing on to his mother's warm lap, where suddenly the cold wind of sermonising drove him away, back to his Indian ayah.

In his marvellous war writings – *The Long Week-End* and the posthumous *War Memoirs 1917–1919* – among many dreadful traumas, the worst was perhaps the wounding and death of his young runner, Gunner Sweeting. The context was the crucial upcoming battle for Amiens. Bion, commander of a group of tanks, and his men were exhausted. With Sweeting, he was on his way to the meeting point, where he was due in fifteen minutes. There was fog and, suddenly, incoming shell-fire. The tank he had been in moments before had been blown up. Bion was anxious that he had got lost, that he had sent his tanks in the wrong direction, not as intended towards the enemy but towards their own lines, and that he and they were in the wrong place for the strategic rendezvous. Sweeting and he had dived or had fallen into a shell-hole that seemed to offer some relief from the intense fire. Bion writes sardonically that it was as good a place as any to wait. 'Bion felt sick. He wanted time to think . . . He tried to think.' He 'compelled Sweeting to look back and see the road. He asked him what it meant. Sweeting agreed that it must be the Amiens-Roye road' – that is, that they were indeed in the wrong place; Bion must have got his compass readings wrong.

'Pale with fear, Sweeting again buried himself as deep as he could into the shell-hole, clutching closely to Bion's side for further shelter.' This was when Bion heard him trying to talk to him, barely audible above the barrage. (Bion here writes about himself in the third person.)

> Bending his ear as close as he could to Sweeting's moving lips, he heard him say, "Why can't I cough, why can't I cough, sir? What's the matter, sir? What's the matter?"
>
> Bion turned round and looked at Sweeting's side, and there he saw gusts of steam coming from where his left side should be. There was no lung there. Bion began to vomit unrestrainedly, helplessly . . . The boy's lips were moving again. "Mother, Mother, write to my mother. You'll remember my address, sir won't you? 22, Kimberly Road, Halifax. Mother, Mother, Mother, Mother." "Oh, for Christ's sake, shut up," shouted Bion.
>
> And then I think he died. Or perhaps it was only me.

When Bion emerged from the shell-hole, in bright sunlight and quiet, it turned out that in the fog they had mistaken tall grasses for the 'waving poplars of the Amiens-Roye road'. They were in fact in the right place. Objectively, there had been no need to tell Sweeting to look. He thought: '"Well, thank God he's gone", filled with passionate hatred of himself for his hatred of the wounded man.'

By 'perhaps it was only me' who had died, I think Bion meant that in response to the unbearable trauma, which included exhaustion, terror and particularly guilt (had his telling Sweeting to look caused his no doubt fatal wounds? How terrible to have told him to shut up, to have wished him dead!), he had killed off his own self, his own humanity. I suggest that this loss of empathy might have been liable to reoccur for the rest of his life.

* * *

His later-life attempts to put into words that which went beyond K in his analytic work used language imbued with theological associations; or, perhaps more accurately, philosophical language that is typically put to a religious use. By then, alongside 'K', he was using 'O', which stood for 'ultimate reality, the First Cause'. The psychoanalyst should aim at O. Enlarging on the cryptic phrase 'ultimate reality', Bion suggests that it is represented 'by terms such as absolute truth, the godhead, the infinite, the thing-in-itself'. He refers also to 'at-one-ment' with O (with reality, with the Other person). 'O', he continues, 'does not fall in the domain of knowledge or learning . . . it can be "become", but it cannot be "known".'

My suggestion is that Bion's move beyond the language of K into religious or quasi-religious language is an indication of his inner need to counter his tendency to use thought as a substitute for action, as a substitute for emotional engagement. If he restricted his aims to understanding, did he have to strive to avoid becoming cut off? Did he at times watch the patient crawl, as it were, across the lawn?

I worry too: am I entitled to put these thoughts together in this way?

* * *

Some psychoanalysts part company with Bion at this point in his thinking. They suspect he is reifying the 'thing-in-itself'. One question is: how far does his use of the language of O, of ultimate reality and such terms, go beyond metaphor into mysticism? Does he imply the existence of a 'something' beyond the grasp of the human mind, but which we get inklings or hints of but can only approach? In another life, but not this one, we might, as Paul says in his famous letter to the Corinthians, 'see not through a glass darkly, but face to face'.

It seems to me that Bion does here go beyond what he earlier implied in advocating negative capability and the giving up of memory and desire. I suggest he has the idea that, since by setting aside our often constraining and limiting frames of mind we may succeed in getting closer to the essence of the other, if we could give up *all* frames of mind, we could (at the ultimate) glimpse reality (or perhaps Reality) 'face to face'.

* * *

At times, Bion uses an initial capital letter for related terms such as 'Mystic' or 'Ultimate Reality'. As psychoanalyst Ronald Britton suggests, doing this appears to turn these words into Proper Names, implying a definitive description of a unique individual. It is as if we might move from ordinary descriptions in general terms (like 'a man with white hair'), which could apply to many men, to a description so perfect in its capturing the entire, precise, unique reality of that which we are describing; as if a Proper Name could, at this mystical level, be an unambiguous pointing to its essence.

Bion is right to assert that there are always new problems aroused by each developmental step, always further problems, as well as further ways of seeing, further paradigms for description and explanation. We are, as theologians recognise, essentially limited by our embodied state, by our impermanence, and by the fact that our language is 'only' a kind of map. But I think he is wrong to move from this reality into a conclusion that there *must be* an ultimate reality. Further I doubt whether the idea that there could be a place to map it from that is free from the limitations that any particular map-projection imposes is really, when spelled out, capable of being conceived or thought.

Wittgenstein raises a similar question, but comes to a different answer. He asks whether there is a rock-bottom endpoint to one's investigations. 'If I have exhausted the justifications, I have reached rock-bottom and my spade is turned. Then I am inclined to say: "this is what I do".' Wittgenstein is not denying that at a later date he or someone else may go further than he has gone. Rather he is saying that, if he can (at this point) go no further, all he can rely on is that this is where he gets to, this is what he (or we) do, this is what counts for us as truth or fact in the language games we play.

Unlike Wittgenstein, Bion is a Platonist. He believes that truths exist prior to their being discovered. Paradoxically, finding a truth, or something that is on the way towards truth, does not, he states, require creativity, as it is already there waiting to be experienced. He also refers to 'invariants' in common to all instances of a concept: the invariant is a Platonic Form (capital letters creep in again). Wittgenstein by contrast speaks of 'family resemblances', suggesting that there may be *no one thing in common, but a series of threads* that run through the cases, related (as in families) more or less closely to other threads. Thus, within the concept of a game there are ballgames, card games, boardgames, psychological games, each with overlapping similarities to and differences from instances in the other categories.

Bion's 'transformations in O' go beyond 'transformations in K'. That is, there may be developments (in the analyst–patient relationship) that involve growth towards O, growth towards being at one with a psychic reality that is forever beyond our reach. To my mind, he conveys an attempt to cross over from isolation and separateness towards some form of being-at-one with the patient's soul. There is a longing to overcome isolation, to get beyond all impediments to perfect, truthful intimacy.

I would say that we are inevitably isolated; this is part of our being ourselves. We may put ourselves in the shoes of another, get to know and love another, imagine our way into their minds, be more alert to the moves and vibrations of their hearts; but we have to mourn the impossibility of being in any literal sense 'one with another'. No man is an island – maybe; but everyone's emotional life, each person's death, is uniquely personal.

*   *   *

Bion's teaching and exegesis is demanding. It represents his struggles to overcome dishonesty, superficiality, falseness. He has a deep goal of going beyond the 'sensual', beyond the ordinarily 'known'. One of his aims was to create a language that is abstract enough to accommodate a range of instances, abstract enough to represent these impossible aspirations, this straining towards the sublime, but that also avoids the overtones of language belonging to other spheres of thought. He does not avoid these overtones in his religious talk of O, but tries to invite us to think for ourselves what this language might mean for us.

Bion does not ease the path for us readers or listeners, though later in life he wrote: 'In practice we have to have a feeling about what the patient can stand.' He provokes us, challenging us; his waiting in massive silence and stillness leaves us to take our own steps of thought. Is this frosty? Is it cruel and powerful, refusing to offer us a hand, leaving us to get distressed when, like Parthenope, we long, perhaps need, to be picked up? Or is it a matter of his own spare truthfulness, combined with his giving us the benefit of the doubt; we don't need to be mollycoddled, it is vital for us to come to things for ourselves?

Bion gives us the chance to do this work (though we may simply become traumatised, like me in the front row of Wisdom's lecture). While being aware of the risks (for himself, for the analyst) of megalomania, he at the same time makes clear that the fear of megalomania, the fear that one may 'appear to believe one can *be* God . . . be ultimate reality', may stultify our efforts to go as far as we can.

There is a story about Bion, possibly apocryphal. He makes an interpretation. The patient says, 'Would you mind repeating that please?' He says: 'The moment has passed.' And perhaps it has. The not hearing, the asking for repetition, creates a new emotional situation. Perhaps the river of Heraclitus that you can't step into twice is also the river of the ever-changing, kaleidoscopic emotional moment. It's possible you can't step into the same river *once*.

Bion certainly became something of a prophet, declaring Jeremiah-like that there is something wrong in psychoanalysis, and in particular in psychoanalysis as practised in England during his time. Echoing the phrase used by Jesus, 'A prophet is not without honour but in his own country', Bion writes of the prophet who, 'loaded with honours, sinks without trace'; he was aware of the risk of being politely 'kicked upstairs' like someone who, apparently promoted by being elevated to the House of Lords, is thereby rendered ineffective. The 'honours' in his case were both eminent positions and polite acclamations. I think the responsibilities that arise out of being honoured not only distracted him, and took up too much time, but also, if he was not careful, or for that matter if he was too careful, might induce him to refrain from thinking afresh, might turn him into a 'fashion', or a copy of himself, take him further from the sublime. He was constantly aware of the temptation to evade difficulties rather than face them. He may also have felt that he risked coming to bask in his honours as if he had possession of the truth, seeing his ideas as gospel rather than as partial but important insights on the route to new problems, and to new questions. 'The answer is the disease, or misfortune, of the question,' he once said, quoting Maurice Blanchot.

Perhaps it was considerations of this kind that drove him, in his seventies, to accept an offer of living and working in Los Angeles. He stayed there for eleven years, returning in September 1979. He then became ill, dying in Oxford on 8 November.

I would imagine that his UK colleagues were inspired, puzzled and intimidated by him. We admire a prophet provided he is not in our own country, our own house, provided he doesn't leave us too worried that we are foolish or second-rate. We are embarrassed at being unable to decide whether the latest art is deeply meaningful or a matter of pretentiously finding rhythm in a matchbox. We are uncertain whether he has the truth and should therefore be acclaimed as saviour, or is a deluded megalomaniac who should be crucified (or at least disempowered by elevation).

* * *

My view is that Bion the puritan takes a part for the whole. His earlier view seems to have been that the essence of being a psychoanalyst is to be found in this move from minus K towards K, first (usually) in the analyst and then in the patient. Later, he finds this K-target insufficient, and he aspires to help the patient move towards O. And both these aims or efforts are to be engendered through the transference, through the patient's feelings about, perceptions of, and behaviour towards, the analyst.

I am inclined to think that, even within psychoanalytic treatment, this arduous route to self-knowledge and to whatever O symbolises is not the only truthful, fruitful one. To think so is itself a matter of seeing through a limiting lens. Focusing on the live transference is central to our work. But it is not the be-all and end-all.

As James Strachey wrote, even if currants are what defines a currant cake, the cake itself needs many other ingredients. There are times when an interpretation is more applicable to my patient's relationship with his daughter, say, than to his relationship to me. I may believe the hot point and the potential learning point is to be found in a revision of the patient's past, or in her marriage, or whatever. Reviewing her life may be crucial to a patient's growth and change; in insisting on the absolute priority of the immediate transference relationship, the analyst may fall into narcissism and narrowness.

Moreover, as Neville Symington says, the transference is strong enough to survive some excursions away from this home base.

At times I wonder if I'm drawn to Bion's kind of thinking for questionable reasons of my own, to do with admiration for so singular a man, with my childish envy for the devout, for the advocate of the sublime. I also worry that it is presumptuous of me to link Bion's lifelong striving to develop with the traumatic impact of his early life. Or is it a valid effort to see him in the round?

✳ ✳ ✳

Even if I'm right that Bion mistakes the part for the whole, that 'part' *is* central to psychoanalysis. We are all liable to lose sight of, be distracted from, the predominant emotional message from the patient to ourselves as analyst at any given moment. I may be carried off on what Edna O'Shaughnessy calls an 'excursion', into the byways of the past and the patient's external life, and fail to keep in mind the immediate inter-personal emotional message that is often, as Bion regularly reminds us, hard to receive, notice and give voice to. But O'Shaughnessy also refers to an enclave, where one is shut up in a closed space that refers only to analyst and analysand.

Reading Bion refreshes me in my analytic identity. I may well be puzzled by him, but often I am revitalised. I get a sense that I am in the footsteps of a master, I am an apprentice in the presence of a true psychoanalyst, of the man whose processes of thinking come closest to the real thing. Reading him *is* inspiring, in something close to the word's original meaning. He breathes into one a feeling of sublime possibilities for psychoanalysis and for being a psychoanalyst. He restores and strengthens faith in the process of psychoanalysis. Bion is a guide as well as a challenge, an ongoing reminder of the value of this faith.

He even has a symbol that approximates to Faith: 'F'.

CHAPTER 13

STARING INTO THE FIRE

Joseph Conrad, criticised for an over-long novel, responded: 'The whole story might have been written out on a cigarette paper . . . The history of men since the beginning of ages may be resumed in one phrase of infinite poignancy: They were born, they suffered, they died. But . . . I am not capable of such detachment.'

Bede, known as 'The Venerable', offers a cigarette paper image of life on earth: it is like the flight of a sparrow across a king's warm mead-hall, entering through hail and snow at one end, flying out into hail and snow at the other, all a brief interlude, over in the blink of an eye. 'As for what comes before or after,' he adds, 'we know nothing.'

The *Bhagavad Gita* offers an answer to that bleak vision and that unknown. It commends the notion of *shraddha* – unflinching trust in the unknown. A boy twin is lamenting to his sister their discomfort in the womb. His sister consoles him: 'We'll soon be leaving this place for a world with so much space and opportunity.' The boy remains sceptical, for him this is a fanciful notion. She says: 'Sometimes in the silence I hear a voice saying, "I am your mother, and I'm waiting to welcome you in the next phase of your life."'

Where do we stand on this, with the boy or the girl?

People also vary in the degree to which they follow Pascal in having a literal or metaphorical skull on their literal or metaphorical desks, to remind them of mortality. But we all have our moments and mementos. And we all, with differing degrees of intensity, not only fear death but wish for it.

Four score years is now perhaps the equivalent of the former three score and ten. This means that I, born in 1942, cannot any longer trick myself out of the category of old age. And passing this landmark makes more acute, even at times more urgent, anxieties about death and dying.

Old age is not for the faint-hearted but feels better than the alternative. As with ageing cars, maintenance is increasingly called for and costly. Our dents need patching up. One condition complicates another. There are many ways our bodies, not to mention our minds, may go wrong, even if they haven't yet. We work better in reverse than going forward. Alongside Susan Sontag's related Kingdom of Illness, there is a Kingdom of Old Age.

We cannot altogether avoid a sharper recognition of the approach of death.

One element came home to me when five or so years ago I went to an event that brought together several former cricketers, some of whom I hadn't seen for decades. Most discussions began as organ recitals: the prevalent organs being hips, knees, backs, shoulders; eyes and ears.

One opponent from the distant past was Norman Gifford, the Worcestershire and England slow left-arm bowler who also captained his county. I had hardly known him in a personal way. But I had a strong impression of him as a competitor who would give everything on the field. In my picture, he was covered in dust, his shirt and flannels stained – red (from polishing the ball for the quick bowlers), green (grass stains from diving in the field) and beige (sweat); his face burned red from the sun, he may have been tired, frustrated by bad luck, by umpires who didn't agree with him about lbws, by obstinate batters, by the shortcomings of his own side, but he would willingly bowl all day.

Is there just one beat of the sparrow's wings in this image of indefatigability, of labour and strain combined with high craft and total commitment? Of his pride in honest and skilful work, too? But now, in our seventies, we compare notes about ageing bodies. Mutual (I think) respect for how we were, but also for our current vulnerabilities.

I'd been lucky, a few broken bones and joint problems, but, at the time of my meeting with Norman, nothing worse than creaking joints to refer to. I can't remember what his were, only that he had some. Cupping our ears (my children say I need not one but two ear trumpets), we laughed as we recognised this fact: time reclaimed, time so different.

* * *

As for illness, I entered its kingdom on discovering, by lucky chance, in late 2019, that I had a lymphoma. In the spring, I had had a deep vein thrombosis. That autumn, at my annual meeting with the endocrinologist Professor Bouloux, whom I see for check-ups related to a pituitary tumour I had twenty years before, he mentioned, in a 'by the way' tone, that some DVTs are caused by undiagnosed tumours; it might be worth getting a full body scan to investigate.

Mana and I arranged for this to be done soon after we arrived in India in mid-November. On the technical front the unit was excellent. But their personal treatment of me was worse than inconsiderate. The lack of communication about what was happening was not simply a matter of language difficulties, as I knew both from their earlier use of English and from their rudeness to a local patient, an elderly Gujarati woman with no English, who was even more obviously confused and alarmed than me. At one point, after the scan and a long wait, I was told I would have a second scan. No explanation. A small plastic cup and two one-litre bottles of yellow liquid were plonked in front of me. For all I knew, the stuff in the bottle could have been urine.

When I tried to find out if I was to drink this enormous volume of dubious liquid, and why I was being called back for the second scan, I was fobbed off. When I protested, the doctor in charge became defensive. Several hours later, as we were about to leave, this doctor appeared along the corridor. We asked him if he had seen any results. He threw his words over his shoulder: 'It was good we did a second procedure.' What did he mean? He smiled, smugly. 'You'll get the report,' he said and disappeared. This sadism put me firmly into the category of the dependent and worried ill.

Almost all the doctors and medical authorities I've had dealings with in India have been excellent, on emotional as well as operational levels. But there is also in this richly varied country a bureaucratic tradition that can be cold and impersonal. This often has to do with the relentless pressure caused by the numbers of people seeking help or information. Some attribute the difference in attitude to rural as opposed to urban settings – the latter population being more used to full explanations, the former being more docile and less expectant. But I was in the urban category, and this unit was in a city.

Here, at the scanning clinic, was one lesson about becoming ill: we are vulnerable to callousness. I'm reminded of Tom Main's remark that patients who don't recover – or, I could now add, who refuse to behave like sheep – may receive barbarous behaviour disguised as treatment. An American friend was haunted for a long time by her father's embarrassment, a few weeks before his death, by the door of an ambulance being left open when he was undressed inside. She was appalled at the fact that no one, including herself, had anticipated his humiliation.

In my case, the verdict of subsequent careful consultations and testing, after minor delays and misdiagnoses, was that I had a form of non-Hodgkin's lymphoma. This would require chemotherapy over several months. When I reported this to Prof Bouloux by email, he told me that University College Hospital was a world centre of excellence in this field. He mentioned one of the consultants by name – Dr Chris McNamara. It was clear that we should return to London as soon as possible.

A few days later, making our way towards the Macmillan Cancer Centre at UCH in early December, we met a man who looked desperately ill, pallid and sweaty. He was trying to find the same place. In the lift, during that awkward moment of silence among strangers, an old woman, equally pale, tried to hurry the doors; pressing the wrong button, she prevented them from closing. She said, 'I never get that right.' A man experienced in the life of this kingdom told me about observing two brothers going through treatments. He called them 'grotesque' – the treatments, not the brothers. A brave new world. People hanging in or on. As I was about to become. I had hardly any symptoms yet, but would soon, more from the chemical cure than the illness itself.

The night before, I had dreamed of *playing cricket in a Test match. The batting order had changed. I was supposed to be captain but this didn't seem right. I scored a few runs, but against more or less joke bowlers. The main ones were not to be wasted on me. I was no longer really in charge.* The batting order reminded me of a comment made long ago at a cricketer's funeral: 'the one thing we don't know is the batting order'. I think the joke bowlers were wishful thinking on my part – the really hostile bowlers could come on at any time. But wishing for an easy ride, I put myself down. I was evading my fear, as when I made jokes. I suspect I was too frightened to feel fear.

We learned from Dr McNamara that if I were to have no treatment, I would probably be dead by September. I started the chemotherapy on Christmas Eve.

The day after this consultation, I had another dream. *It's a bright sunny day. I'm on a green grassy path, near a cliff edge. The path narrows ahead of me, perhaps towards a dead end. I'm afraid of falling, or of jumping off the cliff.* The dream seemed to be saying that the prospects were relatively sunny, the path promisingly green – the consultant had been optimistic, though also, it seemed to me, realistic: 70 per cent of those treated for this particular form of cancer not only survive but are cured. At the same time the prospects were also frightening, as the dead end and the cliff edge implied. But jumping? If I get too close to the edge, will I obliterate myself? Am I already jumping towards death, or jumping away from my real situation?

The chemo was, as I had been warned, drastic in patches. It destroys not only 'bad' cells, but also quick-growing healthy ones, including hair-follicle cells, and many in the mouth and the digestive tract. I felt more tired than before. I suffered, and to a small extent still do, in these areas, as well as from neuropathy of the hands and feet, a condition in which these parts tingle with pins and needles, sometimes feeling as if covered by metal boots or gloves, or as not really belonging to me. I was (and am) less dextrous than before.

The first casualty of war is truth: ditto of illness, at least in my reactions. I was unsure if I was under- or over-estimating the seriousness or extremity of my condition and symptoms; it seemed difficult to be simply honest. And though consciously I wanted to be given all information, how much could I really have borne to know?

When I felt seriously unwell, especially during those weeks when my immunity was lowest (the middle week of each three-week gap between chemotherapy infusions), I was not always confident how to assess my discomfort, or my lack of appetite and taste. On one occasion, my long-suffering wife was trying to find at least one kind of food that I might be able to swallow. She hit, with some enthusiasm, upon a baked potato. At that moment I felt not only that I didn't want to eat anything, a potato or anything else, except just possibly ice cream, but also that I couldn't bear even to think about the question. That too seemed an unappetising, even distasteful, burden. Was I exaggerating? Was I really so physiologically devastated as not to be able, however weakly, to give minimal consideration to this challengingly existential question? Sometimes mental space is so oppressed that there feels to be no room even for a putative potato.

One image came to my mind at that low point: I had the idea that this exhausted capitulation was how some of Napoleon's soldiers, marching back in abject defeat and freezing cold from Moscow, might have felt when they lay down in the snow; that the last thing in the world they wanted to do was to take another step (and for many this was the last thing they did in this world). Thinking about a potato felt like one more step in the snow. I remembered a friend who told me of her impulse to surrender to death during a frightening period of being unable to breathe properly.

Mountains and molehills, mistakes in either direction. But in both distortions, I was preoccupied with all the details of the experience.

* * *

I am inclined to think, though this idea is controversial in psychoanalysis, that there are in us all forces towards life and forces towards death. In this context, death may refer not mainly to biological death, rather to a psychological deadening. We have passages of thought and emotion like Keats's 'half in love with easeful death'. To attain this ease, we enter moods 'where but to think is to be full of sorrow'. Ease of this kind comes from limiting our life force.

It's also true that if our drive towards life involves mania, or (in Nicola Abel-Hirsch's phrase) 'outrageous growth', we need the capacity to oppose it, even to negate it. We need to restrain our arrogance or triumphalism in thinking we can face any potential outcome.

As one might expect, death wishes take many forms. In one case, they may be primarily a form of self-protection; it may also be more a matter of a sneering at life and at the vulnerabilities that living a life entails.

261

Here are two examples of people, one of them fictional, who have in different ways and spirits shut down on central aspects of living.

* * *

After, a story of Guy de Maupassant's, tells of a conversation one evening between an old countess (who is bringing up her three grandchildren after the early deaths of her son and daughter-in-law) and her friend the priest. After her guest's affectionate goodnight to the children, she sensitively opens up a big question: 'You are fond of children, M. le Curé . . . Has your solitude never weighed too heavily on you?' The priest hesitates. 'But I was never made for ordinary life . . . I was made to be a priest.' The countess wonders aloud how this came to be.

The priest is reluctant to speak. At this point, the narrator tells us he is 'a good man, benevolent, friendly to all, gentle and generous'. He is also tender: 'he laughed readily, and wept also, on slight provocation'.

The priest tells his story. His childhood was unhappy. His parents loved him 'more with the head than the heart', more with a view to his following them in their business successes than from an awareness of what really suited him. Homesick at the hated boarding school to which he was sent from a young age, he was unhappy also when at home.

An abandoned or lost dog, a spaniel with long ears, crawls towards him on a country lane. They become inseparable friends, their love mutual. He even finds the courage to assert himself against his parents, taking the dog in and feeding it with food from his own plate.

One terrible day the dog is run over and killed by a coach and horses in front of his eyes. He 'resolved to sacrifice possible joys in order to avoid sure sorrows'. Becoming a priest would admit of a 'milder form of emotion . . . I could not have seen one of my children die without dying myself'.

His story, almost a confession, ends. The countess responds that she herself could not envisage life without her grandchildren.

Both are deeply moved. M. le Curé is filled with regret, despite the compensations from the course his life has taken. He stares into the fire, into the mystery, as if seeing there 'the unknown of the existence he might have passed, had he been more fearless in the face of suffering'.

I read that story at school and have remembered it ever since. Only recently have I located it and re-read. My memory was accurate, and full. I'd forgotten his desperately lonely schooldays but remembered the rest.

Did the priest say no to life? Or was he saying yes to the best choice he could realistically make? Is this a case where compromise is better than risk? Maupassant leaves the question open. We feel the poignancy of his regret, along with the reality of his dread. We don't judge.

Maybe he knew himself best; that he was right to think that for him to have chosen otherwise would have been arrogance, like (it has been suggested) Oedipus' in assuming he was strong enough to deal with any result of the investigation into the causes of the blight and plague that was ravaging Thebes. Oedipus wasn't, and nor was Jocasta. And perhaps Maupassant's priest would indeed have been destroyed by the devastation of the loss of a loved child.

He has come to the conclusion that for him, after the dog died, it was better never to love than to have loved and lost.

* * *

Fred withdraws from contact with others; his aim, too, is to avoid an existential threat. But in his turning away from life there is also a scorn for those who try to help him.

I heard about Fred in a seminar, from a colleague who was treating him in analysis. He was around fifty, the oldest of three. There had always, it seemed, been neglect in the family, from both parents. He was the one to look after his siblings.

One scene from early childhood was referred to repeatedly: an early memory of driving his favourite toy, a big yellow truck, while his mother was sitting on a chair in another part of the garden.

His mother regularly threatened to leave the family, which she eventually did when he was eighteen; on the day they moved, she simply didn't turn up at the new house. The children came to know that she had set up with another man.

In his current life, Fred lived with his long-term partner in her flat. Despite her physical disability, she was the one who worked and paid for everything. Fred was a sort of housekeeper/carer, but seemed to be offering less and less. In his twenties and thirties, he had had various forays into work, but each effort had tailed away. Nowadays, whenever a question came up of his trying to get a job, he was contemptuous of any suggestion.

He had been gifted in painting. Now he would occasionally lay out his paints and paper. He simply stared at them.

The analyst reported that he had hardly ever looked her in the eye. Like the small boy on the truck, he stayed in another part of the garden. Though he attended scrupulously, he had withdrawn more and more from contact with her. She came to feel that he was going through the motions in analysis, as he was in the rest of his life. He turned inwards, away from the world, from herself as from other people.

His analyst frequently felt paralysed by this negativity. She wondered whether she should find a way of ending an analysis that felt to be increasingly, numbingly futile. It seemed he was repeating with the analyst his efforts to keep the mother from leaving by making fewer and fewer demands on her. She felt that he had to be half dead in order to survive; coming alive would have alienated the analyst by his needs.

He reported a dream, itself a rare event. *He was with an older woman, who seemed to represent the analyst. She was in a garden. She was offering some vegetable and flower seeds for him to plant. In the dream he knew he could take them, and grow them in his own little garden. But he immediately knew that he would never do this. He spoke as if from a superior place, looking down on the woman and on any inclination in himself to take her gift.*

While the dream aroused hopes in his analyst, it also created forebodings – he 'knew' he would never take the offered seeds. What's more, he showed in subsequent sessions no curiosity or willingness to struggle with the dream, no engagement with the analyst's attempts to understand it with him. He refused to take and plant the dream-seeds, too.

In the seminar we agreed that he also looked down on these efforts by the analyst, and by himself in the first part of his dream, to engage him in life. He sneered at any idea of coming alive, at any opportunity to do so. He seemed to be telling his analyst, in effect, that his refusal of her help was not only self-protective, but also a matter of his asserting his power to trump all her efforts to help him come alive. Perhaps he was punishing his parents through the analyst.

As the analyst predicted, her decision to end the analysis confirmed for Fred that any potential mother would leave him in the end, preferring another, as his actual mother had eventually done. Attempting to mitigate this disaster, she offered a period of once-weekly therapy, with her in a more supportive rather than analytic role. But he declined. She had to work through her guilt and disappointment.

* * *

Is 'denial of life' an accurate phrase to describe the choice of vocation of Maupassant's priest? Certainly, it seems to be a correct description of Fred's increasingly negative attitude.

The death wish, or death drive, is most obviously revealed in suicide or in murder (sometimes in both combined, as in suicide bombers). But there are other forms of suicide (itself murderous) in which life, of a kind, lingers on, as Hermann Hesse wrote: 'The true suicide is not necessarily the person who killed himself, but the person in whom the mental and emotional processes are deadened.' This kind of denial of life, this deadening, may be primarily self-protective (as with the priest), an at least temporarily necessary retreat. But it may also be twisted, perverse, even cruel (perhaps as with Fred, or when a person who kills himself enjoys the idea of the other suffering from guilt for the rest of their lives). In all such cases, a crucial question is, can the person recognise his (or her) turning away from life, and struggle with it? Or are they bound to it in an unending repetition?

Maupassant's story ends as follows. The countess has seen the priest off, his 'tall shadow . . . disappearing through the gloom of the night. Then she came back and sat down before the fire, and pondered over many things we never think of when we are young.'

Like her, I ponder about death and deathliness more than when I was young. But I reflect also that I was so taken by this story that I remembered it for sixty-five years, every now and then making an effort to track it. Even when I read it at fifteen, it glimmered with meaning for me. I also remember, from a year or two later, the motion of a school debating society, though I never, then or later, participated in formal debating. The motion was: 'This house believes it is better to have loved and lost than never to have loved at all.'

Indeed, loving opens one up to real dangers. This fact rang painfully true for the priest, for Fred, and weighs heavily on anyone inclined to vote against the motion. Hope, trust and emotional attachment are indeed hazardous. It's not the rejection that hurts, people say, it's the hope. Hope, like love, is a hostage to fortune, as is having children. All three create the likelihood of disappointment, of loss, of disillusion. For some people, as Virgil wrote: 'The only hope for the doomed is no hope at all.'

So, what was it about these two, M. le Curé and Fred, that made them so memorable to me? Why do they stick in my mind while so many others have disappeared from consciousness?

I think I must have been dimly aware of my timidity, my own tendency to shy away from emotional venturing. Though I have never been literally suicidal or chronically depressed, I have long been aware of a fascination with death and dying, a fascination that suggests both a fear of it and a pull towards it. I find myself drawing back from a too direct confrontation with the skull on Pascal's desk.

And however much I'm charmed by the vision of the sister in the *Bhagavad Gita*, her *shraddha*, I can't share it.

＊　＊　＊

Physical decline is inevitable, relentless and unnerving. But my greatest conscious fears lie in the area of mental decline. Occasionally when working with patients, I catch myself mentioning something from the past to reassure myself that my memory is still functioning. When I can't remember, I wonder if this is the beginning of the disaster, though so far there has been, I'm sure (or does everyone think this?), only ordinary, slow memory decline, in some ways compensated for (I hope) by increased freedom of mind, and broader comprehension.

Relatives, friends, teachers, admired colleagues, ex-cricketers – so many have died, but so many too have had disabling strokes, dementias, brain tumours that did not instantly kill them. People whose minds and personalities were rich and wonderful are departing from the shared world while still alive. ('Our cohort is under fire,' a friend writes.) We miss them. We are in effect saying goodbye gradually and prematurely, as the essential persons they were fade away. We realise how precarious life is, how outcomes are not under our control. If our brains turn to straw in one way or another, we as persons will eventually join the living dead.

We, we of this realm of the old, may feel out of place. We are slower, our expectations and suppositions less nimble than younger people's, our hearing less sharp. We both over- and undervalue the habits and values of our own heydays. We feel excluded partly because we exclude the young. Either way, excluded or excluding, or both, we have become outdated, past our sell-by date.

Traditional attitudes of respect towards the old have declined. But when younger I too felt impatient with members of the previous generation, meeting whom could be something to be got through in order that we, the forceful young, could get back as soon as possible to the conviviality and assumptions of our contemporaries. A small but shameful episode returns to me. I was talking intently with fellow university students in our Ealing house when my father came home from work. I remember feeling proud of not allowing myself to be distracted by his return. In other words, I froze him out, my genial, friendly father, pleased to get home after his day's work, happy to see me and my friends in his home.

Nowadays, the old are likely to be even more marooned than in the past, lonely in solitary flats, cut off in particular from small children for whom great age is of interest and not itself a marker of inferiority. ('Do you have snow on your head?', a five-year-old in Ahmedabad asked me, earnestly, not long ago, having intently studied my hair for some minutes.)

CHAPTER 14

IT CAN'T BE ME

Last scene of all, as Shakespeare tells us, is 'second childishness and mere oblivion; sans teeth, sans eyes, sans taste, sans everything'. We who live long have much to mourn before we die. But what about death itself? I'm struck by two diametrically opposed 'takes' on the prospect of death; at least for someone like me who regards belief in life after death as wishful thinking.

On one view, there is no loss as great. We are to be deprived of all that we have, all that we are. We will be no more. After each earlier loss, we are there to mourn it, to come to terms with it as well as we can, to have at least some memories of better days, of friends 'hid in death's dateless night'. On this view, not to be afraid of death would be a sign of our dementing, or of our self-protective evasion of reality. But we may (or some may) see the situation in an opposite way. What is there to fear? Nothing. We did not 'miss' the millions of years before our birth; why then should we worry about aeons of time to come when we will be no more? Moreover, we may, like leaves in autumn, be ready for death. We may be tired of life, especially if living has become too painful or difficult. Ripeness, or readiness, is all.

* * *

As someone whose parents were both more or less swiftly, and before that, gradually, insidiously, disabled by Alzheimer's, I have long been all too aware of the possibility of some such disaster striking me down. The German analyst Gabriele Junkers reports a cautionary tale of an ageing analyst falling ill, almost dying, slowly recovering to the extent of being left with failing memory and mental decline. His last training patient, required to be in her training analysis until qualification, hung on for him. She eventually saw him in the rest home where he lived. He would not or could not see that he was no longer in a fit state to do this work. Rather than helping his patient, he was using her to bolster his own threatened identity.

When I was training, our student group realised that one teacher, a warm and gifted psychoanalyst, was becoming repetitive and not fully present in the seminars. I told my progress advisor about the group's worry. Having no doubt heard similar stories, she had to tell him, in as kindly a way as she could, that he had to stop. I learned much later that the man taking our seminars had been her analyst.

To make a commitment to become someone's analyst is to be prepared for a long haul, that is, at least for five years or so. Seven or eight years ago, I decided not to take on new, open-ended, intensive cases. I took Junkers' warnings seriously. I have also reduced my caseload, doing my therapy and supervisory work on three days a week.

At the same time, I realised, and I hope still accurately realise, that I can do useful work with shorter-term patients, and with colleagues who come for supervision. I made another decision, that I could, with proper consideration for each person, take a two-month sabbatical every winter, when Mana and I could spend time in India, and I could write. Before embarking on this arrangement, I had been asked if I might follow another analyst in applying for an honorary four-month fellowship in Kyoto. Our daughter Lara challenged me. 'If you can think of going to Japan for a few months, you could do that in India, you know!' So now I can enjoy India, and give Mana, who has lived outside India for more than forty years to be with me, the pleasure of more extended, and joint, stays in her home country.

Turning over the Pebbles is the fourth book to emerge from this change of routine. This has been a life-enhancing shift for me, not least in the writing itself, but also in enabling me to work to integrate different facets of my life.

As long as memories remain, they may also enrich, and stimulate gratitude and significance, though I was struck by Kazuo Ishiguro's novel *The Buried Giant*, which leaves us uncertain whether unearthing buried memories will release terrible old conflicts and polarisation, or a more mature ability to accommodate them. If we can move on, we have our shared pasts to return to with others. With each of my grandchildren I have been struck by how, whenever we meet, they intuitively bring up with me exchanges that are special to the two of us, reminders of shared jokes, games, interactions, playfulness. And that is also true with old friends. Some early memories foreshadow later fulfilments; they are the seeds that give rise to flowering or indeed weed production.

* * *

My experience of psychoanalysis, both as patient and analyst, has resulted in my being closer than I might otherwise have been to a state in which the past can be restored, gaps filled, meanings deepened.

Dreams, even nightmares, help.

A colleague tells me a dream of hers: *She drives to Whitestone Pond, (up the hill between Hampstead and Golders Green); in her dream there is a restaurant and a large car park next to the pond. She is on her way to give a webinar with a senior person in her area of specialism. They are due to meet at her father's house at the bottom of the hill. The webinar is due to start in five minutes. Rather than drive on, she turns towards the car park, away also from the pond. She then spends ten minutes ordering a takeaway from the restaurant. She is now very late for the webinar, past the hour at which it should have started.* She wakes in panic.

She says she has never been so pleased to realise, on waking from a dream, that she had been dreaming, not acting in the real world. The dream reminded her of a saying, that 'the best way to get writing is to sit by a pond, letting one's mind go free'. The image of the take-away led to her realisation that she has allowed herself to be 'taken away' from her priorities, that she has been too easily distracted from her work. The message of the dream seemed to be that of a helpful superego admonishing her for not getting things done on time. She said that having had these thoughts her mood had changed; she was able to sit quietly and listen to what she had inside herself. Within twenty minutes, she had written, with fluency, the introduction to the webinar that had been troubling her for days.

I told her my associations to her dream. She had turned away both from the pond and from her important appointment down the hill at her father's. Instead, she went to the tarmacked car park. To me, the take-away was a quick meal, a set of ideas she was relying on getting from someone else rather than having access to herself, sitting by a pond. We both understood the dream as a realistic and helpful jolt towards realism – awakening her creativity and fluency.

Struck by the similarity to my dream of being in Japan, in which I was unable to find my way to the airport and thus home, I told her mine, how in that state I felt I could understand nothing. She commented on the productive aspects of my dream, too. It may at times be a good thing not to understand, to be in the dark, to allow this state of mind. Seeds grow in fallow ground, in winter. Persephone goes down to Hades for six months of each year. She mentioned too the presence of the potentially helpful figures, one who could translate, and another who had lived life fully until his death, and had in his bag-mind a lot of resources.

We commented on how fortunate we are to have this capacity, developed by long experience and practice with our own and others' dreams and thinking processes, to begin to own our terrors, to come to terms (more or less) with our limitations, errors and the damage done; to our many blessings, and be reminded at the same time of real strengths and resilience, all of which enable us to recover more quickly from disruption than before.

We may, too, through psychoanalysis and other influences and examples, have been helped to broaden our arc of interest and concern, so that we care, in old age, for the young, for the next generations, for the planet, for projects, disciplines and fields that we have been part of but soon will not be. We may have emerged with a more generous rather than envious attitude to those whose chance of life will, normally, extend far beyond our own. We have retained or even expanded our curiosity. Psychoanalysis (among other things) has enhanced our internal resources.

If we're not too self-important or self-denying, we may still have something to offer the younger generation.

* * *

Shortly before he died, Wittgenstein said, 'Tell them I've had a wonderful life.' He also said that fear of death is a sign of a life not well lived.

At a dinner, I once sat next to Cicely Saunders, who had started the hospice movement. Recently I heard on the radio a story about Saunders's first encounter with the plight of someone dying in an ordinary hospital ward in the early 1950s. The dying person was David Tasma, a Polish Jew in his thirties who happened to have been in England when the war broke out. His entire family had been murdered. He now had an inoperable cancer. Cicely came to talk to him frequently in his last two months. Tasma's emotional and spiritual pain had a profound effect on her.

Tasma felt he was dying before he had lived. Utterly alone, he would leave not a ripple on the waters of life. The conversations led her to her life-changing 'revelation': that she might develop the possibility of a different form of treatment for the dying, focusing on giving patients the opportunity to be themselves, not simply to have their physical pain suppressed or their time prolonged. She emphasised the quality of life rather than the quantity. It turned out that Tasma had received a legacy. Before dying, he signed the £500 over to Cicely; he would 'be a window in your home'. She used it to further her idea. Now a room at the first hospice is named after him. He made a ripple after all, and not only with his bequest.

* * *

We may be too frightened of reality, too false in our living of life, to admit the fact of our own impending death. In Tolstoy's story 'Master and Man', Vasily has refused an offer to stay in a comfortable house rather than drive on through a snowstorm in order to clinch a dodgy deal before a rival gets in first. After further misadventures and hardships, he is totally lost, riding the now-exhausted horse. He encounters long stems of wormwood, a bitter aromatic shrub, a symbol in the Bible for the bitter taste and poisonous effects of sin, misery and grief; as in his life, he keeps mistaking these tall plants for markers of the lost path. But soon he can no longer reassure himself with self-congratulatory memories of business successes, or with his sense of superiority over peasants, business rivals and others. He is in terror of death, which is indeed close at hand. Until now, this superiority and self-satisfaction have precluded him from experiencing in any felt way either the suffering of others, or the inevitability of his own death. Now the latter takes him over.

This story reminds me of Tolstoy's short novel *The Death of Ivan Ilyich,* and of that character's inability or refusal to recognise how serious, indeed fatal, his illness is. His life, too, has been false; he does not feel he has really lived. Only at the very end, with the help of his kindly and forbearing servant, Gerasim, who eases Ivan's pain by allowing him to rest his legs on his shoulders for hours during the night, can he begin, almost at the last gasp, to face this reality. Gerasim himself contemplates the inevitability of his own death equably, even in good cheer.

Ilyich makes me think of a bleak joke. Philip meets an old college friend forty years on. In response to his questions about the other man's life, he discovers that in every department there has been disaster – the man's wife ran off with another man, his daughter is ill, his grandchild died, his business collapsed. To each of these reports, Philip responds, 'It could have been worse . . .' Eventually his former friend gets furious; 'What do you mean, it could have been worse?' Philip replies: 'It could have been me.' I suspect we all feel this at some level. The news of the death of a friend may quicken, or even deepen, my appetite for life, but at the same time I may, like Ilyich, secretly doubt whether such a thing could happen to me, who, like Ivan, 'was little Vanya', his 'mother's favourite', who 'loved playing with a stripey ball'? Ilyich's hopes are vain both in the sense of empty (he will die, and soon) and in the sense of self-centred (all men are mortal except me, I am the great exception).

∗   ∗   ∗

I have not been brought face to face with the full realisation of my own impending death. The lymphoma might have gone the wrong way, of course; it might have killed me; but I told myself I'd be in the 70 per cent who would survive.

It's hard to know how we will be when death is inexorably near, when 'there it will be, "the distinguished thing"', as Henry James described it on his deathbed. Should we console ourselves with

Hamlet's thought that 'There's a special providence in the fall of a sparrow. If it be now, 'tis not to come; if it be not to come, it will be now; if it be not now, yet it will come. The readiness is all'? We don't after all mourn the time when we were not yet born. Is there anything to fear, then, from the abyss of the future after we are dead? Sleep, perchance *not* to dream.

For all losses *within* life, we are there to mourn them afterwards; this most extreme loss we mourn, if at all, only in advance. (And not so devastatingly, we hope, as to preclude the joys that remain.)

Nevertheless, the loss of one or other faculty or accomplishment – sight, hearing, the ability to walk, to sleep or to talk, disabling as even one of these losses is – pales beside the loss of *everything*. When we're dead, our whole world will have gone. It's hard to imagine, partly because imagining ('centrally' imagining, as Richard Wollheim put it) often implies being there, as when we imagine being present at our own funeral, hovering above our coffined self. In such ways we smuggle ourselves back into the picture, removed, to be sure, but present. Trying to assert our absolute death, we thereby deny it.

And is not the terror of the wormwood, the instinctive clinging on to life, the gut-wrenching panic on hearing the worst diagnosis, universal (or nearly so)? I once saw a short film of an Ambrose Bierce Civil War story ('An Occurrence at Owl Creek Bridge'). In the instant of a man's being executed on a bridge, he has a fantasy of escape: he miraculously manages to dive into the river, and dodges, or avoids, the bullets. I suspect that such life-asserting, life-demanding, intensities in the immediate prospect of the inevitable, the undistinguished, offensive thing, are likely to play a part.

I think I *am* afraid. Perhaps the fear of 'nothingness' gets its content from the fear of becoming a vegetable, or a stone, or a block of wood, no longer a person. But in general, am I too comfortable, too complacent, perhaps even too frightened, to allow it house-room, to encounter it?

So far, my physical illnesses and injuries have felt like shots across the bows. I was lucky with my cancer. The Vanya-me was sufficiently confident that my life would carry on for me not to feel really scared. Indeed, it might even be an opportunity for me robustly to see off the Grim Reaper, to prove to myself that I am the exception. I was apprehensive, cautious, immensely grateful to my excellent doctors, nurses and family; but hardly ever terrified. I was not *forced* to alter my complacent view that wormwood – death – is a condition for others. A friend of mine wrote to me as he moved into his fourth decade that his 'twenties had not prepared him for his thirties': has my fortunate life prepared me for the terror of dying and of death?

* * *

We/I have 'left undone those things which we ought to have done, and done those things we ought not to have done. We have followed too much the devices and desires of our own hearts'. But there *is* (also) health in us (in me) – I have struggled with these things, in analysis, in my own work and in everyday life. I can still lose sleep from shame or guilt or anxiety; but I am generally aware of how lucky I am in my family and personal relationships, friendships and (a lot of the time) with my own company. My work fascinates me. I am busy and more open to my heart and mind than I used to be. I have had a good, full, multi-faceted life.

The older I get, the sadder I am at landmarks, or rather time-marks, passing. The beginning of May, the summer solstice, the autumn equinox. Will there be another? For me? And yet, no two minutes are exactly alike. Perhaps I can be alive at my own death.

In the end, as Edgar tells Gloucester:

> Men must endure
> Their going hence, even as their coming hither;
> Ripeness is all.

SELECTED BIBLIOGRAPHY

Note: The references in each chapter are put in the order of their appearance in, or relevance to, the narrative.

I Am Me
Mildred Batchelder, *The Adventures of Chippybobbie and his friend Mr Field-Mouse*, 1927.
William Ernest Henley, 'Invictus' in *Oxford Book of English Verse*, 1900.
Nina Coltart, *Slouching towards Bethlehem*, 1992.
Mike Brearley (with Dudley Doust), *The Return of the Ashes*, 1978.
Mike Brearley (with Dudley Doust), *The Ashes Retained*, 1980
Richard Holloway, *Waiting for the Last Bus*, 2018.
George Eliot, *Middlemarch*, 1871–2.
William Shakespeare, *Sonnets*.

Chapter 1 'If You Carry on Like This . . .'
Donald Winnicott, *Playing and Reality*, 1971.
Michael Apted (films), *Seven Up*, 1964; *Collected Series*, 2018.
Harold Pinter, *The* Caretaker, 1960.
Evelyn Waugh, *Decline and* Fall, 1928.
William Shakespeare, *Julius Caesar*.
C. P. Snow, *The Two Cultures*, 1959.
W. H. Davies, *Collected Poems*, 1916.
Jonathan Lear, *A Case for* Irony, 2014.
Michael Henderson, *That Will Be England Gone*, 2020.

Mike Brearley *The Art of* Captaincy, 1985.
Plato, *Republic*.

Chapter 2 Foot-Hat or Head-Shoe?
William Shakespeare, *A Midsummer Night's Dream*.
Rebecca Solnit, *Orwell's Roses*, 2021.
Meg Harris Williams, 'Shakespeare and Personality
    Development', 2012.
William Shakespeare, *Julius Caesar*.
Wisden Cricketers' Almanack, 1978.
Theophrastus, *Characters*.
Homer, *Odyssey*.
Mike Brearley, *On Form*, 2017.
W. H. Davies, *Collected* Poems, 1916.
Ernest Hemingway, *Old Man and the* Sea, 1952.
Aeschylus, *Agamemnon Trilogy*, 458 BCE.
Euripides, Alcestis, 438 BCE.
Sophocles, *Oedipus Trilogy*, 429 BCE.
Heraclitus, *Fragments*.
Renford Bambrough *Reason, Truth and God*, 1969.

Chapter 3 More Things in Heaven and Earth
William Shakespeare, *Hamlet*.
Melanie Klein, *Envy and Gratitude*, 1957.
W. B. Yeats, *Selected Poems*, 2000.
Aristophanes, *Frogs*.
Homer, *Iliad*.
Melanie Klein, *Envy and Gratitude*, 1957.
Common Worship: Pastoral Services, 2011.
Homer, *Iliad*.
Mike Brearley, *Spirit of Cricket*, 2020.
La Rochefoucauld, *Maxims*, 1678.
The King James Version (KJV) Bible, 'Ezekiel'.
Priscilla Green, 'The Poet and the Superego: Klein,
    Blake and the prophet Ezekiel', *Journal of Child Psychotherapy*,
    2002.
D. W. Winnicott, *Playing and Reality*, 2005.
T. S. Eliot, *Four Quartets*, 1943.
Rowan Williams, *Writing in the Dust*, 2002.

Marilynne Robinson, *Jack*, 2020.
Marilynne Robinson, *Home*, 2008.
Ivo Andrić, *Signs by the Roadside*, 1976.

Chapter 4 'No, No, No, No . . . No, on the Whole No'

John Wisdom, *Philosophy and Psycho*-analysis, 1953.
Plato, *Meno*.
Ludwig Wittgenstein, *Tractatus Logico-Philosophicus*, 1921.
Ludwig Wittgenstein, *Philosophical Investigations*, 1953.
Ray Monk, *Ludwig Wittgenstein: The Duty of Genius*, 1990.
Pearl King and Riccardo Steiner, *The Freud-Klein Controversies 1941-45*, 1992.
Brian Magee, interview in *New Statesman*, 2018.
David Kynaston, *On the Cusp: Days of '62*, 2021.
David Kynaston, *A Northern Wind: 1962-5*, 2023.
Karl Britton, *Philosophy and the Meaning of* Life, 1969.
Nadezhda Mandelstam, *Hope Against Hope*, 1989.
F. R. Leavis, *The Great Tradition*, 1948.

Chapter 5 Henry James's Ruined Shoes

Mary Fairclough, *Miskoo the Lucky*, 1947.
Richmal Crompton, *Just William*, 1922.
Hugh de Sélincourt, *The Cricket Match*, 1924.
H. G. Wells, 'The Truth about Pyecraft', 1903.
Ambrose Bierce, *A Horseman in the Sky*, 1889.
Sigmund Freud, 'Letter to Fliess, September 1897' in Jeffrey Masson, *The Complete Letters of Sigmund Freud to Wilhelm Fliess, 1887–1904*, 1985.
Henry James, *The Portrait of a Lady*, 1881.
Henry James, *The Europeans*, 1878.
F. R. Leavis, *The Great Tradition*, 1948.
Giuseppe di Lampedusa, *The Leopard*, 1958
Henry James, *Autobiographies*, 2016.
Colm Tóibín, *The Master*, 2004.
Richard Wollheim, *Germs: A Memoir of* Childhood, 2004.
Alan Hollinghurst, 'The Digested Tract', *Guardian*, 2004.
Elizabeth Lowry, 'Open wounds', *Guardian*, 2008.
Henry James, *The Ambassadors*, 1903.
John Scholar, *Henry James and the Art of Impressions*, 2020.

Edmund Gosse, *Aspects and* Impressions, 1922.
Leo Tolstoy, *War and Peace*, 1869.

Chapter 6 'Please Look After my Dog'
Marion Milner, *On Not Being Able to Paint*, 1950.
William Shakespeare, *Hamlet*.
John Wisdom, *Philosophy and Psycho-analysis*, 1953.
Oliver Sacks, *The Man Who Mistook His Wife for a Hat*, 1985.
Hanna Segal, 'Notes on Symbol Formation' in *The Work of Hanna Segal*, 1981.
Sigmund Freud, *The Question of Lay Analysis*, 1926.
Ken Robinson, 'A Brief History of the British Psychoanalytical Society', 2015.
Paula Heimann, 'On Counter-transference' in *International Journal of Psychoanalysis (IJPA)*, Vol. 31, 1950.

Chapter 7 Haydn's Duck Quartet
Juliet Rosenfeld, *The State of Disbelief*, 2020.
Richard Flanagan, *The Narrow Road to the Deep* North, 2013.
Bob Dylan, *Chronicles: Volume One*, 2004.
Roger Kennedy, *The Power of Music: Psychoanalytic explorations*, 2020.
Donald Tovey, *Essays in Musical Analysis*, 1935.
Francis Grier, 'The Inner World of Beethoven's ninth symphony: Masculine *and* Feminine?' in *International Journal of Psychoanalysis (IJPA)*, Vol. 101, 2020.
C. L. R. James, *Beyond a Boundary*, 1963.
John Kay and Mervyn King, *Radical Uncertainty: Decision-making for an Unknown Future*, 2020.
Malcolm Gladwell, *Blink: The Power of Thinking Without Thinking*, 2005.
Hans Christian Andersen, *Fairy Tales*.
David Sylvester, *London Recordings*, 2003.
T. S. Eliot, *Four Quartets*, 1943.

Chapter 8 'A Straight Ball, Michael, has a Certain Lethal Quality'
Colin Cowdrey, *M.C.C.: The Autobiography of a Cricketer*, 1976.
Mike Brearley, *Phoenix from the* Ashes, 1982.
Mike Brearley, *The Art of Captaincy*, 1985.

Chapter 9 The Cracked Vase
Sigmund Freud (1914): 'Remembering, Repeating and Working Through', *Standard Edition*, Vol. 12, 1958.

Willian Shakespeare, *Troilus and Cressida*.

Melanie Klein, *Love, Guilt and Reparation*, 1975

Sándor Ferenczi, 'Child analysis in the analysis of adults' in *International Journal of Psychoanalysis (IJPA)*, Vol. 12.

Harrison Birtwistle and Fiona Maddocks, *Harrison Birtwistle: Wild Tracks*, 2014.

Leo Tolstoy, *War and Peace*, 1869.

Melanie Klein, *Narrative of a Child Analysis*, 1958.

Sigmund Freud (1917), 'Introductory Lectures in Psychoanalysis', *Standard Edition*, Vol. 17, 1958.

Joe Sandler and Anne-Marie Sandler, 'On the Development of Object Relations and Affects' in *International Journal of Psychoanalysis (IJPA)*, Vol. 59, 1978.

Tom Main, *The* Ailment, 1989.

Sigmund Freud (1915), 'Transference Love', *Standard Edition*; Vol. 3, 1958.

Nina Coltart, *Slouching towards Bethlehem*, 1992

Salman Akhtar, *Tales of Transformation*, 2022.

T. S. Eliot, *Four Quartets*, 1943.

William Shakespeare, *King Lear*.

Chapter 10 A Picture Held Us Captive

Ludwig Wittgenstein, *Philosophical Investigations*, 1953.

Plato, *The Republic*.

Plato, *Phaedo*.

Platro, *Phaedrus*.

Ludwig Wittgenstein, *Tractatus Logico-Philosophicus*, 1921.

John Locke, *An Essay concerning Human Understanding*, 1690.

Wilfred Bion, *Notes on Memory and Desire*, 1967.

Sigmund Freud, (1923) 'The Ego and the Id', *Standard Edition*; Vol. 19, 1958.

Samuel Beckett, *Waiting for* Godot, 1952.

Helmut Thoma, 'Transference and the Psychoanalytic Encounter', *International Forum of Psychoanalysis*, Vol. 18, 2009.

Sigmund Freud (1914), 'Remembering, Repeating and Working Through', *Standard Edition*; Vol. 12, 1958.

Wilfred Bion, *Experiences in Groups*, 1961.

George Eliot, *Middlemarch*, 1871–2.

Sigmund Freud (1915), 'Instincts and their vicissitudes', *Standard Edition*, Vol. 14, 1958.

Lolita Chakrabarti, *Red Velvet*, 2012.

David Bell, 'Projective identification' in Cathy Bronstein, *Kleinian Theory: A Contemporary* Perspective, 2001.

Sigmund Freud (1917), *Mourning and Melancholia, Standard Edition*, Vol. 14, 1958.

John Wisdom, *Philosophy and Psycho-analysis*, 1953.

Antonino Ferro, *Seeds of Illness, Seeds of Recovery*, 2005.

Jonathan Lear, *Wisdom won from Illness*, 2017.

Samuel Beckett, *Waiting for Godot*, 1952.

Irma Brenman Pick, *Authenticity in the Analytic* Encounter, 2018.

George Berkeley, *A Treatise Concerning the Principles of Human Knowledge*, 1710.

Chapter 11 'That Ain't Going Nowhere'

James Rebanks, *The Shepherd's Life*, 2015.

Wilfred Bion, *A Long Week-End, 1897–1919*, 1982.

Roger Deakin, *Wildwood*, 2007.

Leo Tolstoy, *Anna Karenin*, 1878.

George Herbert, 'The elixir', 1633.

Sally Weintrobe, *Psychological Roots of the Climate* Crisis, 2021.

Chapter 12 Prophet to a Profession

Chris Mawson., ed., *The Complete Works of W. R. Bion*, 2014.

Joan and Neville Symington, *The Clinical Thinking of Wilfred* Bion, 1996.

Wilfred Bion, *Experiences in* Groups, 1961.

Wilfred Bion, *Brazilian Lectures*, 1990.

Wilfred Bion, *Memoir of the* Future, 1975.

Wilfred Bion, *The Long Week-End, 1897–1919*, 1986.

W. H. Auden. 'In Memory of Sigmund Freud', 1940.

Pearl King and Riccardo Steiner. *The Freud-Klein Controversies 1941–45*, 1991.

Wilfred Bion, *Elements of Psychoanalysis*, 1963.

John Keats. Letter to his brothers. 1817.

Sigmund Freud (1912 and 1911), 'Recommendations to physicians practising psychoanalysis' and 'Formulation of the two principles of mental functioning', *Standard Edition*, Vol. 12, 1958.

Nicola Abel-Hirsch, *Bion 365 Quotes*, 2019.

Wilfred Bion, *A Memoir of the Future*, 1975.

Wilfred Bion, *The Long Week-End, 1897-1919*, 1986.

Johan Huizinga, *Homo Ludens*, 1938.

John Steiner,

Wilfred Bion, *Four Discussions with W. R. Bion*, 1978.

Robert Macfarlane, *Mountains of the Mind*, 2003.

Francesca Bion, 'Envoi' in W. R. Bion (Editor: Chris Mawson), The *Complete Works of W. R. Bion*, Vol 2., 2014.

Wilfred Bion, *War Memoirs 1917-1919*, 2015.

Wilfred Bon, *Learning from Experience*, 1962.

Wilfred Bion, *Transformations*, 1965.

Ronald Britton. Review of James Grotstein's A *Beam of Intense Darkness* (2007) in *Fort Da*, Vol. 14, 2008.

Maurice Blanchot,

James Strachey. 'The nature of the therapeutic action of psychoanalysis' in *International Journal of Psychoanalysis (IJPA)*, Vol. 15, 1934.

Neville Symington (1985), 'John Klauber, Independent Clinician' in *Becoming a Person through Psychoanalysis*, 2007.

Edna O'Shaughnessy. 'Enclaves and excursions', in *International Journal of Psychoanalysis (IJPA)*, Vol. 73, 1992.

Heraclitus, *Fragments.*

Chapter 13 Staring into the Fire

Joseph Conrad, *Chance*, 1913. (Foreword to later edition, 1925.)

Venerable Bede, *Ecclesiastical History of the English People*, 731.

The Bhagavad Gita.

Blaise Pascal, *Pensées*, 1670.

Susan Sontag, *Illness as Metaphor*, 1978.

Tom Main, *The Ailment*, 1989.

Guy De Maupassant, 'After', 1900.

John Keats, *The Complete Poems*, 1977.

Nicola Abel-Hirsch, 'The life-instinct', in *International Journal of Psychoanalysis (IJPA)*, Vol. 91, 2010.

Hermann Hesse, Steppenwolf, 1972.

Virgil, *Aeneid.*

Chapter 14 It Can't Be Me

Willian Shakespeare, *As You Like It.*

Gabriele Junkers, *The Empty Couch*, 2013.

Kazuo Ishiguro, *The Buried Giant*, 2015.

Ray Monk, *Ludwig Wittgenstein: The Duty of Genius*, 1990.

Cicely Saunders, *Care of the Dying*, 1976.

Leo Tolstoy, 'Master and Man', 1895.

Leo Tolstoy, *The Death of Ivan Ilyich*, 1886.
Henry James in Leon Edel, 'The Deathbed Notes of Henry James', 1968.
William Shakespeare *Hamlet*.
Richard Wollheim, *The Thread of* Life, 1984.
Ambrose Bierce, 'An Occurrence at Owl Creek Bridge', 1890.
William Shakespeare, *King Lear*.
John Keats, *The Complete Poems*, 1977.

ACKNOWLEDGEMENTS

This is a memoir, as my editor Andreas Campomar puts it, a 'memoir of the mind'. Or rather of *my* mind. Part of its motivation is to let our grandchildren, two children each of Mischa and Lara, know something of my life. They know it in their own ways; in ways appropriate to nineteen-, thirteen-, six- and three-year-olds. But, like our children too, they may all, perhaps when they too are in their eighties (or even before), want to know about, and from, this particular grandfather, and find something in the book to interest them.

I'm constantly struck and moved by how intense and fascinating grandparent relationships are. As a child, I had little of that experience. Two of my four grandparents had died before I was born, a third when I was eighteen months old. The fourth lived in Heckmondwike, which in those days was experienced as another world, far from London. This grandma, whom I do remember, was formidable; she and I liked each other, I think, but distantly. There wasn't much playing with her, and no being looked after by her. She died when I was ten.

The intimacy, conversations, affection, frankness, playfulness of my grandchildren, so present and in contrast with my earlier lack, explains the dedication. I love them, and would love to see how their lives pan out. I'm fortunate to have seen them so far. They are each unique, and special.

Mischa and Fae, Lara and Jaco too. And we're quite an Indian family. All have lived for periods with Mana and me. In relation to the writing of this book, all too have made comments, given me ideas and thoughts, each in their own ways.

And, of course, my parents, Horace and Midge, did and gave much to make me what I was and am. Both were maths teachers, both keen on sport, both warmly supportive. My sisters, Jill and Margy, younger than me, and close to each other in age, were for most of my childhood 'the girls', and as such subjected to a degree of superiority from me. I here apologise, for what that's worth! (My fifth-form class teacher, Rev C. J. Ellingham, growled at us one day that he had had enough of our empty 'Sorry, Sir's.) Most family rows started with some squabble between 'the girls' and me which led to parents taking sides along broadly Oedipal lines; my mother supported me, my father my sisters, and then they would have a bigger, longer and more silent argument.

This is a book to which many, many people have contributed. It would be impossible to mention them all, and even harder to know who they all are. Some are mentioned in the text, but most aren't. Many are now dead. When I started to make a list, I soon saw that any list, while remaining invidious, quickly became too long. I hope that my friends, teachers, colleagues, team-mates will understand my not mentioning names except where they come into my telling of the story. They, you, are present in my thoughts, and in who I am.

I will mention by name four people who read parts of the book and made helpful comments. All have written their own memoir-like books recently.

David Kynaston, a distinguished writer and historian, read an earlier version of the chapter on Bion and encouraged me to keep it in despite it being somewhat specialised. David and I have frequent conversations about cricket, the humanities, politics, history and writing. In what feels to me a labour of love, he proof-read the whole book, averting errors and infelicities.

Second, David Millar, a psychoanalyst-colleague, who has published his own memoir, *A Connecting Door.* We are more or less of an age, and have our own, I think overlapping, things to say about the life of a psychoanalyst, and the kind of difference that has made for us. We are members of a small CPD group that meet monthly to discuss clinical ideas (the others are Nick Temple and David Bell).

Third, Hugh Brody, anthropologist, filmmaker, writer and friend; his memoir is called *Landscapes of Silence: From Childhood to the Arctic.* We have long shared our moments of doubt and of elation about writing. 'Why should anyone want to hear about my childhood?' was one night-time feeling of Hugh's.

Fourth, Irma Brenman Pick, another psychoanalyst, whose CPD seminar group I've been part of for about thirty years. (The members of this group, whom I can't name individually, have also been important.) I have gained a lot about life and psychoanalysis from Irma, who has also been one of my supervisors and a good friend.

I must refer more fully to my esteemed editor, Andreas. (Others from Little, Brown, especially Holly Blood and Henry Lord, have also been helpful and have gone beyond the call of duty. I have been grateful to have Matthew Hamilton as my agent, too.) Andreas and I have now done four books together. We talk freely, for much of the time without focus on the particular problems of writing. But then arrive his, sometimes sharp, mots: 'May we have at least one chapter without psychoanalysis; it keeps creeping in like a garden weed.' 'Sometimes it's like you and me sitting at opposite ends of a dinner table trying to have a conversation, while everyone between us keeps talking. Speak directly.' 'Make it simple. Make it lighter; then it will be heavier.' At one time I got shirty and said, 'Why don't you write the book and I'll do the editing?'

Much the same can be said of Mana, my wife. Editors, (mid) wives, psychoanalysts – sensitive, empathic, robust. I'm lucky with mine. She too has a healthy suspicion of psychoanalysis, having lived through not only my training but also, as a child, her mother's. She combines the garden weed view with a readiness to offer her own share of interpretations. She generously gives me time and space, and her own special setting. I'm a very lucky man.

INDEX